# Death Rituals and Politics in Northern Song China

MIHWA CHOI

OXFORD
UNIVERSITY PRESS

# OXFORD

UNIVERSITY PRESS

Oxford University Press is a department of the University of Oxford. It furthers
the University's objective of excellence in research, scholarship, and education
by publishing worldwide. Oxford is a registered trade mark of Oxford University
Press in the UK and certain other countries.

Published in the United States of America by Oxford University Press
198 Madison Avenue, New York, NY 10016, United States of America.





Library of Congress Cataloging-in-Publication Data
Names: Choi, Mihwa, author.
Title: Death rituals and politics in Northern Song China / Mihwa Choi.
Description: New York : Oxford University Press, 2017. |
Includes bibliographical references.
Identifiers: LCCN 2017015725 | ISBN 9780190459765 (alk. paper)
Subjects: LCSH: Funeral rites and ceremonies, Confucian—China—History—To 1500. |
Confucianism and state—China—History—To 1500.
Classification: LCC GT3283.A2 C52 2017 | DDC 393/.930951—dc23
LC record available at https://lccn.loc.gov/2017015725

1 3 5 7 9 8 6 4 2

Printed by Sheridan Books, Inc., United States of America

*For my grandmother*

*Hwadan Kim*

# Contents

# *Acknowledgments*

PERHAPS MY INTEREST in the topic of this book began with my childhood memories, in which Confucian death rituals were a core thread in the fabric of family life. My grandmother's twenty-seven-month-long daily offerings, often accompanied by her formulaic and improvised wailings at the altar of my grandfather, felt very long to a five-year-old girl. In addition to the annual memorial service to each ancestor, collective offerings to recently deceased ancestors were the high points of major seasonal festivals until my grandmother left the world twenty years later. It is now a lost tradition in my family, as in so many other households in my home country, Korea. This book takes us back to the time when Confucian death rituals began to take solid root within the circle of learned elites and to be further extended to the life of commoners in centuries to come.

The project grew out of my study as a graduate student at the University of Chicago, where I was privileged to work with many great teachers. The late Martin Riesebrodt introduced me to historical sociology, which became a foundation for this project. The late Anthony Yu, my mentor, suggested I gather solid textual evidence for the entire project before I began to write a chapter, which turned out to be excellent advice. Bruce Lincoln kindled my interest in the subject, and I wrote the first draft of Chapter 3 of this book in his class, "Ritual Theories." All three teachers played crucial roles in developing my research agenda, and thoroughly read and presented feedback to the dissertation version. Conversations with Steven Collins helped me develop the notion of "social imaginary" central to this project. Donald Harper and Edward Shaughnessy trained me to pay attention to detail in the reading of classical Chinese texts. Judith Zeitlin's class on Chinese ghost stories influenced me on including rumors and strange stories in Chapter 4. Wu Hung was a great resource for me to learn about mortuary culture in China, and I wrote a section of Chapter 5, "Eternal Happiness Bought with Money" in his graduate seminar course, "Chinese Tombs."

I was fortunate to study Confucianism with William Theodore de Bary and the late Irene Bloom at Columbia University, which reset the direction of my academic interest to Confucianism. Wendi Adamek and Angela Zito inspired me to include cultural studies and social theories in the study of Chinese religions. My teachers at Seoul National University introduced me to a wonderland of religious studies; I am particularly grateful to Hakjin Rah, Chinhong Chung, and Jangtae Keum.

A fellowship of the Center for Chinese Studies at National Central Library in Taiwan allowed me to conduct research in the initial stage of dissertation writing. I would especially like to thank Vera Yu- Chen Ma, Lily Wu, and Li-chun Keng for their warm and welcoming support. A Kyujanggak fellowship of Seoul National University made it possible for me to use holdings at the Kyujanggak Institute and to participate in various academic conferences in Korea. I want to give special thanks to Tae-koo Huh, Paekchol Kim, and Ji Won Song at the Kyujanggak Institute for sharing their knowledge in Korean studies and for their friendship. I would like to extend my appreciation to many faculties at Seoul National University for providing great opportunities for me to present my work in various venues: Chong-Suh Kim, Dong-shin Nam, Eun-su Cho, Sem Vermeersch, Weonjae Jeong, and Youn-Seung Lee. I would like to express my special gratitude to Young-Min Choi, CEO of Hanshin Machinery Co., for his generous donation to the Yangwoon fellowship which sponsored my study at Pacific School of Religion.

Many friends at the University of Chicago not only nourished my intellectual growth but also assisted me in numerous ways: Jacob Nussim, Matthew Vincenz, Larisa Masri, Paul Han, Stephen Wang, Jaeyeon Yim, Dongfeng Xu, Patrick Hatcher, Ari Sato, Melanie Barrett, Jerry Keys, and Fr. Paul Mariani. My friends since high school days, Heeja Kang and Yeonhee Chae, have been cheerleaders in various stages in my life. Friends in academia offered listening ears and emotional support: I want to give special thanks to Kyung-Hwan Mo, Suk Choi, Bongrae Suk, Chansoon Lim, Wilburn Hansen, Anne Donadey, and James Frankel. I am grateful to David Nikkel, Jeffrey Geller, and Ray Sutherland for reading parts of this book and presenting feedback. I thank José Angel Hernández for his critical reading of my book proposal and for sharing his tips about book publication.

I am deeply indebted to Keith Knapp for his close reading of the entire manuscript and for providing helpful suggestions and directing resources, which improved this book significantly. Two anonymous reviewers' constructive criticism and corrections of my translations also contributed to improving this book. All oversights and errors are mine. I would like to express my appreciation of Daniel McNaughton for his copyediting of my manuscript. I am grateful to Jen-der Lee, editor of *Asia Major*, for extending permission to reproduce Chapter 3 in its present form; it appeared as "Sima Guang's Thoughts on Death Rituals" in *Asia Major* (3rd Series) 29. 1 (2016): 45–72. I appreciate Howard I. Goodman, copyeditor of *Asia Major*, for his suggestions and corrections of errors. I would like to express my special gratitude to my editor, Cynthia Read, and the staff at Oxford University Press, Hannah Campeanu, Lincy Priya, and Steve Dodson.

My family deserves special mention. My sisters, Miyoung and Miseon, have always been there for me, especially in times of travail. I am grateful to my brother, Daeyoung oppa, for his financial support of my study, and my younger brother, Juyoung, and my mother, Aesoon Lee, for their love and encouragement. I dedicate this book to my late grandmother, who lived a life of the last generation of *shi* family, raised me with love, and instilled in me an unquenchable desire to learn.

# *Introduction*

IN TRADITIONAL CHINA, the funeral and ensuing death rituals, including burial and memorial services, presented critical moments for the immediate family members of the deceased to fulfill their filial piety, a core value of the society. At the same time, death rituals were social occasions: people with a connection to the deceased were expected to visit with donations for other people's funerals. Their social nature was most prominent in the observance of the "three-year mourning" (*sannian sang* 三年喪) for the death of a parent. For either twenty-five months or twenty-seven months,[1] people would wear mourning garments made of unprocessed hemp cloth, abstain from participating in joyful social activities, and even take a leave of absence from their job.[2] Death rituals were also channels for the outward statement of belief in a religiously pluralistic society. During the eleventh century, the growing cultural influences of Buddhism and Daoism were especially visible in the practices of death rituals both at the imperial court—for deceased royal family members—and throughout the realm as people desired to improve the soul's placement in the next life or in the world-beyond.

In the early eleventh century, some high-ranking officials also adopted Buddhist elements in their death rituals. For example, Wang Dan 王旦

---

1. Whereas the *Liji* 禮記 and *Xunzi* 荀子 describe the length of the "three-year mourning" as being twenty-five months, Zheng Xuan 鄭玄 (127–200 CE) interprets it as being twenty-seven months. During the eleventh century, it was customary to have it for twenty-seven months. For discussion of the length of the period, see Guolong Lai, "The Diagram of the Mourning System from Mawangdui," *Early China* 28 (2003): 57–59.

2. Influential works discussing Confucian death rituals include Miranda Brown, *The Politics of Mourning in Early China* (Albany: State University of New York Press, 2012), and Norman Kutcher, *Mourning in Late Imperial China: Filial Piety and the State* (New York: Cambridge University Press, 1999).

(957–1017), Grand Councilor, left a will stating that he would be buried with his head shaved and clothed in a Buddhist monk's robes.[3] Economic disparities of households were also revealed in performing or omitting death rituals, as they entailed costly expenses such as buying a burial plot and coffin, as well as human resources for performing a funerary procession. Whereas many poor people had no choice but to adopt cremation, some wealthy people constructed luxurious tombs containing exquisite burial items.

Against this background, in the mid-eleventh century death rituals became the subject of bitter, interminable disputes at the imperial court. The chief points of contention among officials were interpretations of the classical texts that treated rituals, interpretations that served as the basis for criticism of the emperor's ritual practice and for charges brought against officials for their violations. As death rituals became an arena for political contention, they developed into a subject of state control through the implementation of criminal laws. As such, in the eleventh century death rituals became a point of convergence for individual psychological concerns, social values, and state policies. Political contentions over the adequate performances of death rituals took place in tandem with the revival of Confucianism, a trend that was observed in renewed interest in applying the canonical ritual prescriptions of antiquity to current practices. This book examines how the politics surrounding death rituals in eleventh-century China, or the mid-Northern Song dynasty (960–1127), contributed to a revival of Confucianism, which laid the groundwork for the emergence of Neo-Confucianism, or the Way of Learning Confucianism (*daoxue* 道學), in the twelfth century. Neo-Confucianism became the dominant system of thought throughout East Asia, with its influence being felt in the spheres of ethics, religion, and politics, among others.

## *Historical Background and Guiding Questions*

It is generally held that the centralized bureaucratic system of the Song government took a leading role in the revival of Confucianism. Its expansion necessitated an increased number of state officers, and thus widened opportunities for the Confucian classics-based education gearing toward preparation for the civil service examinations. Thus, a great deal of previous scholarship has been devoted to the study of diverse aspects of civil service

---

3. Suzanne Cahill, "Taoism at the Sung Court: The Heavenly Text Affair of 1008," *Bulletin of Sung and Yüan Studies* 16 (1980): 33.

examinations as the primary impetus for cultural and social changes.[4] In particular, the increased number of participants in the varied levels of examinations was seen as the major factor contributing to the revival of Confucianism, because they internalized Confucian values and transmitted the cultural heritage of civilization to local communities.[5] This explanation by and large holds true as far as it is concerned with moral and intellectual aspects of Confucianism in which learning played a significant role in the moral transformation of individuals. Given that, this project turns its attention to changes in cultural patterns, especially in the performance of death rituals. Rather than take cultural transformation as a natural result of Confucian learning, I will inquire into political conditions and the historical process of making the movement of ritual reformation possible by examining some scholar-officials' efforts to establish Confucian rituals as the sole orthopraxis and to minimize Buddhist and Daoist influences in ritual practices within society.

The emergence of scholar-officials as a major social force was established through the first emperor's statecraft of expanding the power of the central government. Zhao Kuangyin 趙匡胤 (927–976), Palace Guard Commander of the Later Zhou State (951–960), having usurped the throne from the last king of the Later Zhou and founded the Song state, succeeded in bringing an end to the period of disunity known as the Six Kingdoms period through constant military campaigning.[6] During his reign as Emperor Taizu, the first emperor of the Song state, from 960 to 976, he emphasized the building of the highly centralized bureaucratic structure in order to effectively impose influences of the central state onto local areas and to minimize the potential influence of illustrious clans in local regions, as had been the case in the previous era.

---

4. Peter Bol, "The Sung Examination System and the *Shi*," *Asia Major* 3, 3rd series, no. 2 (1990): 149–172, and "The Examinations and Orthodoxies: 1070 and 1313 Compared," in *Culture and State in Chinese History: Conventions, Accommodations, and Critiques*, eds. Theodore Huters, R. Bin Wong, and Pauline Yu (Stanford, CA: Stanford University Press, 1997), 30. Influential works on state examinations of the Song Dynasty include John W. Chaffe, *The Thorny Gates of Learning in Sung China: A Social History of Examinations* (Albany: State University of New York Press, 1995), and Winston W. Lo, *An Introduction to the Civil Service of Sung China* (Honolulu: University of Hawaii Press, 1987).

5. Bol, "The Sung Examination System and the *Shi*," 167.

6. F. W. Mote, *Imperial China: 900–1800* (Cambridge, MA, and London: Harvard University Press, 1999), 92–98; Lau Nap-yin and Huang Kuan-chung, "Founding and Consolidation of the Sung Dynasty Under T'ai-Tsu (960–976), T'ai-tsung (976–997), and Chen-tsung (997–1022)," in *The Cambridge History of China*, vol. 5, part 1: *The Sung Dynasty and its Precursors, 907–1279*, eds. Denis Twitchett and Paul J. Smith (New York: Cambridge University Press, 2009), 208–242.

Taizong (r. 976–997), the younger brother of Taizu, expanded the civil service examinations as a recruitment tool for talented civil officers, who in turn constituted a new social group.

Despite this turn to centralization operated by bureaucrats equipped with a Confucian classics-based education, the policies of the early Northern Song under Taizu and Taizong were intended to create a climate in which the major religions could thrive without coming into conflict.[7] It was hoped that this would maximize the rulers' religious authority, vital to the construction of the new dynasty.[8] As part of his efforts to portray himself as a benign and legitimate ruler, Taizu sought to take advantage of the widespread adherence to both Buddhism and Daoism. For its part, institutional Buddhism saw an opportunity to regain its influence on society and its organizational power, which had been sharply diminished by the Later Zhou state's unfavorable policies. Buddhist discourse thus attempted to forge a close link between Buddhism and Taizu by portraying him as the anticipated legitimate ruler. Taizong also sought the backing of the hierarchies of the major religions in order to legitimize his emperorship, because he had violated the general custom of the patrimonial inheritance of rulership and was suspected of having been involved in the unnatural death of Taizu's son.[9] The two emperors, however, did not fail to place both Buddhist and Daoist institutions under state authority by retaining control over the ordination of clergies of both religions.[10] As a result, the court rituals of the early Song were highly eclectic. In addition to the regular seasonal imperial rituals based on Confucian ritual texts, the imperial court facilitated ad hoc rituals such as the offering of prayers to produce rain by drawing from multiple traditions. Sometimes civil servants were separated into groups for different religious services held in Buddhist and Daoist

---

7. For general information on this topic, see Chikusa Masaaki, "Sōsho no Seiji to shūkyo 宋初の政治と宗教," in *Collected Studies on Sung History Dedicated to Professor James T. C. Liu in Celebration of His Seventieth Birthday*, ed. Tsuyoshi Kinagawa (Kyoto: Tohosa, 1989), 179–195.

8. Huang Chi-chiang, "Imperial Rulership and Buddhism in the Early Northern Sung," in *Imperial Rulership and Cultural Change in Traditional China*, eds. Fredrick P. Brandauer and Chi-chiang Huang (Seattle: University of Washington Press, 1994), 144–187.

9. Cahill, "Taoism at the Sung Court," 38; on Taizong's policies on Buddhism, see Huang Qijiang, *Bei Song Fojiao shi lungao* 北宋佛教史論稿 (Taipei: Taiwan shangwu yinshuguan, 1997), 31–83.

10. Yang Weisheng et al., *Liang Song wenhua shi yanjiu* 兩宋文化史研究 (Hangzhou: Hangzhou University Press, 1998), 592–595 and 629–669; Wang Shengduo, "Songdai dui Xi Dao erjiao de guanli zhidu 宋代對釋道二教的管理制度," *Zhongguoshi yanjiu* 2, no. 6 (1991): 130–139.

temples and shrines for cultic figures.[11] In other instances, members of the Buddhist and Daoist clergies prayed together at the same ritual altar.

Whereas Emperors Taizu and Taizong chose to keep their personal religious propensities a private matter, Emperor Zhenzong 眞宗 (r. 997–1022) let his personal beliefs determine his policies by instituting many new public rituals that were in line with Daoist practice. During his reign, a few court officials challenged the state's ritual programs, but their critical voices remained a minority. However, immediately following Zhenzong's death, officials backing Confucian ritual practice moved quickly to bring an end to the dominance of those key officials who were instrumental to engineer and implement Zhenzong's Daoist ritual programs at the imperial court. During the reign of Renzong 仁宗 (r. 1022–1063), Confucianism emerged as the sole dominant intellectual and liturgical paradigm within the imperial court, and further expanded its influence on the life of civil officers. Behind the process of this change, there were a series of fierce political contentions over the imperial rituals that often polarized officialdom in the imperial court. The state increasingly turned death rituals into a domain subject to state control by making the observance of the "three-year mourning" a requirement for all civil officers and also by regulating details of burial, which brought many charges against civil officers for their violation of the laws. Nevertheless, the central government did not mandate Confucian rituals exclusively for public rituals, but rather facilitated Buddhist and Daoist memorial services for the general public by continuing its historical valorization of religious pluralism. Some scholar-officials also had liberty in adopting those religious practices for memorial services for their family members and in inserting prevailing cultural customs into traditional Confucian death rituals.

The main social agents presented in this study are leading scholar-officials who filled the vacuum in political and social spheres created by the near demise of formerly illustrious clans.[12] They held high-ranking offices both in the capital and in local regions, were involved in court politics, and had

---

11. Examples of such events found in the primary texts are: CB 86.1982, 84.1999, 88.2014, and 97.2248. Related secondary articles are Wang Shengduo's "Songchao li yu Fojiao 宋朝禮與佛教," *Xueshu yuekan* 252 (1990): 52–58, and "Songchao li yu Daojiao 宋朝禮與道教," in *Guoji Songdai wenhua yanjiu taolunhui lunwenji*, ed. Sichuan daxue, Guoji zhengli yanjiusuo (Chengdu: Sichuan daxue chubanshe, 1991), 35–49.

12. Nicolas Tackett argues that prominent Tang aristocratic families survived until the late ninth century. Nicolas Tackett, *The Destruction of the Medieval Chinese Aristocracy* (Cambridge, MA: Harvard Asia Center, 2014), 187–234.

national and capital-centered social networks.[13] Not only were they leaders of political opinion and advocates for public policies, they also shaped the contour of intellectual trends for *shi* 士, civil officers in varied official ranks and their family members who were familiar with Confucian teachings.[14] *Shi* at large are also included in this study, as producers, transmitters, and recorders of rumors and gossip and as ritual agents. Scholar-officials practiced ritualized decorum and performed Confucian rituals, as these were their cultural identity markers, despite the varied extent of their commitment to those rituals.

Another new social group, the grand merchants, stood in competition for seeking status by adopting ostentatious consumption patterns, including the lavish funerary rituals that had been practiced by aristocrats in earlier times.[15] Despite wealth accumulated from accelerated commercial activities, merchants were placed lower than farmers in the traditional social classificatory system and thus were barred from participating in state examinations by the Northern Song laws.[16] However, they could have generational upward mobility in the social classificatory system by investing in education for their sons to take government offices and by arranging intermarriage with scholar-officials.[17] On the other hand, scholar-officials had to grapple with potential generational downward mobility due to limited access to civil offices, even though low-ranking "protection" offices were conferred on their descendants.[18] Against this background, a group of scholar-officials took the lead not only in reviving the Confucian canonical rituals both in the imperial court and in the family life of scholar-officials but also in condemning non-Confucian rituals, "lavish burials" in particular. In their envisioning, a social

---

13. Hartwell and Chaffee called them "professional elites," James Liu "intellectuals." Robert Hymes, "Sung Society and Social Change," in *The Cambridge History of China*, vol. 5, part 2: *Sung China, 960–1279*, eds. John W. Chaffee and Denis Twitchett (Cambridge: Cambridge University Press, 2015), 627–650.

14. For a definition of *shi* of the Northern Song period, see Peter Bol, *This Culture of Ours: Intellectual Transition in T'ang and Sung China* (Stanford, CA: Stanford University Press, 1992), 34.

15. Qi Xia, *Zhongguo jingji tongshi* 中國經濟通史, vols 10–11, *Songdai jingji juan* 宋代經濟卷 (Beijing: Jingji ribao chubanshe, 1999), 1253–1289; Christian de Pee, "Purchase on Power: Imperial Space and Commercial Space in Song-Dynasty Kaifeng, 960–1127," *Journal of the Economic and Social History of the Orient* 53, no. 1 (2010): 149–184.

16. Chaffee, *Thorny Gates of Learning*, 54–56.

17. During the Southern Song, sons of nouveau riches merchants entered candidacy. Chaffee, *Thorny Gates of Learning*, 60.

18. Beverly Jo Bossler, *Powerful Relations: Kinship, Status, and State in Sung China (960–1279)* (Cambridge, MA: Harvard Asia Center, 1998), 53–55.

order hierarchically organized in accordance with official ranks nicely dovetailed with the premise of Confucian rituals that demarcated official ranks through ritual elements.

Against this background, this project investigates how polarizing debates about death rituals introduced new terrain for political power dynamics in the process of molding statecraft between monarchy and officialdom, and between groups of politically and intellectually divided court officials. Since Renzong's reign, scholar-officials had tended to share a vision of building a society based on Confucian ideals, but they disagreed on details. Factional strife among scholar-officials has drawn scholarly attention in identifying their differing views on policies, intellectual justifications of their differences, and shared common elements among leading figures or the factions led by them.[19] Built upon previous scholarship, this project broadens the parameter of their contention by presenting how their theorizing, politicizing, and regulating rituals not only derived from their differing Confucian visions of social and political order but also served their factions' political interests. It attempts to explain how political, intellectual, and legal disputes on death rituals and cultural campaigns against "heterodox" practices contributed to the revival of Confucianism by demonstrating that those disputes necessitated the study of various classical and traditional ritual texts as the authoritative source for guiding orthopraxis, and created a social ethos to take the observance of Confucian rituals as a hallmark of scholar-officials. This project thus will fill a gap in previous studies of Confucian rituals by presenting the missing link of explaining how classical Confucian rituals revived during the eleventh century, after the prevalence of Buddhist death rituals and before the appearance of Zhu Xi's *Family Rituals* (*Jiali* 家禮), an authoritative text for defining Confucian orthopraxis to a broad audience.[20]

## *Social Imaginaries and Rituals*

Why, then, had death rituals in particular become a point of political contestations and a channel for disseminating Confucian values at this time? Many

---

19. See Ari Daniel Levine, *Divided by a Common Language: Factional Conflict in Late Northern Song China* (Honolulu: University of Hawaii Press, 2008).

20. For a translation and annotation of the text, see Patricia B. Ebrey, *Chu Hsi's "Family Rituals": A Twelfth-century Chinese Manual for the Performance of Cappings, Weddings, Funerals, and Ancestral Rites* (Princeton, NJ: Princeton University Press, 1991). For discussion of the production, circulation, and cultural impact of the text, see Patricia B. Ebrey, *Confucianism and Family Rituals in Imperial China: A Social History of Writing about Rites* (Princeton, NJ: Princeton University Press, 1991).

death rituals imply the social imaginary of the world-beyond in which supplicants wish to ensure the well-being of the deceased. Even death rituals that deny the existence of the imagined world-beyond or choose to remain silent about it imply some kind of social imaginary; one concern is how the deceased will be incorporated into the social world in the memory of the living. The present study is an attempt to establish a relation linking ritual, social imaginary, and social reality, which may find broad applications in the field of history of religions. More concretely, it inquires into how rituals enact diverse types of social imaginary, how the social location of a group influences social imaginary, and how contestations over social imaginaries manifested in rituals imply ritual agents' envisioning of power relations.

Those who have taken up social imaginary as a theoretical concept have approached the topic in a number of ways and have offered a wide variety of definitions.[21] Some scholars, however, have employed the term without finding it necessary to provide a (rigid) definition.[22] The French word *imaginaire* has been used in recent scholarship with the meaning of roughly "what is imagined" or "the contents of the imagination." Imagination refers to the mental faculty of imagining, and *imaginaire* is its product. As there is no equivalent for *imaginaire* in English, I translate, in this study, *imaginaire* as "social imaginary," which I define as being "a world-frame, or the conditions of its possibilities, in terms of which imaginative events and states may appear and be rendered coherent."[23]

Thanks to Paul Ricoeur and Cornelius Castoriadis, we are able to see social imaginary as a component of a blueprint for the social world, as well as for imaginary worlds that have no grounding in reality.[24] Castoriadis in *The Imaginary Institution of Society* offers a broader concept of social imaginary

---

21. Richard Kearney examines diverse approaches of imagination and social imaginary—phenomenology, existential philosophy, hermeneutics, and poststructuralism—in *Poetics of Imagining: Modern to Post-modern* (New York: Fordham University Press, 1998); see also Jean-Jacques Wunenburger, *L'imaginaire* (Paris: Presses Universitaires de France, 2003), 5–29.

22. For example, Serge Gruzinski, *The Conquest of Mexico: The Incorporation of Indian Societies into the Western World, 16th–18th Centuries,* tr. Eileen Corrigan (Cambridge, MA: Blackwell, 1993); Bernard Faure, *Visions of Power: Imagining Medieval Japanese Buddhism,* tr. Phyllis Brooks (Princeton, NJ: Princeton University Press, 1996).

23. A similar point is made by Edward Casey in his description of "imagined content": *Imagining: A Phenomenological Study* (Bloomington and London: Indiana University Press, 1979), 107.

24. Paul Ricoeur, "Imagination in Discourse and in Action," in *Rethinking Imagination: Culture and Creativity,* eds. Gillian Robinson and John Rundell (London and New York: Routledge, 1994), 118–135; Cornelius Castoriadis, *The Imaginary Institution of Society,* tr. Kathleen Blamey (Cambridge, UK: Polity Press, 1987).

as the source of symbolic significance through which society constitutes its identity, its understanding of the world, and its relation to the world. Serge Gruzinski, on the other hand, studies different types of social imaginaries presented by two opposing groups in his *The Conquest of Mexico* and *Images at War*.[25] He contends that colonialism as a social imaginary was the real cause of such confrontations, and that images were the means of expressing political consciousness. However, Gruzinski chooses not to inquire into the sociopolitical impact of conflicting images beyond the domain of human consciousness.

Building upon Gruzinski's observation, this book will examine how conflicts over the material presentation of different social imaginaries can rearrange prevailing power relations, as well as why the position of a particular group in a society prompts its members to opt for a particular social imaginary. When social imaginaries convey the fundamental orientation of society or a social group, the forms of their material presentation, such as narratives, rumors, songs, rituals, and visual images, often become the objects of censorship. These signifiers of social imaginary not only imply social conflicts, but often also have political consequences as a result of contention concerning the signifiers. I therefore argue that social imaginary not only has a societal origin but also the capacity to position social groups and to articulate relationships between these groups.

From this perspective, this book will confront issues related to the ritual embodiment of social imaginary. In the field of history of religions, myth has often been viewed as solving an intellectual conundrum for which rational argument is not able to offer an answer; ritual enacts such mythological ways of thinking.[26] Scholars who accept this conceptualization of myth tend to highlight the universality of mythic themes addressing cosmological and ontological questions. In contrast, J. Z. Smith emphasizes sociohistorical particularity, which gives rise to a specific myth and ritual. He argues that when people experience "incongruity" between the social ideal and social reality, they invent a new ritual and reconcile the two through ritual practice.[27] He rightly pinpoints what people expect from ritual, but he neither clarifies how this reconciliation

---

25. Gruzinski, *The Conquest of Mexico*, and *Images at War: Mexico from Columbus to Blade Runner (1492–2019)*, tr. Heather MacLean (Durham and London: Duke University Press, 2001).

26. Mircea Eliade is a representative scholar of this position. Mircea Eliade, *Myth and Reality*, tr. Willard R. Trask (New York: Harper & Row, 1963), and *The Myth of the Eternal Return: Cosmos and History*, tr. Willard R. Trask (Princeton, NJ: Princeton University Press, 1971).

27. Jonathan Z. Smith, *Imagining Religion* (Chicago: University of Chicago Press, 1982), 90–101.

happens through ritual practice specifically nor addresses the social outcomes of performing such rituals. This project addresses the issues of how ritual is used as a locus to narrow the gap such "incongruities" represent, as perceived differently by diverse social groups, and what social consequences they wished to ensue in the wake of ritual performance.

In order to pursue these inquiries, I will make a two-layered analysis. First, I will delineate the social imaginaries implied in three different types of death rituals: royal ancestor veneration, Confucian family ritual, and non-Confucian rituals ("lavish burial" in particular). These rituals are "ideal types" in the Weberian sense, because there was no rigid consensus among ritual agents on what constituted each type of ritual. Because each of these rituals operated in different spheres—private or public, personal or official—I will draw from diverse arrays of theoretical tools those that are suitable to each case. Secondly, I will inquire into the sociopolitical ramifications of conflicts brought by performing different types of death rituals in eleventh-century China. For this inquiry, I share concerns with "practice theories" of ritual, in Catherine Bell's terms, that "are explicitly concerned with what rituals do, not just what they mean, particularly the way they construct and inscribe power relationships."[28] From this stance, the present study will show that diverse social groups practiced different kinds of rituals, invented new ones, and inserted new elements into existing practices to advance their interests. It will also examine how these practices were enmeshed in the struggle over social imaginaries between groups as they envisioned different constructions of social reality.[29]

## *Resources for the Study and the Organization of the Book*

By applying methods developed within the Annales School, this book will examine structural changes in ritual practices roughly spanning about eighty

---

28. Catherine M. Bell, *Ritual: Perspectives and Dimensions* (New York: Oxford University Press, 1997), 83.

29. My approach diverges from previous studies on death rituals that presume that the meanings and purposes of funerals are shared by ritual participants and emphasize the solidification of identity through ritual performance. One of the most influential books on funeral ritual, *Death and Regeneration of Life*, edited by Maurice Bloch and Jonathan Parry (New York: Cambridge University Press, 1982), also subscribes to this idea. Despite its emphasis on particular sociohistorical contexts of ritual performance, it highlights exclusively the idea that the meanings of rituals and the roles of practitioners are prescribed in ritual by a dominant social group. The work pays scant attention to the fact that ritual agents often invent new ritual practices and ascribe new meanings to existing practices.

years, from 1008 to 1085, or from the Heavenly Text affair (1008) to the end of Emperor Shenzong's reign (1067–1085). Synchronically speaking, it covers rituals practiced by diverse social strata, from the imperial family to scholar-officials and, to a lesser extent, grand merchants and other wealthy literati without official ranks. This project draws on a wide array of sources in order to grasp the breadth of the subjects at hand. The *Xu zizhi tongjian changbian* 續資治通鑑長編 (*A Sequel to the Comprehensive Mirror for Aids in Governance in Detailed Version*) and *Songshi* 宋史 (*A History of the Song*) are the standard sources of official dynastic historiography. Close examinations of these texts enable us to trace the emergence and consequences of the political and legal debates concerning rituals at the imperial court. In addition, the sections on ritual affairs in the *Songshi*, the *Song da zhaoling ji* 宋大詔令集 (*Collections of the Government Edicts during the Song*), and the *Song huiyao jigao* 宋會要輯稿 (*Collected Manuscripts on the Various Aspects of the Song Dynasty*) contain information on state regulations, policies, and the practices of various rituals. Collections of personal writings by various individuals, including essays, letters, and memorials, yield valuable information often left out of the official historiography. These writings are quite informative with regard to individual and collective ritual practices, the responses by scholar-officials and literati to state regulations, and criticism of other individuals. More informal writings called "jottings" or *biji* 筆記 often draw on free-floating rumors, gossip, regional events, family affairs, and the author/recorder's reflections on them. These writings are a valuable resource for deciphering the mentalities that acted upon social imaginaries. Unfortunately, not many local gazetteers are available for this period, which makes it hard to focus on a particular area.[30] As for ritual practices, Sima Guang's *Shuyi* 書儀 (*Letters and Rituals*), a leading Confucian manual, presents ideal prescriptions for scholar-officials and literati, standards for ritual reform, and rationales for his criticism of "heterodox" practices. Archaeological reports include details of actual burial practices of individual ritual agents that written texts may have neglected to mention.

This book consists of five main chapters that link politics, ritual, and social imaginaries. The first two chapters narrate the history of the debates at court. Chapter 3 presents a prescription of Confucian death ritual. Chapters 4 and 5 delineate the contesting social imaginaries of the world-beyond and of the social world expressed in popular narratives and burials, respectively.

---

30. James M. Hargett, "Song Dynasty Local Gazetteers and Their Place in the History of Difangzhi Writing," *Harvard Journal of Asiatic Studies* 56, no. 2 (1996): 405–442.

Chapter 1, "The Adaptation of Ancestral Ritual to Serve the Royal Imaginary," introduces the Heavenly Text affair (1008) and the nationwide cult of the Sacred Ancestor. After the Song government signed the humiliating treaty with the "barbarian" Liao state, a "Heavenly Text" declaring the legitimacy of the imperial family to rule mysteriously appeared on top of a palace gate. This incident marked the beginning of a new era during which the imperial court invested heavily in various ritual performances as a major way of solving practical issues. After offering the historically rare *fengshan* 封禅 imperial ritual giving thanks for dynastic prosperity, ironically in the wake of exposing military weakness, the imperial government invented the myth of "the Sacred Ancestor," claiming that the progenitor of the Song royal clan was an incarnated Daoist god. Afterward, the central government institutionalized the cult of the Sacred Ancestor with Daoist undertones both as one of the most significant and most frequently performed rituals at the imperial court and as a nationwide civil ritual to be observed by people at large.

Chapter 2, "'How Does Heaven Come to Speak?': The Contesting Discourse and the Revival of Confucian Death Rituals," explains the historical revival of Confucianism by focusing on the strategic use of discourse in death rituals. After the death of emperor Zhenzong, scholar-officials challenged the legitimacy of the Heavenly Text and the related myths and rituals. Extracting a critical citation from the *Analects* reading, "How does Heaven come to speak?," they argued that, because there was no way that Heaven could speak through the proposed revealed text, the Heavenly Text was fabricated. In the end, a consensus was reached between Emperor Renzong and officials that only Confucian canonical rituals would be legitimate as imperial death rituals, and the cult of the Sacred Ancestor should be reduced to a private ritual of the royal family.

Later, the distribution of power between the emperor and officials divided the latter into two factions: one supported stronger monarchical power, while the other saw the bureaucratic system as the ultimate locus for political power. The former believed that the emperor, exercising his role above and beyond the bureaucratic system, had a right to adjust the stringent regulations of the ancient Confucian rituals for contemporary imperial ritual practices. In contrast, the latter maintained that ancient Confucian ritual laws were endowed with an authority that was even higher than the royal authority commanding the bureaucracy, and so they could cite Confucian classics in criticism of an emperor who would attempt to violate these regulations. I argue that the various debates and the legal cases related to death rituals stimulated the study of ancient canonical rituals, and thereby fostered the revival of Confucianism as an intellectual and sociocultural movement.

Chapter 3, "Ordering Society through Confucian Rituals," is an in-depth analysis of the *Shuyi*. Its author, Sima Guang 司馬光 (1019–1086), was the pivotal figure in opposing the New Policies (1069–1076) that aimed for comprehensive social, military, and economic reforms. The author believed in the moral reformation of society through the dissemination of Confucian ritual norms. He maintained that rituals were the locus in which the hierarchical social order could be manifested according to official rank. He especially objected to lavish burials performed by wealthy commoners in the belief that such burials implied a social imaginary of the wealthy where status could be improved by material investments in ritual performance. Sima Guang's conception of ritual testifies to his vision of society or social imaginary in which official ranks are the fundamental basis of social hierarchy.

Chapter 4, "Social Imaginaries and Politics in Narratives of the World-beyond and the Supernatural," attempts to answer a broader question posited in this book: How did social imaginaries of the world-beyond come to have political implications during the eleventh century? After the death of Wang Anshi 王安石 (1021–1086), the chief engineer of the New Policies and a supporter of stronger monarchical power, a series of eyewitness accounts of his ill fate in purgatory were widely spread via rumors. In contrast to the purgatorial limbo of Wang Anshi, Han Qi 韓琦 (1008–1075), a critic of the New Policies, was reported to have become the perfected in glory who was in charge of the other-world tribunal court. During the period when official and public discourse was frequently used for political purges, these stories about the affairs of the world-beyond written in the form of rumor were used as a convenient vehicle to deliver political messages, since the authorship and the veracity of the content could be neither confirmed nor refuted.

Chapter 5, "Burial: Contested Site for Social Imaginaries," asks why burials had become a focal point of some scholar-officials' efforts to build a socio-moral order based on Confucian norms. During this time, many scholar-officials took issue with the previously tolerated negligence of burials, not only by imposing moral accountability to responsible individuals but also by taking care of neglected burials with the establishment of a public graveyard for the poor. The "simple burial," idealized by scholar-officials, used a simple pit tomb with minimal burial items, based on the mainstream Confucian tradition of rejecting literary or material expression of the social imaginaries of the world-beyond. Its focus was on a tomb inscription tablet highlighting the public accomplishments and virtue of the deceased by which they would remain within social memory among the living. On the other hand, many rich merchants (and large landholding literati) were able to conduct a "lavish burial," against the government's prohibitions, believing that the material furnishing of the tomb would actually influence the soul's transitional process and its well-being in the world-beyond. Nevertheless, there were some exceptional cases that did not fit into the general pattern of correlations between social groups and burial practices, which suggests that tombs tended to remain as private spaces where individual souls could rest in peace in accordance with their beliefs and self-identity.

I argue that death rituals functioned as a stage on which practitioners not only revealed their imaginings of the world-beyond and their positions within that imaginary world, but also located themselves within the hierarchical relations of the contemporary social world. I maintain that those disputes and institutional censorship of death rituals not only contributed to rearranging power relations between emperors and officialdom as well as between different factions within officialdom, they also fostered the revival of Confucianism.

*I*

——————

# The Adaptation of Ancestral Ritual
# to Serve the Royal Imaginary

DURING THE REIGN of Zhenzong (998–1022) of the Song, and especially the era of the Great Central Tally of Auspiciousness (*dazhong xiangfu* 大中祥符, 1008–1016), ritual discourse and practice focused on royal ancestry became the center of life within the imperial court. The Heavenly Text (*tianshu* 天書) blessing the imperial rule mysteriously appeared in 1008, which became a defining moment of the reign. This event was hailed in 1009 by the performance of the *fengshan* ritual, the most prestigious, large-scale, and costly imperial thanksgiving ritual, after a lapse of 282 years. Afterwards, Zhenzong developed a dynastic myth of the divine origin of his family by borrowing from Daoist theology and cosmology.[1] The first ancestor of the royal clan was worshipped as an incarnation of the Yellow Emperor rather than as an apotheosized deity. Furthermore, the cult of the Sacred Ancestor introduced a new approach to the commemoration of late emperors, who were venerated either independently from or accompanied by Daoist deities both in official court rituals and in civil rituals to be observed at all levels of society. This new cult of the Sacred Ancestor became one of the most significant religious activities during the Song dynasty and continued to prevail until abolished by the Mongols of the Yuan dynasty in 1292.[2]

——————

1. For a study of the history of Chinese emperors' use of talismans and other signs for justifying their receiving the Heavenly Mandate, see Anna Seidel, "Imperial Treasures and Taoist Sacraments: Taoist Roots in the Apocrypha," in *Tantric and Taoist Studies in Honor of R. A. Stein*, Vol. 2, ed. Michel Strickmann (Brussels: Institut Belge des Hautes Etudes Chinoises, 1983–1985), 291–371.

2. Yang Weisheng, et al., *LiangSong wenhua shi yanjiu* 兩宋文化史研究 (Hangzhou: Hangzhou University Press, 1998), 612.

Historians hardly fail to mention the descent of the Heavenly Text affair in their description of Zhenzong's reign.[3] His personal commitment to Daoism is also well known. Both traditional and modern historiographies question to what extent the emperor was involved in the fabrication of the alleged revelation.[4] In her study of the descent of the text and the performance of the *fengshan* ritual, Suzanne Cahill argues that the emperor made conscientious political choices in pursuing those affairs based upon his belief in Daoism, rather than having been manipulated by "evil ministers." Agreeing with her position, for our understanding of religious landscape and state policies of religion in early Northern Song, this chapter will not only fill gaps in previous renditions on the affair of the descent of the Heavenly Text and the *fengshan* ritual performance, but also further extend this topic by laying out the historical development of the invention of the myth of the Sacred Ancestor and the ensuing nationwide ritual programs, which have yet to receive close attention. This chapter will engage the question of what social imaginary was implied in the new myth and rituals in ways that generated the intended political impacts. How did the newly invented death rituals with a strong Daoist undertone serve the intended political interests better than the classical imperial rituals?

## *The Crisis of Royal Authority and the Fabrication of Revelation*

The Heavenly Text affair in 1008 was a landmark in the history of Zhenzong's reign. A scroll appeared, hanging on a gate, with text that proclaimed the legitimacy of the Zhao family, blessed by Heaven. The finding of the scroll ushered in a new era in which the imperial court expended a great deal of energy in various imperial ritual performances. How did this supposedly revelatory text bestowed by Heaven appear at the very center of the state? Who were the human agents possibly involved in its appearance? Why and how was this text perceived to benefit those human agents at this particular time of history?

---

3. Suzanne Cahill, "Taoism at the Sung Court: The Heavenly Text Affair of 1008," *Bulletin of Sung and Yüan Studies* 16 (1980): 23–44; Lau Nap-yin and Huang K'uan-chung, "Founding and Consolidation of the Sung Dynasty under T'ai-tsu (960–976), T'ai-tsung (976–997), and Chen-tsung (997–1022)," in *The Cambridge History of China*, vol. 5: *The Sung Dynasty and its Precursors, 907–1279, Part 1*, ed. Denis Twitchett and Paul J. Smith (New York: Cambridge University Press, 2009), 260–278; Edward L. Davis, *Society and the Supernatural in Song China* (Honolulu: University of Hawaii Press, 2001), 67–69.

4. Cahill, "Taoism at the Sung Court," 26 and 35–42.

Emperor Zhenzong (998–1022), facing a losing battle with the Liao state, entered into the Shanyuan Alliance 澶淵同盟 in 1005—a military treaty that relegated the Song state to a "younger brother" status vis-à-vis the Liao, whose origins traced back to a set of nomadic tribes. Under the Shanyuan treaty, the Song had to pay a tribute to the Liao of 100,000 taels of silver and 200,000 bolts of silk, estimated to be about 0.3 to 0.5 percent of the state's expenditure.[5] A faction in Song officialdom supporting the treaty argued that the demanded tribute was less than the cost of continuing to wage a war that the state was losing. Despite some initial hesitation, the Song state accepted it for purely pragmatic reasons, and hailed the alliance as a diplomatic victory. But the Song people found the affair a bitter and unsettling reversal. Historically, the Chinese government had set the terms of such agreements with countries like Korea and Vietnam as the recipient of tribute. Now they were obliged to take on the unprecedented and humiliating task of paying tribute to what they had considered a "barbarian" state—a great wound to Chinese national pride.

The declining strength of the Song can be linked to a prior, opposing swing of the historical pendulum. In the opinion of former emperor Taizu (r. 960–976), during the Tang dynasty (712–756) the central government failed to control military generals who had grown too powerful, which ultimately led to its downfall.[6] Now, after deliberate attempts by Taizu to shift support from the military to government bureaucrats, Zhenzong found himself emperor of a weakened state. Profoundly ashamed and depressed, the emperor sought a way to restore national pride without waging a ruinous war on the Liao.

The historical records do not indicate that anyone challenged Emperor Zhenzong's authority on the basis of the treaty. An undisputed source for that authority came from the politico-religious tradition, holding that the emperor received the Mandate of Heaven as its agent on earth, and was thus in charge of the order of the human world. This tradition, however, also offered a chance

---

5. Lau Nap-Yin and Huang K'uan-chung, "Founding and Consolidation of the Sung Dynasty," 268. For a review of modern scholarship on the political and diplomatic implications of the treaty, see Hoyt C. Tillman, "The Treaty of Shanyuan from the Perspectives of Western Scholars," *Sungkyun Journal of East Asian Studies* 5, no. 2 (2005): 135–156; Don J. Wyatt, "In Pursuit of the Great Peace: Wang Dan and the Early Song Evasion of the 'Just War' Doctrine," in *Battlefronts Real and Imagined: War, Border, and Identity in the Chinese Middle Period*, ed. Don J. Wyatt (New York: Palgrave Macmillan, 2008), 75–109; Karl F. Olsson, "The Structure of Power under the Third Emperor of Sung China: The Shifting Balance After the Peace of Shan-Yuan" (PhD diss., University of Chicago, 1974), 139–186.

6. F. W. Mote, *Imperial China: 900–1800* (Cambridge, MA, and London: Harvard University Press, 1999), 102–104.

to question the ruler's moral quality in the face of natural disasters and losses in war. On the other hand, various auspicious natural phenomena were often presented as divine acknowledgment of the emperor's achievements. Although Wang Dan 王旦 (957–1017), Grand Councilor, pointed to certain auspicious natural phenomena in support of Zhenzong,[7] the reality of circumstances left the ruler vulnerable in maintaining the expected royal authority.

Against this backdrop, in the eleventh month of 1007, Wang Qinruo 王欽若, Director of the Bureau of Military Affairs (*zhi shumiyuan shi* 知樞密院事), approached the emperor. From the time he assumed this prominent position in 1006, he soon began to have equal political power with Wang Dan. Here, Wang Qinruo devised a demonstration of more explicit heavenly sanction. A *History of Song* (*Songshi* 宋史) reads:

> The Khitans call their ruler heaven and his wife earth. They make sacrifices to heaven innumerable times a year. A flying wild goose caught by hunting and a bustard falling on the ground by itself are all referred as heaven's granting. They make offerings and boast about them.[8]

This account roughly coincides with Sima Guang's 司馬光 (1019–1086) description:

> Recently, the state has wished to subjugate the Khitans, which it has not been able to accomplish. The barbarian's nature reveres Heaven and believes in spirits. Now, if the state were to abound with auspicious talismans and introduce the Mandate of Heaven for self-esteem, barbarians wouldn't dare belittle China by hearing this.[9]

A celestial blessing, achieved through the arrival of heavenly signs, would be necessary in order to elevate the status of China in the eyes of the Liao by appealing to its deep-seated religious culture. A plan hatches in the following exchange between Qinruo and the emperor:

---

7. Li Tao, *Xu Zizhi tongjian changbian* 續資治通鑑長編 (hereafter CB) (Beijing: Zhonghua shuju, 1979–1993), 70.1578 (the first number indicates the *juan* in the original edition; the second number indicates the page number in the reprinted edition). Regarding Wang Dan's antiwar stance during Zhenzong's reign, see Wyatt, "In Pursuit of the Great Peace," 75–109.

8. Tuo Tuo, *Songshi* 宋史 (A *History of the Song*) (hereafter SS) (Beijing: Zhonghua shuju, 1977), Benji 8, 8.172.

9. Sima Guang, *Sushui jiwen* 涑水記聞, 1st series, 7:6.80.

> If Your Majesty does not seek to use military force, then you must accomplish a great task. You might be able to conquer the whole world and show off China to the barbarians." The emperor said, "What can be called a great task?" Qinruo said, "It is none other than the *fengshan* ritual.[10]

The *fengshan* ritual in particular would best suit their purposes. Various accounts unanimously state that Wang Qinruo was the architect of this scheme and that the emperor was not comfortable with Wang's suggestions.[11] It might be true that the emperor was genuinely uncomfortable because his father, Taizong, had dismissed a similar proposal.

Modern scholars generally believe the *fengshan* ritual to be the most solemn imperial ritual in traditional China.[12] Chinese emperors conducted the ritual on the peak of the highly sacred Tai Mountain, in present-day Shandong Province. The origin of the ritual is unknown, because it does not appear in any of the Confucian classical texts. However, it appeared in the *Shiji* 史記 (The Grand Scribe's Records) as having been performed by the First Emperor of the Qin State in 219 BCE.[13] According to legend, Tai Mountain was the place where spirits descended from Heaven, and also where Heaven and Earth met.[14] The ritual involved traveling to the mountain and a sacrificial offering to the highest deity within indigenous Chinese cosmology. After the Han dynasty (206–220 CE), elements of Confucianism were steadily incorporated into the *fengshan* ritual. As a result, the purpose of the ritual was to

---

10. CB 67.1506; SSJBM 22.128; SS Benji 8, 8.172.

11. The *Songshi jishi benmo* records that Wang Qinruo was jealous of the success of Kou Zhun 蔻準, who had played a significant role in the Shanyuan Alliance process. It states that Qinruo initially conceived of using the Heavenly Text as a way to improve his own standing at the court.

12. For a review of previous scholarship on this subject, see Howard J. Wechsler, *Offerings of Jade and Silk: Ritual and Symbol in the Legitimation of the Tang Dynasty* (New Haven, CT, and London: Yale University Press, 1985), 170–172, and Mark Edward Lewis, "The Feng and Shan Sacrifices of Emperor Wu of the Han," in *State and Court Ritual in China*, ed. Joseph P. McDermott (Cambridge: Cambridge University Press, 1999), 49–52.

13. Sima Qian, *The Grand Scribe's Records*, vol. 1: *The Basic Annals of Pre-Han China*, ed. William H. Nienhauser, Jr., trans. Tsai-fa Cheng et al. (Bloomington: Indiana University Press, 1994), 138, and "Shih Chi 28: The Treatise on the *Feng* and *Shan* Sacrifices," in *Records of the Grand Historian: Han Dynasty*, tr. Burton Watson (New York: Columbia University Press, 1993), vol. 2, 13–65.

14. Wechsler, *Offerings of Jade and Silk*, 173.

confirm the legitimacy of the emperor as one who had received the Mandate of Heaven.[15]

Although clearly offering the *fengshan* ritual had the potential of elevating the status of a ruler, the relative infrequency and the context in which the ritual had traditionally been performed made it an unlikely choice for the reluctant Zhenzong. It typically was performed only in times of great prosperity and peace as an offering of thanksgiving to Heaven for granting such blessings. As a practical matter, this made perfect sense, since the emperor had to take the substantial risk of leaving the capital city for one-and-a-half months of travel. Prior to Zhenzong, only five emperors in Chinese history had performed it. The last emperor to do so was Xuanzong 玄宗 (r. 712–756) during the Tang dynasty. The ritual carried a psychological burden for a reluctant Zhenzong, and the emperor's discomfort with the idea of performing the *fengshan* ritual revealed his conscientious questioning of the quality of his accomplishments, according to standard historiography.

In addition to general prosperity, auspicious signs such as supernatural phenomena were considered as signals that the ritual should occur. In particular, as a precondition to performing the *fengshan* ritual, it was required to obtain a text sent by Heaven, called *fu* 符 (tally), that bestowed the Mandate of Heaven on an individual. The idea that Heaven revealed its intent through signs and text emerged during the Western Han dynasty (206 BCE–9 CE) and began to be utilized by both presiding and would-be emperors for justifying their rule after the reign of Emperor Ai (r. 7–1 BCE). This idea, however, did not become a part of mainstream Confucianism, as later scholarship condemned it along with the government's frequent prohibition of the allegedly revealed body of literature, the so-called Prophetic and Apocryphal Texts (*chenwei* 讖緯), in fear of invoking new leadership, yet this idea remained influential till the Six Dynasties Period (220–589 CE).[16] Now Zhenzong found himself in need of a revealed text to grant him permission to hold the *fengshan* ritual. Key questions hinged on the extent of human intervention permissible in the emergence and presentation of auspicious signs. Wang Qinruo, a devout Daoist, offered the view that

---

15. Wechsler, *Offerings of Jade and Silk*, 172–174.

16. Jack L. Dull, "A Historical Introduction to the Apocryphal (Ch'an-wei) Texts of the Han Dynasty" (PhD diss., University of Washington, 1966), 113–167; Zongli Lü, *Power of Words: Chen Prophecy in Chinese Politics AD 265–618* (Bern: Peter Lang, 2003), 13–110; Tiziana Lippiello, *Auspicious Omens and Miracles in Ancient China: Han, Three Kingdoms and Six Dynasties* (Sankt Augustin: Monumenta Serica Institute, 2001), 51–65.

"Heavenly signs can be obtained."[17] He stated: "In the past, there were cases in which humans caused the signs to appear. If people have a profound belief in what is declared [to be true] and venerate it, it is tantamount to a heavenly sign."[18] Referring to the River Chart (*hetu* 河圖) and the Luo Text (*luoshu* 洛書)[19] as examples, Wang argued that although people believed them to be revealed texts containing the spirit's words, in fact they were none other than tools that the sage used for teaching. He implied that all supposedly revealed texts were in fact human-made, and that this could apply to those auguring the *fengshan* ritual. Not entirely convinced, another night the emperor alone asked an old scholar (老儒), Du Gao 杜鎬 (938–1013), how he thought of *hetu* and *luoshu*. Not knowing the emperor's intention, he answered that these texts were none other than what the sage used the spirit's words for teaching.[20] His answer happened to agree with Wang's argument, which helped Wang persuade the emperor. Some people believed the agreement of Wang Qinruo and Du Gao as to the divination texts was itself an auspicious sign.[21] On the ninth month of the year, however, Du Gao was fined for mishandling objects used in the death ritual held at a palace shrine, signaling ongoing conflict between the camps within the palace.[22]

About two months after the discussion with Wang Qinruo, in the first month of 1008, the emperor reported a mystical experience that allegedly happened on the night of the twenty-seventh of the eleventh month of 1007. An account of his experience reads:

> When I was about to go to bed, all of a sudden I saw that one room was very bright. In surprise I looked at it and saw a divine being (*shenren* 神人). He told me, "You should establish a ritual enclosure

---

17. For Wang's biography and his commitment to Daoism, see Huang Qijiang, "Wang Qinruo yu Daojiao" 王欽若與道教, *Jiangxi Shehui kexue*, no. 5 (1994): 59–61.

18. CB 67.1506.

19. For the historical origins of Hetu and Luoshu, see Anna Seidel, "Imperial Treasures and Taoist Sacraments," 257–302; Stephen L. Field, "The Numerology of Nine Star *Fengshui*: A *Hetu* 河圖, *Luoshu* 洛書 Resolution of the Mystery of Directional Auspice," *Journal of Chinese Religions* 27 (1999): 13–33; Lippiello, *Auspicious Omens and Miracles in Ancient China*, 51–65. As for its being accepted as a legitimate Confucian text, see Dull, "A Historical Introduction," 397.

20. SSJBM 22.129; CB 67.1507.

21. CB 67.1506–1507.

22. CB 70.1562.

for Yellow Register Purgation (*huanglu zhai* 黃籙齋) in the Audience Hall for one month: thereupon, three pieces of the Great Central Tally of Auspiciousness (*dazhong xiangfu* 大中祥符) will descend. Do not reveal Heaven's plan." When I quickly stood up to address him, he had already disappeared.[23]

The emperor added that he had adopted a vegetarian diet and observed a ritual fast since the first day of the twelfth month. As the emperor himself credited the mystical prophecy and had already prepared for its fulfillment, the imperial court moved quickly to prepare for a notable event as soon as his report was done. Three pieces of the auspicious tally ought to appear throughout his reign. The Daoist ritual enclosure was established. A carved wooden carriage decorated with gold and jewelry was made. As they continued to make offerings for divine blessings until the first month of 1008, the first piece of the Great Central Tally of Auspiciousness appeared.

A gatekeeper reported that on the left of the Chengtian gate, a yellow silk cloth was flying, hanging on top of a roof tile. Officials reported to the emperor: "It is a silk cloth about two feet long, sealed like a scrolled book. It is tied three times with blue cloth. Where it is sealed, there are faint writings." The emperor thought about it and said, "Doubtless, it is the text descended from Heaven to which the divine being referred." The officials hailed the event as attributed to the virtue of the emperor. The opened silk cloth contained the text:

The Zhao family received the Mandate of Heaven and arose during the Song dynasty. The Mandate will be handed down to eternity. It resides in *ritual vessels* and is preserved within the legitimate line of succession. Its succession will be assured for seven hundred and ninety-nine generations (趙受命興於宋付於恒。居其器守於正。世七百九九定).[24] [italics added]

Emulating the style of the *Daode jing* 道德經, the most authoritative Daoist text, the text continued praising the emperor's filial piety and frugality, and it laid on blessings for his descendants in eternity.[25] After reading the text, they put it into a golden casket. Numerous officials came into the palace to congratulate the emperor. At the Audience Hall, a banquet was held where the emperor and officials ate vegetarian dishes to commemorate the occasion.

---

23. SSJBM 22.129.

24. CB 68.1519.

25. CB 68.1519.

An examination of the text reveals the ideology set forth by the emperor emphasizing the desire of the Zhao family that the legitimacy of its rule be unassailable. "Ritual vessels" referred to imperial rituals that were exclusively designated as the duty of the emperor. The text also confirms a prevailing notion that the criterion of political legitimacy of a ruler in a dynasty was the direct line of succession (*zhengtong* 正統) of the imperial family.[26] Therefore, the text echoed the idea that the classical ritual dedicated to Heaven (and Earth) could serve as an important criterion for dynastic legitimacy.[27]

Given the way the text, at least on the surface, focused on a more personal and genealogical level with respect to the Zhao family, it could serve political ends subtly. At the same time, such a celestial nod favoring the emperor elevated a mood suffering from guilt over the war, which was going badly, and the ensuing treaty. There is no historical mention of how the text appeared on the gate, nor of any investigation into its origins. Little incentive existed for such an investigation given how it aptly, and not coincidentally, met the desire of the emperor and his officials for heavenly signs. Desire itself was incentive enough to lead any one of them not privy to the truth to accept that it was indeed divine in origin. Suzanne Cahill pinpoints that standard historical sources differ in their presentation on the issue of to what extent the emperor was cognizant of the fabrication of the text, while they unanimously point to Wang as the grand architect of the scheme.[28] Historical sources indeed betray bias in historians' commentaries on the event of the appearance of the text and differ in the details of description, yet they are coherent in the descriptions of the overall course of the events and policies ensued after the descent of the Heavenly Text in which the emperor played an active role.

The emperor soon issued an edict to announce the "descent" of the Heavenly Text. He sent officials to perform the ritual of reporting this event to the deities at the Imperial Ancestral Shrine (*zongmiao* 宗廟) and to the Shrine of the Gods of Land and Agriculture (*sheji* 社稷), which were "great sacrificial rituals" (*dasi* 大祀) in the canonical tradition. Then he declared a new era, beginning with the year 1008, called the Great Central Tally of Auspiciousness, and announced five days of official holidays to celebrate this event. The year 1008 in the lunar calendar started with the affair of the Heavenly Text, which was merely a prelude to what would come later.

---

26. Wechsler, *Offerings of Jade and Silk*, 15.

27. Wechsler, *Offerings of Jade and Silk*, 17.

28. Cahill, "Taoism at the Sung Court," 26.

## *Performing the* Fengshan *Ritual*

As the conversation between the emperor and Wang Qinruo indicated, the appearance of the Heavenly Text simply laid the groundwork for performing the *fengshan* ritual, as the allegedly revealed text declared the ideology that underlay the ritual.[29] The emperor and his staff moved forward to orchestrate public sentiment in favor of performing the ritual. Additional auspicious signs were reported continuously, while the imperial palace did its best to enact the textual prescriptions of the ritual in order to best demonstrate royal authority as designated and blessed by transcendental authority.

As the authenticity of the Heavenly Text was accepted, and celebrated as such, opinion in favor of performing the *fengshan* ritual grew quickly within a certain segment of society. Support for conducting the ritual also came on the thirteenth day of the third month of 1008 from 1,287 residents, consisting of Elder (*fulao* 父老) Lǚ Liang and others, of Qianfeng County 乾奉縣, where the Tai Mountain was located. Their sentiment was recorded thus:

> The state received the Mandate of Heaven for fifty years. It has already brought about great peace. Recently Heaven sent down an auspicious tally to make your great virtue manifest. Therefore it is appropriate to undertake the sacrificial ritual at Tai Mountain in order to give thanks to Heaven and Earth in return.[30]

Historical sources do not indicate how they were mobilized other than specifying the name of an elder, otherwise unknown. Because such a large group's long-distance trip to the capital city demanded considerable resources and meticulous plan, it is very possible that there were some officials maneuvering this seemingly voluntary activity. No matter who were backing this somewhat populist-initiative meeting—central or local officials—residents of the region could expect the material benefit of hosting a long inactive ritual, such as the tax break that we shall see later. If rewards were not material, at least it would raise the profile of the region, and of local officials for facilitating the event.[31]

---

29. Lewis, "The Feng and Shan Sacrifices," 50–65; Sima Qian, "Shih Chi 28: The Treatise on the *Feng* and *Shan* Sacrifices," 13–22.

30. CB 68.1528.

31. Sarah Schneewind presents a case that diverse actors acted on their agenda in the event of presenting an auspicious object to the throne, and in the interpretation of the object and

The emperor's response did not imply that he would decline the request, but exhibited due caution: "This huge business cannot be discussed lightly."[32] Perhaps realizing that more support was needed for the radical invocation of the *fengshan* ritual, Grand Councilor Wang Dan, in the third month of 1008, led a public meeting at the palace to request the emperor to perform the ritual. At the meeting, over 24,300 people, including both civil and military officials of various ranks, low-ranking officers at local governments, Daoist and Buddhist clergies, leaders of ethnic groups, and respected elders requested that the ritual be held.[33] This public meeting orchestrated by the highest-ranking official not only justified the cause of the ritual performance but also made it appear to receive a broad support from diverse segments of society. Later we shall see that some people from these diverse groups were involved in the logistics of the ritual performance, and were rewarded afterwards.

Another piece of the Heavenly Text was discovered at the palace in the fourth month, just as the first tally prophesized two more would appear. This appearance of the second tally further bolstered the necessity of the performing the ritual.[34] The pragmatic business remained of getting enough fiscal backing for the proposal. The emperor first asked Ding Wei 丁謂 (966–1037), Provisional State Finance Commissioner (*quansan sishi* 權三司使), about the cost of the ritual, and he responded with the favorable opinion, "For a great plan, certainly there is extra money."[35] After such deliberation, the emperor decided to perform the *fengshan* ritual in the tenth month of the year.[36] The emperor appointed several special commission offices for the preparation of the ritual performance: for Wang Qinruo became the Commissioner of Great Ritual (*dalishi* 大禮使), and Wang Dan the Commissioner of Ritual (*liyishi* 禮儀使).

---

the related events. *A Tale of Two Melons: Emperor and Subject in Ming China* (Indianapolis, IN: Hackett Publishing, 2006).

32. The text is not clear whether his answer was a typical initial declining of a compliment for the sake of virtue only to accept the offer another time, or an indication of genuine reluctance. Xu Song, *Song huiyao jigao*, 宋會要輯稿 (hereafter SHY) Li (Beijing: Zhonghua shuju, 1957) 22.2a; CB 68.1528.

33. CB 68.1530.

34. Cahill notes that most historical sources did not mention this occurrence. Cahill, "Taoism at the Sung Court," 27–28.

35. CB 68.1531.

36. CB 68.1531.

In the sixth month of 1008, Wang Qinruo went to the County of Qianfeng in order to make preparations for the *fengshan* ritual, and reported, "At Tai Mountain, a sweet spring bubbled up and at Xi Mountain, an azure dragon appeared."[37]

Wang's report was followed by a more dramatic event.

At Tai Mountain, a wooden worker saw a yellow cloth hanging on a plant. There was writing on it but he was illiterate. He reported it to an officer, Wang Juzheng 王居正. Seeing the emperor's name on it, the officer rode to Wang Qinruo. Afterwards, Wang brought the text to the palace.[38]

This report marked the third occurrence of the descent of the Heavenly Text. After hearing about this newly found text, the emperor announced publicly that in the previous month (the fifth) he had had a dream in which the divine being from his earlier mystical experience appeared again. The divine being told the emperor that he certainly would receive the Heavenly Text at Tai Mountain during the first ten days of the following month. The presumed coincidence of the two separate events led the emperor to identify the newly acquired text as that which the divine being foretold.

The text was treated as a sacred object. It was read in public with great reverence; a part of it went as follows:

You have served me with respect and filial piety, and nourished peo-ple and spread blessings. I have granted you a blessed sign so that commoners would know [my blessing]. Secretly guard these words and comprehend what I mean. The dynasty's reigning years will be extended to eternity, and your lifespan will be very long.[39]

By focusing on the emperor individually, rather than the Zhao family more generally, the new text with a personal tone, narrated by the divine being, intimated why the ritual should be undertaken by this particular emperor. In addition, these blessings of longevity undoubtedly provided just the kind of message regarding the stability of the state that the emperor wished to get across to doubters and potential challengers in his domain.

---

37. CB 69.1542, 1543.

38. CB 69.1549.

39. CB 69.1550.

In another account in the *Songshi jishi benmo*, the historiographer does not omit to mention that the emperor in fact told Wang Qinruo in private that he had had the dream in the fifth month.[40] This statement intimated that it was Wang Qinruo who had made the Heavenly Text and put it in the foretold place. After this reading, it is reported that additional auspicious phenomena, including extraordinary natural phenomena, were said to have occurred. For example, immediately after the second "descent" of the text, Wang Qinruo presented 8,000 pieces of fungus, viewed as auspicious. Another individual presented a five-colored golden jade cinnabar and over 8,700 red fungi.[41] Many other auspicious objects arrived from around the country, to the extent that "it was impossible to record them all."[42] These additional reports about various auspicious signs provided sufficient rationalization, which had been lacking before, for performing the ritual. Although the third Heavenly Text received less attention than the first, it helped reconfirm the project already under way. Wang Juzheng, who reported its discovery, was rewarded with promotion.

The court officials in charge did their best to follow the prescriptions of the ritual text regarding *fengshan* protocol so that the ritual's prestige would be magnified. Because it had been 282 years since the last performance of the ritual by Emperor Xuanzong of the Tang dynasty in 726, it was necessary to study the ritual texts. In the fifth month of the year, the Office of Codification (*xiangding suo* 詳定所) reviewed the ritual texts, and set forth all the details about the size and array of the altar and other spaces.[43] In the sixth month, when the office presented a ritual text, *Commentaries on the Fengshan Ritual* (*Fengshan yizhu* 封禪儀注), to the emperor, the emperor asserted, "This ritual has long not been performed. If the ceremony is not adhered to precisely, how can it achieve its aims?" Court officials, for example, argued over the kind of material that should be used for brewing ritual liquor according to references in the various classical texts.[44]

As the day of the ritual drew near, preparations by the imperial court intensified. The emperor personally rehearsed the ritual at the Hall for Venerating Governance (*chongzheng dian* 崇政殿).[45] Soon the ritual taboo was proclaimed.

---

40. SSJBM 22.130.

41. *Songshi* records that this occurred in the ninth month after the Heavenly text was presented at the Imperial Ancestral Shrine or *taimiao*.

42. SSJBM 22.130.

43. CB 69.1543; SHY Li 22.4–5.

44. CB 70.1564–1565.

45. CB 70.1566; SS 7.137.

For a month after the seventeenth day of the ninth month, the slaughtering of sacrificial animals and the playing of music were prohibited nationwide. And those who were supposed to participate in the *fengshan* ritual were required to keep days of ritual fasting and take ritual baths. These people included high officials, musicians, officers handling the ritual vessels, horsemen, and soldiers.[46] In the ninth month, a ceremony offering the Heavenly Text took place at the Imperial Ancestral Shrine, *taimiao* 太廟, the place for the classical imperial ritual.[47] More auspicious signs were reported from surrounding areas. In the tenth month, the emperor adopted a vegetarian diet in preparation for the ritual, although Wang Dan suggested giving it up because the procession would be arduous given the winter weather. Meanwhile, an imperial astrologist reported auspicious stellar movements.

The much-awaited procession set off with great fanfare. On the fourth day of the tenth month, the procession departed from Qianyuan Gate. The Heavenly Text was at the front, loaded on a large jade chariot. Yellow flags borne aloft followed it, surrounded by drummers and flutists. Daoist liturgists and Commissioners of Assistance followed right after them. High-ranking officials bowed reverently to the procession below the hall. After a while, the emperor joined the procession by taking a seat in the chariot. The size of the procession spoke to the significance of the event. For this day alone, the number of men on horseback bearing flags, recruited from military offices and ritual offices, totaled at least 1,962.[48] The number of Daoist liturgists employed during the procession on the road was 30 per day, and 100 on the days of departure from the palace and arrival at Tai Mountain.[49]

While the procession was en route, the participants observed additional auspicious signs. For example, they observed that a divine aura arose on top of the Heavenly Text carved in jade.[50] Wang Qinruo again brought over 8,000 auspicious fungi on the eighteenth day of the procession. The ascent of Tai Mountain, 1,545 meters in height, was perilous. In a display of enthusiasm and piety, the emperor chose to walk up the notoriously steep mountain when the horses refused to proceed any further, despite the staff's suggestion that he ride by chariot. His enthusiasm far exceeded that of his officials, in that he alone kept to a strict vegetarian diet.[51]

---

46. SHY Li 22.16.

47. CB 70.1560; SS 7.137.

48. SHY Li 22.10.

49. CB 69.1545.

50. CB 70.1569.

51. Sima Guang, *Sushui jiwen*, 7.96

On the twenty-fourth day of the month, or twenty days after the departure from the palace, the entourage was finally able to perform the *fengshan* ritual. The emperor presented an offering to the Supreme Thearch of August Heaven (*haotian shangdi* 昊天上帝) accompanied by Taizu and Taizong at the round altar. The emperor ordered a group of officials to make offerings to the Thearchs of the Five Directions and other deities at the *fengshan* altar. The ritual in most ways followed what the ritual texts prescribed and how it had been performed in the Tang dynasty. It reflected the main purpose of the ritual, which was to credit Heaven and the royal ancestors for the current emperor's accomplishments.

However, the ritual was significantly augmented by references to the Heavenly Text. Officials of the honor guard presented the Heavenly Text on the left side of the Supreme Monad (*taiyi* 太一). Acting Vice Director of the Secretariat (*nie zhongshushilang* 攝中書侍郎) Zhou Qi 周起 read the writings of the Heavenly Text carved in jade. As the emperor delivered the ritual offering for the participants to share, the acting Vice Director requested that Wang Dan kneel down and proclaim:

Heaven has granted the emperor a celestial tally of the Supreme Monad. Accomplish it and start again; and eternally safeguard [your] people.[52]

Immediately upon the completion of the ritual, the emperor and his staff made a strategic effort to cast it as his great accomplishment. Observing auspicious natural phenomena around the ritual altar, the whole entourage took them to be a celestial blessing of the ritual.

Following after the ritual, the emperor was congratulated by various groups of people, including both civil and military officials, royal family members, foreign guests, respected elders, and Daoist and Buddhist clergies.[53] Because a large number of people from these groups requested that the *fengshan* ritual be performed at the meeting organized by Wang Dan, their appearance in this honorable scene could be read as a reward for their petition.

The emperor, the Son of Heaven, then primarily presented himself as the granter of blessings. First, he proclaimed a wide amnesty and three days of national festivities as well. He awarded special benefits to both civil and military officers who participated in the ritual. Those prefects through which the procession had passed received the benefit of tax and corvée reductions for the

---

52. CB 70.1571; SS 7.138.

53. CB 70.1572.

following year. Those local residents who petitioned to perform the *fengshan* ritual now could see that the whole communities were rewarded. The emperor also elevated the status of the space where the ritual took place. The County of Offering to Heaven (*qianfeng xian* 乾奉縣) was renamed the County of Venerating the Talisman (*fengfu xian* 奉符縣). The emperor also exercised his authority in the area of religion by granting titles to the deities of temples and shrines which he visited on the return to his palace. The foremost example was his visit to Qufu, Confucius' hometown near Tai Mountain. The emperor granted Duke Wen of Zhou (Zhou Wengong 周文公), the paragon of the ruler-sage idealized by Confucius, the title of the King of Dedication to Letters (*wenxian wang* 文憲王) and ordered a shrine to be built for him in Qufu. At the shrine of Confucius, the emperor made the generous gift of three hundred thousand taels of copper cash and three hundred bolts of cotton cloth to the forty-sixth-generational descendant of Confucius who was the caretaker of the shrine.

Furthermore, the emperor added two more characters to Confucius's previous title proclaimed in the Tang dynasty, so that the latter's official title became the King of the Mysterious Sage, Proclaimer of Letters (*xuansheng wenxuan wang* 玄聖文宣王).[54] The word *xuan* meant mysterious and dark, which was one of the most prominent terms in Daoism. The *Xu zizhi tongjian changbian* (*A Sequel to the Comprehensive Mirror for Aids in Governance in Detailed Version*) gave two textual references for why such a title was given to Confucius.

> *Chunqiu yankong tu* 春秋演孔圖 reads, "Confucius' mother was visited by the Dark Emperor in a dream and gave birth to Confucius; therefore he is called the Dark Sage." In *Zhuangzi* 莊子, there is a passage which reads, "Tranquil and peaceful is the Dark Sage; he exemplifies the Way of the simple-minded ruler."[55]

Here, Zhenzong did not just present himself as a patron of Confucianism, but went one step further in positioning himself as the granter of a title to Confucius, one with a strong Daoist association. The Confucian apocryphal text *Chunqiu yankong tu* presents a clue for justifying the title.[56] This move

---

54. CB 70.1574.

55. CB 70.1574. The passage in the *Zhuangzi* has nothing to do with Confucius. Therefore, although the comments explain the origin of the word *xuansheng* 玄聖, the author fails to link the word with Confucius.

56. For the portrayal of Confucius' supernatural birth and supernormal physique in the *Chunqiu yankong tu*, see Dull, "A Historical Introduction," 519–521.

symbolically represented the emperor's combining Confucian and Daoist liturgical traditions for various state rituals in the years to come.

The *fengshan* ritual represented a symbolic conquest, not only in the domestic realm but also in international relations. First of all, the primary motivation for conducting the ritual was to promote the notion that the Song was superior to the Liao. As the result of a treaty, the Song had lost significant ground in its battle to maintain the supreme position that China had held in East Asia. Because the Song paid tribute to the Liao, many other states shifted their tribute from the Song to the Liao, implicitly recognizing that there had been a shift in power.[57] Not long after making the decision to perform the ritual, Sun Shi 孫奭 (962–1033), Vice Director of the Capital Officials Section (*duguan yuanwailang* 都官員外郎), was sent to the Liao state to deliver a letter informing the Khitans of the ritual. Ironically, Sun Shi had led the faction that objected to the performance of the *fengshan* ritual and various nonclassical rituals. As such, Sun Shi's words carried more weight in underscoring the legitimacy of Zhenzong's performance of the ritual as well as the significance of the ritual itself. However, he received the following response:

> "China herself performs the great ritual. Why does she bother to report about the ritual? [The Khitans'] gift for the ritual is considered to be a violation of the conditions of the alliance [of the two states]. The Khitans cannot dare to give away a gift openly."[58]

This response indicated that the Khitans had grasped the Song government's purpose behind the ritual performance and refused to acknowledge it as a proof of Song superiority.

Although the Song government failed to obtain the desired recognition from the Liao state through the ritual, it did receive cordial congratulations and gifts from other states. On the fifth day of the eighth month of 1008, the Song government sent word of the ritual performance to other neighboring states.[59] As the procession was underway, ambassadors of vassal states arrived with gifts, which included Champa, the Tsong-kha Tibetans, Tajik, the Uighur qaghan of Ganzhou, and Srivijaya.[60] An envoy from Tajik met the entourage

---

57. David Curtis Wright, *From War to Diplomatic Parity in Eleventh-century China: Sung's Foreign Relations with Kitan Liao* (Leiden and Boston: Brill, 2005).

58. CB 69.1548.

59. SHY Shihuo 41.32.

60. SS Benji 7, 7.140.

in the middle of the procession and presented a jade ritual tablet, saying, "May [Your Majesty] accept this gift. Your Excellence Sage Lord of China performs the *fengshan* ritual. We have therefore come from afar to present this." [61] Once the emperor returned to the palace from forty-seven days of journeying, the previously indifferent Khitans also sent ambassadors to offer their congratulations.[62] The Song believed these visits were a diplomatic achievement which created a momentum confirming the state's alliance with other states.

As such, the *fengshan* ritual transformed the emotional zeal garnered from the event of the Heavenly Text into more practical political capital. In the episode of the Heavenly Text, the emperor did not specify which supernatural agent had granted the Heavenly Text—Heaven or the Jade Emperor—nor did he identify the spiritual being who appeared in his dream. In the absence of clear textual reference to validate the supernatural agent or the event itself, the *fengshan* ritual legitimated great emperorship within the imperial ritual tradition.

## *The Mythmaking of the Divine Origin of the Royal Family*

The *fengshan* ritual was one of the imperial rituals that delineated the relation between Heaven and the imperial family, though not included in the classical ritual texts. However, this concept was nothing new and lacked the power to appeal to the general public on a long-term basis. It was a one-time event, one that could not be repeated during the reign of an emperor. Against this background, the myth of the Sacred Ancestor was developed three years after the *fengshan* ritual. This was based on the emperor's other mystical experiences, which provided a strong theoretical justification for other ensuing ritual events during his reign.

In the second month of 1009, the then little-known ritual specialist (*fangshi* 方士) Wang Jie 王偡 (997–1022) came up with an interesting story.[63] He claimed that he had encountered a Daoist master whose last name was Zhao, coincidently the same as that of the imperial family. From him, Wang learned the art of alchemy and received a divine sword. Wang asserted, "Doubtless, he is the Lord of Immortality and the Commissioner of Destiny (*siming zhenjun* 司命眞君). He is none other than the Sacred Ancestor (*shengzu* 聖祖)." Liu

---

61. CB 70.1570.

62. SS 7.139.

63. SSJBM 22.131; CB 71.1593–4.

Chenggui 劉承珪 (949–1012),[64]a high-ranking eunuch, heard the story and confirmed its veracity. Based on this story, the Sacred Ancestor received the title of *Siming zhenjun*. The successful storyteller Wang benefited substantially from this report. He was appointed to the new government post of General of the Left Military Guard (*zuo wuwei jiangjun* 左武衛將軍). From that time, Wang's star continued to rise.[65]

While the official recognition of Wang Jie's mystical encounter was a milestone in the formulation of the identity of the Sacred Ancestor, in the tenth month of 1012 there was another significant development in the construction of this myth. This time, it was none other than the emperor who claimed to have a mystical experience. The emperor announced to the high officials that he had had two notable dreams on successive nights. The *Songshi jishi benmo* records the account of the emperor as follows:

> I dreamed that a divine man delivered the order of the Jade Emperor, saying, "In the past, I ordered your ancestor Zhao Yuanlang 趙元朗 to give you the Heavenly Text. Today, I ordered him to see you again." Next day, I dreamed that the divine man delivered the Sacred Ancestor's words. "My seat is in the Western Dipper. Set up six seats and wait." That day I set up a ritual enclosure at the Hall of Extended Mercy with musicians playing five drums and one flute. First, I smelled an unfamiliar fragrance. After a short while, yellow light filled the hall. The Sacred Ancestor arrived. As I made obeisance to him repeatedly below the hall, all of a sudden six people arrived. As I bowed to the Sacred Ancestor, all of them sat down. The Sacred Ancestor ordered me, saying, " I am one of the nine rulers of theocrats. I am in fact the earliest ancestor of the Zhao clan. I am none other than the Emperor of Xuanyuan 軒轅 [i.e., the Yellow Emperor] who repeatedly descended [to the earth]. During the Later Tang period [923–936], I descended again to take charge of the Zhao clan. As of today, it has been one hundred years. The Emperor [i.e., Zhenzong] is excellent at protecting and nourishing people. Do not neglect my previous order." Thereupon, he left the seat. He mounted clouds and disappeared.[66]

---

64. Later his name was changed to Liu Chenggui 劉承規.

65. Isabel Robinet, *Taoism: Growth of a Religion* (Stanford, CA: Stanford University Press, 1997), 212–213.

66. SSJBM 22.134–135, 20.2a–2b; CB 79.1797–98 records the same incident with minor variations.

This account established the identity of the divine being, who had appeared to the emperor in his mystical experience just prior to the affair of the Heavenly Text, as the Sacred Ancestor. It further elaborated upon his identity within the celestial world. First, he was the god of the Western Dipper; and second, he was the Yellow Emperor whose incarnations appeared on earth repeatedly. Furthermore, this report made it clear that it was the Jade Emperor who oversaw the emperor's mystical encounters and dynastic prosperity. In addition, the above account added a new element that emphasized the virtue of Emperor Zhenzong as a precondition for the mystical experiences and celestial blessings.[67]

Another record, the *Xu Zizhi tongjian changbian*, provides us with more details concerning the identity of the Sacred Ancestor.

The Celestial worthy 天尊 said, "I am one of the nine rulers of theocrats. I am in fact the earliest ancestor of the Zhao clan. I am none other than the Emperor of Xuanyuan 軒轅 [i.e., the Yellow Emperor] who descended [to the earth] again. The world understands me as the son of Shaodian 少典; that is wrong.[68] My mother was affected by thunder and dreamed of a heavenly man. She gave birth to me at Shouqiu [at Qufu County in Shandong Province]. During the Later Tang, on the first day of the seventh month, I descended to govern the human world and take charge of the Zhao clan.[69]

The above account pinpoints the birthplace of the Sacred Ancestor to Shouqiu, a birthplace of the Yellow Emperor in the traditional myth.[70]

A more elaborate theory about his birth had emerged. The *Songchao shishi* 宋朝事實 (*Verified Affairs of the Song Dynasty*) describes the thunder that affected his mother. In commentary, it reads:

---

67. Emperor Xuanzong of the Tang dynasty had made the similar claim that Laozi was the ancestor of the Tang imperial family. Charles Benn, "Religious Aspects of Emperor Hsüan-tsung's Taoist Ideology," in *Buddhist and Daoist Practices in Medieval Chinese Society*, ed. David W. Chappell (Honolulu: University of Hawaii Press, 1987), 127–145; Victor Xiong, "Ritual Innovations and Taoism under Tang Xuanzong," *T'oung Pao* 82, nos. 4–5 (1996): 258–316.

68. This passage denies a theory that Yellow Emperor was the son of Shaodian, as recorded in an ancient text. Sima Qian, *The Grand Scribe's Records*, vol. 1, 1.

69. CB 79.1798.

70. Tiziana Lippiello, "The Treatise on Auspicious Omens As Tokens (*Furui zhi*)": A Translation of Chapter 27 of *Songshu*," in *Auspicious Omens and Miracles in Ancient China: Han, Three Kingdoms and Six Dynasties* (Sankt Augustin: Monumenta Serica Institute, 2001), 266.

In the beginning of the dynasty, there was a commissioner [of a government office] who spoke to the emperor as follows: "This state accepted the ruler abdicated by the (Later) Zhou state. The (Later) Zhou takes up the virtue of Wood [*mu* 木] [among the Five Phases]. Wood begets Fire [*huo* 火]. The destiny of this dynasty corresponds to the virtue of Fire. Its color is usually red. On the fifth day of the Ten Heavenly Stems calendar cycle, make offering to the Red Emperor, by taking him as the Emperor of Responsive Birth [*gansheng di* 感生帝].[71]

This account connects his birth with the existing theory of Emperor of Responsive Birth that emerged during the late Western Han dynasty (206 BCE–24CE). According to the theory, each of five celestial deities in turn descends to the human world and through a human mother begets a semi-divine successor, who will establish a new dynasty.[72] This theory justifies dynastic changes by connecting them with the natural and cosmic process explained by the Theory of Five Phases. It also further justifies Taizu's usurpation of the Zhou emperorship, because it, too, was part of this inevitable cosmic process of change.

Immediately after the public announcement of the emperor's dream, the government issued an imperial edict stating that two words associated with the Sacred Ancestor, *yuan* 元 (origin) and *lang* 郎 (an official title), could not be used under any circumstances. The most notable example of adherence to this edict was the permanent changing of the name of a popular deity, Xuanwu 玄武 to Zhenwu 真武, because *xuan* was deemed similar in sound to *yuan*.[73] Moreover, the two words were used interchangeably in different ancient versions of the *Daode jing*.[74] The honorary title previously conferred upon Confucius was also changed from *Xuansheng wenxuan wang* 玄聖文宣王 to *Zhisheng wenxuan wang* 至聖文宣王.[75]

The deification of the first ancestor of the clan also involved the granting of an even longer official title to the Sacred Ancestor. In an account of the first dream of Zhenzong in late 1007, the unknown divine entity was referred to simply as a divine being (*shenren* 神人). In the tenth month, he received the

---

71. Li You, *Sonchao shishi* 1.4 and 7.112. *Songshi* has entry of "*gansheng di*" in Li 3, 100.2461.

72. Lü, *Power of Words*, 84.

73. SHY Li 37.27, SSJBM 22.135. For a history of Zhenwu worship, see Shin-yi Chao, *Daoist Rituals, State Religion, and Popular Practices: Zhenwu Worship from Song to Ming (960—1644)* (London and New York: Routledge, 2011).

74. SHY Li 37.27; SSJBM 22.135.

75. CB 79.1808.

title of the Celestial Venerable, Commissioner of Destiny, and the Upper-level Duke Protector of Life in the Nine Theocrats (*jiutian siming shangqing baosheng tianzun* 九天司命上卿保生天尊).[76] When the myth of the Sacred Ancestor attained its fullest expression, in 1009, the official title of the Sacred Ancestor had sixteen characters: the Great Emperor Heavenly Incomparable, the Sacred Ancestor of the Supreme Spirit and High Way of Nine Theocrats, the Guard of Destiny and Protector of Life (*shengzu shangling gaodao jiutian siming baosheng tianzun dadi* 聖祖上靈高道九天司命保生天尊大帝).[77] In 1014, he was further identified as the god of Eastern Peak or Tai Mountain, and his name was changed to the Perfected Lord of the Sacred, Commissioner of Destiny, and Official of Protection at Eastern Peak (*dongyue siming qingyou sheng zhenjun* 東岳司命卿佑聖眞君).

During this time, the cult of the God of Eastern Peak was quite prevalent, to the extent that some commoner(s) tried to make offerings to the god by illegally melting military weapons.[78] This conflation of the traditional local god of Tai Mountain with the Sacred Ancestor was a clever move to connect the *fengshan* ritual with the newly invented myth. A still extant wall painting, surmised to have been drawn during the Song, at the Hall of Heavenly Blessing in the Dai Shrine (*daimiao* 岱廟) located at the foot of Tai Mountain took Zhenzong as a model of the god of the mountain. The painting entitled "The Figure of God of Tai Mountain Starting the Return Home" splendidly illustrates Zhenzong's hunting excursion to Tai Mountain with a large entourage and his return to the palace on a grand scale. The cult's continuing popularity was well exemplified by the eighteen anecdotes related to the God of Eastern Peak entailed in *The Records of Listeners* (*Yijian zhi* 夷堅志) written by Hong Mai 洪邁 (1123–1202) in the twelfth century.[79]

As this myth emphasized divine conception, the mother of the Sacred Ancestor was also venerated. Her shrine was built at Shouqiu in Qufu County, where she was said to have given birth to the Sacred Ancestor. She began to be called the Mother of the Sacred Ancestor (*shengzu mu* 聖祖母) and assumed the title of Great Sacred Empress of the Primal Heaven (*yuantian da shenghou*

---

76. "Shang jiutian siming shangqing Baosheng tianzun hao zhao" 上九天司命上卿保生天尊號詔, QSW 11:234.393.

77. SHY Li 51.10; CB 79.1800.

78. CB 83.1906.

79. Richard von Glahn, *The Sinister Way: The Divine and the Demonic in Chinese Religious Culture* (Berkeley: University of California Press, 2004), 170–173. Glahn, however, fails to

元天大聖后).[80] In commemoration of his birth, the government changed the name of Qufu County to County of the Immortal's Origin (*xianyuan* 仙源).[81]

In a nutshell, as the Confucian concept of the emperor as the Son of Heaven did not leave room for additional development of an imaginative narrative, Zhenzong for good reason turned to the pantheons and cosmologies developed within Daoism and the traditions of popular religion. In the newly invented myth of the Sacred Ancestor, he wished to promote the concept that there was a point of juncture between the two worlds—incarnation—and that this juncture ran through the blood relations of the imperial family. This concept was the royal imaginary that Zhenzong attempted to derive from the myth, which the *fengshan* ritual had not been able to provide. In the making of this dynastic myth, Zhenzong took the lead by presenting narratives about his own mystical encounters. Other people who contributed to making this myth by adding more believable information also received substantial benefits.

## *Visualizing and Enacting the Royal Imaginary*

The government made concerted efforts to reorient the emperor's dream and mystical experiences from a private experience to one that was known and understood by people from all walks of society. For this purpose, the government desired to establish multiple venues where people could commemorate the myth and venerate royal ancestors both within the palace and throughout the nation. With relative peace after the Shanyuan Alliance, the government spent its financial and human resources on constructing extravagant temples, installing ritual objects, and holding ritual performances.

For Zhenzong, the recognition of the importance of ceremonial architecture as the outward expression of the ideology of the dynasty was immediate, and construction of a monumental temple was begun right after the events of the Heavenly Text and the *fengshan* ritual. The Heavenly Text would be housed in an extravagant government-built temple, the Temple of Reflecting and Responding to the Realm of Jade Purity (*yuqing zhaoying gong* 玉清昭應宮), to be located in the capital city, Kaifeng. Built over a period of six years, the grand temple would prove to be a landmark construction of the Song dynasty, with 2,610 room-units (*qu* 區) in a compound measuring 310 by 413 paces

---

point out that the god was identified as the Sacred Ancestor whose cult was promoted with ideological arguments.

80. SHY Li 51.10.

81. CB 79.1803; SSJBM 22.135; SHY Fangyu 5.16.

(*bu*), or 477 by 636 meters.[82] Support for the temple's construction, however, was mixed. High officials Ding Wei, Li Zonge 李宗諤 (964–1012), and Liu Chenggui believed in the project, but many other ranking officials objected to it. For example, in a critical memorial Wang Zeng 王曾 (978–1038) pointed out that Zhenzong had already used up a great amount of resources in the construction of other temples and shrines.[83] However, Ding Wei, who was in charge of finances, insisted:

> Your Majesty, there is wealth in the nation. Is there any reason not to build a temple to make an offering to the Supreme Thearch (*shangdi* 上帝)? Furthermore, now there is no prince [to inherit the throne]. Building a temple in a dry place within the palace is exactly the right way to pray for such a blessing.[84]

This prioritization of ritual over other aspects of governing reflected an emphasis on ritual as a means of bringing good fortune to the state.

In 1009, the emperor pursued the building construction, despite facing obstacles such as difficult transport of materials, the draining of the military for the purposes of labor, and astronomical costs associated with the exaggerated demands of overseers Ding Wei and Liu Chenggui. Because many of the 340,000 workers per day employed in the building of the new temple were soldiers, the military system of the districts near the capital city ceased to function. All kinds of the finest construction materials were brought in from across the nation.[85] Ding Wei acquired a bad reputation due to his harsh treatment of workers, forcing them to work overnight in order to complete the temple as quickly as possible.[86] Liu Chenggui often made workers redo work even when using gold and jade, which led to astronomical costs.[87]

In addition, in 1013 the government initiated a project of casting sculptural images to be installed in the Temple of Reflecting and Responding to the Realm of Jade Purity upon completion of its construction. Illustrating their resolve in the project despite challenges, the imperial court decided to cast

---

82. Xu Song and Chen Zhicao, *Songhuiyao jigao bubian* 宋會要輯稿補編 (Beijing: Xinhua shuju, 1988), 24–26.

83. CB 71.1612.

84. CB 71.1602.

85. Li You, *Songchao shishi* 7.107–108.

86. CB 71.1611; Li You, *Songchao shishi* 7.109.

87. CB 81.1839.

the bronze sculptures in Jian'an Commandery 建安軍 (present-day Yizheng 儀徵) on the north side of the Yangzi River. After a serious discussion concerning the transportation of the sculptures to the capital city, they finally decided to use boats. The imperial government took the transportation of the revered sculptures as a form of imperial parade, one that attempted to demonstrate the reign's ideological, religious, and social imaginary. The procession of the Sacred Ancestor sculpture featured an imperial boat with a ritual enclosure and carrying four sculptures treated as sacred objects: two of celestial emperors, the Jade Emperor and the Sacred Ancestor, and two of human emperors, Taizu and Taizong. Thus the procession was designed to intertwine royal dignity and supernatural authority. Ten other boats carried various imperial emblems. Chariots with grand titles, like the Chariot of the Sacred Sculpture of the Jade August Supreme Thearch, carried additional sculptures.[88] As many as 2,500 honor guards and 300 musicians walked along the Yangzi river to escort the boats. The sculptures made their way through various provinces and regions in processions featuring entourages of Daoist and Buddhist liturgists and musical bands.

The journey was reported to maintain an active religious aura. The report of an officer, Zhao Zhou 趙州, best exemplified this tendency:

> When the boat carrying the sacred sculptural images and jade stone passed by the stone bridge of the province, the water was shallow and the passage was rough. A black dragon created waves so that the boat could pass [under the bridge]. The river became very rapid. Once the boat had passed the bridge, the river water became shallow and rough as before.[89]

Meanwhile, at the palace the emperor and the court officials were awaiting the arrival of the sculptures with religious fervor.[90] The devout emperor took it upon himself to serve as a visible role model observing a ritual fast at the Hall of Everlasting Spring (*changcun dian* 長春殿), as did other officials who stayed up a whole night at an audience hall at the imperial court.

If not already convinced on spiritual grounds, the extraordinary parade provided, through material inducements or legal compulsion, incentives to

---

88. Song Minqiu and Song Shou, *Song da zhaolingji* 宋大詔令集 (hereafter SDZLJ) (Beijing: Zhonghua shuju, 1997), 149.554.

89. CB 80.1828.

90. CB 80.1825.

accept its ideological premises. The procession carved out a path that enlisted local and surrounding officials and residents, whether enthusiastically or not, as participants. Local government officials met the processions with welcoming banquets. Residents in these areas were legally required to greet the entourage and practice ritual fasting for seven days.[91] People in these areas had their taxes reduced by 10 percent for the summer.[92] The local governments were not allowed to punish criminals for two days as the procession passed through. The central government proclaimed an amnesty, especially for criminals facing the death penalty.

After much fanfare accompanying the completion of the temple in the tenth month of 1014, the Heavenly Text was finally installed within the temple,[93] which also housed the golden sculptural images of the Sacred Ancestor and others.[94] During this time, gold was used in so many ritual items and sculptural images that its price was inflated.[95] A nationwide festival was proclaimed.[96] This temple was open to low-ranking officers and commoners for the first fifteen days in the first month of every year for burning incense.[97] An anonymous scholar who paid a visit to the temple was awestricken:

As for its grandeur and splendor, I cannot describe its image. I look at it from afar and just see the jade tiles that rise up glittering in the air. They illuminate the capital city and the nation. With every beam of sunlight, the floating color of green illuminates. I cannot look at it directly . . . Its expenditure cost several hundred millions. The amount of gold used cannot be even calculated . . ."[98]

To promote the veneration cult of royal ancestors, as represented primarily by their portrait sculptures, a new ritual space called the Royal Image Hall

---

91. Wang Su, *Wenzheng Wanggong yishi* 文正王公遺事, *Quan Song Biji* 全宋筆記 (hereafter QSBJ), 1st series (Zhengzhou: Daxiang chubanshe, 2003), 5:188.

92. CB 80: 1821, 1824, 1825–26; SS Benji 7, 7.153; Li You, *Songchao shishi*, 7.110.

93. This example of the Heavenly Text cast in gold might be the one currently housed in the National Palace Museum in Taipei.

94. Song Minqiu, *Cunming tuicaolu* 春明退朝錄 (Beijing: Zhonghua shuju, 1980), 2.4.

95. Wang Yong, *Yanyi yimou lu* 燕翼藝謀錄, rpt. with Wang Zhi 王銍, *Moji* 默紀 (Beijing: Zhonghua shuju, 1997), 2.20.

96. CB 83.1899 and 1900.

97. CB 83.1903.

98. Tian Kuang, *Rulin Gongyi* 儒林公議, QSBJ, 1st series, 1: 5.92–93.

(*shenyu dian* 神御殿) was created. A ritual of venerating the Sacred Ancestor began when the myth took on its complete form after the emperor's dream in 1012. The emperor issued an edict concerning the installation of the sculpture of the Sacred Ancestor in a hall behind the Jade Emperor Hall within the Temple of Reflecting and Responding to the Realm of Jade Purity, which was partially constructed at the moment.[99] The emperor launched another program of building extravagant temples widely in the territory in which the Royal Image Hall would be located. This new type of temple was called the Temple of Radiant Spirit (*jingling gong* 景靈宮).[100] Among them, the one built in the Royal Image Hall in the capital city played a central role in the ritual veneration. Wang Dan, Grand Councilor, was in charge of the construction of this particular temple, which boasted 1,322 room-units and was completed in 1014.[101] Within the temple, Wang Qinruo installed eighty-four images, including those of the royal family members and immortals listed in the *Daozang* 道藏, the collection of the Daoist texts.[102] In commemoration of the completion of the Shrine of Great Ultimate (*taiji guan* 太極觀) within this Temple of Radiant Spirit, the government granted an amnesty and opened the temple for public view, including for commoners.[103]

The Royal Image Hall was a distinctively Northern Song innovation dating to Zhenzong's reign. In addition to the major temples mentioned above, many Daoist and Buddhist temples housed royal image halls, and some individuals did so in their houses.[104] Although emperors of the previous era drew their portrait paintings, Patricia Ebrey argues that there was no evidence that they were used for ancestral offerings.[105] Although there are a few records of Taizu placing portrait paintings of his parents in two Buddhist temples, it was not until the early years of Zhenzong's reign that the installation of portrait paintings became a common practice. Soon after the death of Taizong in

---

99. CB 79.1800.

100. For the edict of building the *jingling gong* in 1012, see QSW 12: 244.175; concerning the *iingling gong* in local areas, see CB 84.1990.

101. CB 83.1890.

102. SDZLJ 136.479.

103. SDZLJ 180.652 and 144.528.

104. Installing the Royal Image Hall in a private house was later prohibited as a result of officials' criticism. CB 225.5568 and 331.7969; Ye Mengde, *Shilin yanyu* 石林燕語 (Beijing: Zhonghua shuju, 1984), 1.4.

105. Patricia B. Ebrey, "Portrait Sculptures in Imperial Ancestral Rites in Song China," *T'oung Pao* 87 (1997): 49.

997, his portrait was installed at an altar in a Daoist temple that was in the care of the imperial tomb Yongxi Mausoleum (*yongxi ling* 永熙陵). The installation ceremony was so grand that 500 soldiers were deployed.[106] Zhenzong made food offerings in the morning and evening, and burned incense four times a day.[107] In 999, the portrait painting of Taizong was installed in the Founding Sage Monastery (*qisheng yuan* 啓聖院) of Buddhism in Kaifeng, his father's supposed birthplace.[108] Zhenzong made the event a dramatic official event in which he showed his sincere filial piety with emotional outbursts. Seeing his father's portrait, the emperor "bowed and wailed; and everyone therein sobbed."[109] It is noteworthy to mention that Zhenzong had already performed the classical imperial ritual at the Imperial Ancestral Shrine, where imageless spirit tablets were placed in altars. So far, the veneration of the late emperor was not too far from the idea of Confucian classical ritual, apart from placing a portrait, in the place of an imageless spirit tablet, in order to draw out more emotion as Zhenzong staged the installation ritual.

From that time onward, in the first month of a new year, court officials were required to pay a morning visit to the image hall.[110] In the following years, many local Buddhist temples began to build halls for the portraits of Taizu so that commoners could pay veneration to it. In 1005, his portrait was installed in the Jianlong (Buddhist) Temple 建隆寺 in Yangzhou Prefecture.[111] In 1011, the government built a Royal Image Hall for Taizu in the Chan Monastery of Responding to Heaven (*yingtian canyuan* 應天禪院), and another in 1014 in the Abundant Felicity Temple (*hongqing gong* 鴻慶宮) of Daoism at Nanjing.[112] The *Songshi* lists only seven representative image halls for both Taizu and Taizong, and fourteen for Zhenzong in various Buddhist and Daoist temples.[113] However, this list does not exhaust the number of the halls, as recorded partially in "*Shenyu dian* [Royal Image Hall]" in the *Song huiyao jigao* 宋會要輯稿 (*Collected Manuscripts on the Various Aspects of the Song Dynasty*).[114]

---

106. SHY Li 37.27.

107. SHY Li 37.27.

108. SHY Li, "Shenyu dian," 13.1; SS Benji 7, 7.132; TCJBM 18.519; CB 45.962, 51.1107.

109. SS Benji 6, 6.109.

110. CB 45.962; QSW 12:238.27.

111. SS Benji 7, 7.129.

112. CB 75.1716 and 83.1893; Wang Yong, *Yanyi yimou lu*, 2.18.

113. Individual emperors' image halls were established in local areas with which they had particular connections. Ebrey, "Portrait Sculptures," 61–63.

114. SHY Li, 13.

After the establishment of the divine nature of the Sacred Ancestor in 1012, the Royal Image Hall began to function as a place in which to present the dynastic myth. The Temple of Radiant Spirit functioned as the central ritual space for commemorating the deceased emperors' divine origins, and it was here that halls for the Sacred Ancestor, Taizu, and Taizong were built; later, those for Zhenzong and subsequent emperors were added. In 1016, the emperor composed a poem, "Praise to the Temple of Radiant Spirit," which was to be carved in stone.[115] Furthermore, Zhenzong installed the portrait sculptures of deceased high officials, standing near the late emperors whom they had served.[116] Liu Chenggui's sculpture was the first one installed, as an attendant of the two emperors in the Hall for the Two Sages (*ersheng dian* 二聖殿).[117] In addition, the state honored Wang Jie for his contributions to the myth of the Sacred Ancestor by installing his portrait sculpture in the Royal Image Hall. Images of royal ancestors were displayed in a way that which rendered the aura of their semidivinity; this intent was best exemplified by the presence of attendants. Such scenes are typical in Buddhist and Daoist temples where celestial retinues flank the main deity. By borrowing the framework of iconic images and their spatial arrangement from religious liturgies, the cult of the Sacred Ancestor took on a strong religious aura.

As Daoist deities and the concept of the celestial world became the framework of Zhenzong's royal imaginary, he promoted the cult of the Jade Emperor, one of the highest gods in Daoism.[118] Zhenzong also changed the official title of the Jade Emperor from the Great Emperor of Jade August (*yuhuang dadi* 玉皇大帝) to the Great Heavenly Emperor of Jade August, Supreme Creator of Heavens Who Holds Tallies and Imperial Calendar and Contains the True Body of Dao (太上開天執符御曆含眞體道玉皇大天帝).[119] The shortened version of this title was the Great Heavenly Emperor of Jade August (*yuhuang da tiandi*). The word *tian* or heaven was inserted into the old name, *Yuhuang*

---

115. TCJBM 20.15b.

116. Xuanzong of the Tang was the first person who made his own portrait sculpture along with those of other high officials to flank Laozi's sculpture. In addition, he installed his sculpture in a particular ritual hall so that officials would make obeisance to it before they took up their official duties. Benn, "Religious Aspects," 137–138.

117. CB 81.1839.

118. Yamauchi Kōichi, "Hokusō no kokka to gyokko 北宋の國家と玉皇," *Tōhō gakū* 62 (1982): 87–90.

119. CB 83.1894.

*dadi*. Here, Zhenzong wanted to represent the Jade Emperor as the Heavenly Emperor. In the process, he wanted to fuse the Confucian concept of Heaven with the Daoist concept of the Jade Emperor.

In order to honor the Jade Emperor, Zhenzong ordered the building of the Temple of Heavenly Felicity (*tianqing guan* 天慶觀) in various locations in 1012. Local governments were required to build the temple from the ground up on official land or refurbish an existing shrine with the labor of local soldiers.[120] The central government sponsored the maintenance of these temples by providing money from the so-called Heavenly Felicity Fund. After the dream involving the Sacred Ancestor in 1012, the central government decreed that the Hall for the Sacred Ancestor must be built within the Temple of Heavenly Felicity.[121] Through this process, almost all local prefectures throughout the country came to possess a hall for the Sacred Ancestor. Among them, only one in Luoyang was called the *tianqing gong* (lit. the Palace of Heavenly Felicity), signifying its central position.[122]

Early in the first month of 1015, Zhenzong performed the ritual of renaming the Jade Emperor and commanded that all prefectures establish ritual enclosures and all officers and commoners set up incense tables for the Jade Emperor. That same day, he placed the Heavenly Text carved in jade in the Pavilion of the Precious Tally (*baofu ge* 寶符閣) to be venerated as a sacred object.[123] His own writings, carved in stone, were also placed underneath the pavilion.[124] Within the pavilion, his own portrait sculpture in official robes as an attendant serving the Heavenly Text was placed.[125] The emperor personally ascended to the pavilion and made a wine offering. Its message embraced the concept of emperor as the Son of Heaven, or the agent carrying out Heaven's will on earth. At the same time it represented him as a religious medium to receive and guard the revelatory message. The fact that Zhenzong's sculpture stood in the ritual space put forth the idea that he also occupied the space of the royal imaginary.

---

120. TCJBM 20.17a; SHY Li 5.18–19 and Li. 20.12

121. Li You, *Songchao shishi*, 7.110. Having the Temple of Reflecting and Responding to the Jade Purity as a model for space arrangement and ritual objects, they placed the sculptures of the Sacred Ancestor and his attendants. SHY Li 5.18; Shi Su 施宿, *Kuaiji zhi* 會稽志, Yingyin Wenyuange Siku quanshu, vol. 486 (Taipei: Taiwan Shangwu yinshu guan, 1983), 7.

122. Ebrey, "Portrait Sculptures," 52–53.

123. CB 83.1889.

124. SSJBM 22.136.

125. CB 84.1911.

In this way, Zhenzong inaugurated another form of royal ancestor veneration, for which he created nationwide ritual programs and ritual spaces. In this new form of ritual, the ways of venerating royal ancestors were significantly changed. Not only was the Sacred Ancestor worshiped as a god, but also the late emperors were venerated as having divine auras. Although Zhenzong did not make their divinity explicit, late emperors were commemorated as living beings in the celestial world. In this new form, the royal ancestors were presented as if they were alive in the form of sculptures, which was not possible in the classical imperial ritual. Zhenzong hoped that their presence in various temples and shrines and ritual offerings to them would strengthen the legitimacy of the imperial family.

## *Institutionalizing and Disseminating the Royal Imaginary*

As the myths and rituals consistent with imperial ideology had developed to great lengths, Emperor Zhenzong wished to instill their acceptability and implant them in societal memory for all levels of society as part of their daily lives for generations to come. The central government employed various methods in order to ensure the performance of rituals on an annual basis, in particular by designating a new ritual calendar that included festive days. In addition, Zhenzong mandated government officials to participate in and supervise the rituals and festivals. At each stage of the development of the myth, Zhenzong issued edicts to publicize his mystical experiences and other related events and forced the entire population to participate in their celebration.

One of the most salient institutional inventions developed during his reign was the creation of various national holidays to celebrate the myth and the performance of rituals. The *Songshi* reads, "All festive days did not exist in the past. They date from the reign of Zhenzong."[126] Right after the event of the Heavenly Text in 1008, the government proclaimed that the third day of the first month would be the Heavenly Felicity Festival (*tianqing jie* 天慶節), celebrating the descent of the Heavenly Text. The celebration was to be five days long. People were not to work for three days: the day of the festival, the day before, and the day after. In the capital city, lanterns were kept lit in Buddhist and Daoist temples for five days, and street lamps remained lit long into the night. Both officers (*shi* 士) and commoners (*xu* 庶) held banquets as part of the festivities. In the

---

126. SS Zhi 65, 112.2680.

western capital city, Luoyang, ritual enclosures were set up for seven days at government offices and Daoist temples. In all the other provinces, ritual enclosures were to be set up for three days. Butchery and criminal punishments were prohibited for seven days.[127] In 1010, on the festive day, a special ordination of a Daoist master was granted for temples within all circuits in Kaifeng and Luoyang: for each temple, one out of ten was designated for ordination, which demonstrated the religion's close association with the cult of the Sacred Ancestor. This state-initiated public festival resonated with a religious festival that local communities celebrated within Buddhist and Daoist temples, with or without state sponsorship, as seen in the Ghost Festival during the Tang.[128]

The Descent of the Sacred Ancestor Festival (*jiangsheng jie* 降聖節) celebrated the day of the Sacred Ancestor's mystical encounter with Zhenzong (on the twenty-fourth of the tenth month). The proscriptions connected with this festival were basically the same as those of the Heavenly Felicity Festival. In addition, on this day people prayed for a long life for the emperor, which became a common theme during the Song era as expressed through various popular religious practices. In 1013, the government ordered people to wear the Longevity Belt and the Thread of Continuing Life, and present the Protecting Life Wine to one another.[129] In 1021, the ritual of praying for the extension of the emperor's "allotted lifespan" (*benming* 本命) took place in the Hall for Longevity (*wansui dian* 萬歲殿) at the Temple of Radiant Spirit.[130]

The Celestial Ancestor Festival (*xiantian jie* 先天節) celebrated the birthday of the Sacred Ancestor and was held on the first day of the seventh month. Like the other two festivals, it was five days long. In 1013, at Wang Qinruo's request, for these three festivals the government ordered local government officers to establish ritual enclosures and practice ritual fasting both indoors and outdoors just as for the "great sacrificial rituals" (*dasi* 大祀) of the classical tradition.[131] This policy indicated that the government placed the same weight on these three festivals as on the other classical rituals. A month before the festival, government offices and temples recruited entertainers to rehearse the performance at the Office of Public Order (*siliyuan* 司理院).[132] In

---

127. CB 77.1760; SHY Li 57.28; SSJBM 30.1012.

128. Stephen F. Teiser, *The Ghost Festival in Medieval China* (Princeton, NJ: Princeton University Press, 1996), 5 and 35.

129. CB 80.1830.

130. CB 97.2249.

131. CB 81.1849.

132. CB 81.1849–1850.

1014, the government issued an edict prohibiting the use of two words in all government offices during the festivals: "punishment (*xing* 刑)" and "killing (*sha* 殺）."[133] There were moreover other holidays of lesser significance celebrated at this time. The sixth day of the sixth month was the Heaven's Bestowal Festival (*tiankuang jie* 天貺節), which celebrated the descent of the Heavenly Text at Tai Mountain.[134] The first day of the fourth month was the Celestial Auspiciousness Festival (*tianzheng jie* 天禎節) which celebrated the second descent of the Heavenly Text to the Pavilion of Merit in 1008.[135]

In 1017, the government took another step in combining the myth of the Sacred Ancestor with the imperial ritual tradition by proclaiming another new era called the Celestial Blessings (*tianxi* 天禧). This marked the end of major myth and ritual transformation by Zhenzong, and ushered in a period of institutionalization, through repetitive ritual practices, of the commemoration of previous events. Amid political debacle caused by factional fights and the near-bankruptcy of imperial authority, especially in the years of the emperor's failing mental and physical health from 1019 to his death in 1023, ritual affairs were at the center of official functions at the imperial court. Wang Qinruo finally seized the power of his long-time aspiration as he assumed the Grand Councilor's position after Wang Dan died on the ninth month of 1017. Yet it did not last for long, because he was discharged in 1019 and the position was filled by Kou Zhun 寇準 (961–1023), former Grand Councilor who was discharged in 1006 due to Wang Qinruo's criticism against him. Kou himself was discharged in early 1020.[136]

The new era in 1017 began with the inauguration ceremony orchestrated by Wang Qinruo as the official commissioner. The ceremony included the ritual of the ascendance of the Heavenly Text from the Hall for Great Beginning (*tai-chu dian* 太初展) coupled with the ritual of offering the Heavenly Text carved in jade inside the hall. After finishing these rituals, the emperor made an offering of a seamed cotton garment, a ritual gift, and wine at the Hall for the Two Sages. Because Zhenzong wanted these rituals to be celebrated nationwide, the state ordered the establishment of Daoist ritual enclosures throughout the country. In particular, the state required both military and private

---

133. CB 83.1900.

134. During the Celestial Blessing Festival, executions were not allowed for seven days; during the Celestial Grant Festival, for a day. CB 79.1810.

135. SS Zhi 75, 112.2681.

136. Olsson, "The Structure of Power under the Third Emperor of Sung China," 202–237.

places of residence to set up altars for burning incense, and local officers were supposed to supervise them. At the same time, the emperor along with high officials observed the ritual fast at the Temple of Radiant Spirit.[137]

On the fifteenth day of the same month, the emperor held the ritual of the reading of the Heavenly Text. Following that, he offered the Heavenly Text at the Suburban Sacrifices (*jiaosi* 郊祀) or the Heaven and Earth Ritual, a traditional imperial ritual that had been canonized already in the Han.[138] Here, the emperor made offerings to Taizong and Taizu along with Heaven and Earth. This ritual coordinated the new tradition with the old, so that the former would be bolstered by the force of a tradition whose authority was unchallenged. On the same day, the emperor held another ritual in which the Heavenly Text carved in jade was installed in the Hall for Celestial Peace (*tian'an dian* 天安殿). The sculpture of the Jade Emperor was placed with the Heavenly Text on its east side, and the sculpture of the Sacred Ancestor on its west. Not long afterwards the court held the ritual of reading the text in the hall. The emperor stood at the gate facing west, and officials in their court robes one by one recited the Heavenly Text and presented their writings celebrating the text and the emperor's blessed rule.[139]

In addition, in 1017 the central government distributed the two-inch objects called the Precious Tablets of the Apotheosis of the Sacred Ancestor (*shengzu shenhua jinbao pai* 聖祖神化金寶牌) to the symbolically important mountains in the country, as well as to Daoist and Buddhist temples in the capital city.[140] On the front side they read, "Complete construction of the Temple of Reflecting and Responding to Jade Purity; Treasure of [Commemorating] the Celestial Venerable's ten thousand years of boundless longevity." On the back, they read, "Eternal towns of the blessed land; its city walls around them, all arise in a form of dragon's stretch."[141] Distributing the tablets to Buddhist and Daoist temples as well as to the major mountains was a symbolic act by which the cult of the Sacred Ancestor was further integrated into existing religious traditions.

Because the newly invented myth and ritual was without textual support, Zhenzong and his court officials generated a large number of writings on the subject. The emperor's own writings were imbued with a particular authority

---

137. CB 89.2036.

138. For a history of the ritual, see Wechsler, *Offerings of Jade and Silk*, 107–122.

139. CB 89.2036–37.

140. CB 90.2053.

141. CBBM 21.7a.

that often became an object of veneration. In 1018, some of the emperor's writings in praise of the Jade Emperor and the Sacred Ancestor were carved in stone and installed in temples.[142] Earlier, in 1013, the imperial court had sent to the Library of Daoism copies of the emperor's writings: the "Ode of Great Central Tally of Auspiciousness" (*Dazhong xiangfu song* 大中祥符頌), the "Ode of the Perfected's Travel" (*Zhenyou song* 眞游頌), and the "Records of the Descent of the Sacred Ancestor" (*Shengzu jianglin ji* 聖祖降臨記).[143] The emperor in 1019 made the "Records of the Descent of the Sacred Ancestor" in particular more widely available by distributing it to every official in the capital city after he had ordered them to pay a visit to the Hall of the Perfected's Travel.[144] Wang Qinruo, the architect of the Heavenly Text affair, published more writings than anyone else.[145]

Among all the texts of this kind, the Heavenly Text itself was considered to have the most authority and became an object of veneration in various ritual settings. Earlier, on New Year's Day of 1009 (according to the lunar calendar—the year following the events involving the Heavenly Text), the emperor called together his high-ranking officials in order to venerate the Heavenly Text and designated this veneration as an annual ritual henceforth.[146] In 1017, in celebration of the descent of the Heavenly Text, the court decided to hold the imperial court morning veneration ritual at the Temple of Reflecting and Responding to Jade Purity on the fifteenth day of the first month. In the third month of 1019, the new Grand Councilor Kou Zhun reported another descent of the Heavenly Text.[147] This time, many believed it was fraud, but the emperor accepted it and caused it to be celebrated. Therefore the government issued an edict that all high-ranking court officials must pay a morning visit to the Heavenly Text installed along with the sculptural images of Daoist deities at the Hall of the Perfected's Travel (*zhenyou dian* 眞游殿).[148]

---

142. CB 91.2107.

143. CB 80.1830.

144. CB 93.2153.

145. Some of them were the *Records of the Sacred Ancestor's Previous Celestial Life* (*Shengzu xiantian ji* 聖祖先天紀), the *Accomplishment of the Sacred Ancestor* (*Shengzu shiji* 聖祖事迹), and the *Records of the Sacred Ancestor's Celestial Origin* (*Shengzu tianyuan lu* 聖祖天源錄). The *Accomplishment of the Sacred Ancestor* is as long as twenty *juan*. SSJBM 32.722; CBBM 20.57.

146. CB 71.1587.

147. CB 93.2141.

148. CB 93.2144.

In addition, the veneration ritual of the sacred sculptures constituted a part of the official duties of government officers, particularly court officials. In commemoration of the descent of the Sacred Ancestor, a morning veneration ritual at the Temple of Radiant Spirit on the fifteenth day of the tenth month was mandated as a part of court life starting in 1017.[149] If an officer failed to appear on a temple visit, he was supposed to be jailed. In actuality, the government punished him less harshly by ordering him to recite award-winning poems.[150] Later in 1023, after the death of Zhenzong, Wang Qinruo went to Zhenzong's image hall in the Temple of Radiant Spirit to express his gratitude at being reappointed as Grand Councilor. From that time forward, it became customary for a newly appointed Grand Councilor to pay a visit to the royal ancestral hall at the temple.[151]

The Office of Ritual (*liyiyuan* 禮儀院), which oversaw the imperial rituals and undertook textual study concerning ritual regulation, played a supporting role in the validation and development of the newly developed myth and rituals. Potentially, it could have evaluated the legitimacy of nonclassical ritual performance based on textual study. However, its role was by and large limited to supporting the emperor's decisions and providing the details of rituals selected by the emperor and his close staff members. For example, the emperor had already made the decision concerning what kind of clothes were to be used for various rituals; the Office of Ritual then proclaimed his decision and their justification of it using textual sources. It also recommended that the emperor write particular books about the descent of the Sacred Ancestor, and perform rituals of greeting and installing the sacred sculptures.[152] The lack of autonomy on the part of the most important body overseeing ritual affairs allowed the emperor to pursue the invention and dissemination of the myth and ideology of the family's rule unchecked.

In a nutshell, Zhenzong wished to make all people in the state share the imaginary put forth by himself, and to make that imaginary survive throughout time. High-ranking officials further advanced the state's deep commitment to the ritual affairs, as they saw their active support of them as great opportunities for their own career advancement. As a result, the state institutionalized new civil ritual practices to be held at the central and local governments, in public and private spaces, and in civic and religious institutions.

---

149. CB 88.2021.

150. CB 91.2106.

151. Ebrey, "Portrait Sculptures," 57.

152. CB 82.1872.

Various nationwide programs included the circulation of literary works concerning the royal myth, creating new holidays to celebrate it, and building local temples for veneration. As a result, the state's imposition of compulsory participation in the civil ritual practices with strong religious undertones created a chasm in the ritual tradition both of the state and of society at large.

## *Conclusion*

With a deficiency of royal authority and the humiliating diplomatic treaty caused by military insecurity, Zhenzong desired a more powerful religious imaginary of kingship than the traditional Confucian concept of emperor as Heaven's agent. His personal mystical experience had engendered the dynastic myth, one that presented the royal family as direct descendants of a supreme Daoist deity. The transformation from the emperor's personal royal imaginary to a national social imaginary came through the enforcement of civil ritual practices with a strong Daoist undertone in various arenas throughout the state. In contrast with the imageless spirit tablet in the Confucian ritual, the portrait paintings and sculptures of late emperors, installed within a ritual space emulating Buddhist and Daoist platforms, more effectively materialized the imaginary of semidivine kingship in a way that fused the mundane world of politics, religions, and quotidian life with the celestial world. With this arrangement, citizens were now able to participate in death rituals for late emperors, which had been the prerogative of reigning emperors within the Confucian liturgical tradition. By institutionalizing various new civil ritual programs interwoven with the liturgical calendar of the state, the imperial government aimed at generating social integration centering on royal authority to which people at large were to express their subordination in tangible ways. With the emperor's firm belief in the ritual's capacity in securing national defense and engendering blessings to the nation, the government prioritized the ritual performances for the cult of the Sacred Ancestor over the ordinary duties of governance. The cult of the Sacred Ancestor was a showcase that a myth was invented to serve the interest of a particular social group, and was propagated through the systematic operation of institutional power.

*2*

---

# *"How Does Heaven Come to Speak?"*

THE CONTESTING DISCOURSE AND THE
REVIVAL OF CONFUCIAN DEATH RITUALS

IT IS THE scholarly consensus that a revival of Confucianism occurred during the reign of Renzong. This period saw the active political engagement of several influential scholar-officials, such as Ouyang Xiu 歐陽修 (1007–1072) and Sima Guang 司馬光 (1019–1086), who shared the vision that Confucianism should be the mainstay of governing principles. From this time forward, they and other like-minded scholar-officials criticized both Buddhism and Daoism and undertook to develop the discourse of "orthodox" and "heterodox" based on Confucian classical texts and their teachings.[1] This effort was at odds with the religious policy set forth by Taizu, the dynasty's founder, who had proclaimed the equality of the three religious traditions—Confucianism, Buddhism, and Daoism—and had drawn on each of them in various imperial court rituals.[2] Modern scholars of this period have paid little attention to the rapidly changing process from the emphasis of Daoist rituals to classical Confucian ones at the imperial court and to the role of discourse concerning death rituals in the revival of Confucianism following Zhenzong's death. This chapter takes up

---

1. Liu Fusheng, "BeiSong zhongqi ruxue fuxing yundong" 北宋中期儒學復興運動, *Wenxian*, no. 1 (1991): 151–159.

2. Early Song religious policies are the subject of Chikusa Masaaki, "Sōsho no Seiji to shūkyo" 宋初の政治と宗教, in *Collected Studies on Sung History Dedicated to Professor James T. C. Liu in Celebration of His Seventieth Birthday* (劉子健博士頌寿紀年宋史研究論集), ed. Tsuyoshi Kinagawa (Kyoto: Tohosa, 1989), 179–195; Wang Shengduo, "Songchao li yu Fojiao" 宋朝禮與佛教, *Xueshu yuekan*, no. 5 (1990): 52–58, and "Songchao li yu Daojiao" 宋朝禮與道教, in *Guoji Songdai wenhua yanjiu taolunhui lunwenji* 國際宋代文化研討會論文集 (Chengdu: Sichuan daxue chubanshe, 1991), 35–49.

these issues by investigating how critiques of imperial death rituals by court officials contributed to a shift in power relations between the emperors and court officials and between factions within officialdom, and then how those critiques evolved into institutional moves for disseminating Confucian social norms throughout society. In particular, I will focus on the change of rhetoric in officials' criticism of ritual performance at the imperial court, and how the authority of the classical texts was invoked for their effective criticism.

## Critics of the Royal Death Rituals under Zhenzong

As the process of decision-making in the Song imperial court involved open discussion on the part of officials (with the emperor having the final say), Zhenzong's massive ritual project provoked a variety of opinions. Some officials, such as Sun Shi 孫奭 (962–1033) and Wang Zeng 王曾 (978–1038), criticized the emperor's favoring of Daoist ritual practice. Sun Shi, during Renzong's reign, served as the Supervisor of the Academy of Rituals (*pan taichang liyuan* 判太常禮院), which oversaw the various imperial seasonal rituals. During Zhenzong's reign, their criticism represented the view of a minority, however, which did not gain wider support among their fellow officials. The emperor himself by and large disregarded the views of those opposed to his project, but did not go so far as to punish any who held such views. However, this legacy of public criticism drawing on Confucian norms was taken up by succeeding generations, especially during the reign of Renzong (1022–1063).

Ritual critiques employed various kinds of reasoning and accordingly utilized a variety of rhetorical devices. One of the most persuasive arguments was that the state did not have enough funds for those rituals; this had been raised even before the incident of the Heavenly Text.[3] As discussed in Chapter 1, Zhenzong in 1008 convened a meeting to discuss the feasibility of performing the *fengshan* ritual, the greatest scale of imperial ritual, in light of the state's fiscal woes. The Commissioner of Finance, Ding Wei 丁謂, reported that the state always had extra money for such a great plan.[4] Ding's view of what the state should prioritize is clear: he believed that the efficacy of the imperial ritual, in terms of protecting the state, made it a worthwhile expenditure.[5] This

---

3. CB 53.1162.

4. CB 68.1531.

5. He made a similar argument in support of the construction of the Temple of Reflecting and Responding to the Realm of Jade Purity. CB 71.1602.

view was not shared, however, by those who criticized the state's handling of ritual matters, as this group doubted the ability of rituals to have any effect on the security of the state.

This rationale of pragmatic concerns drove Wang Zeng to critique state ritual practice in 1009, specifically the construction of extravagant temples. His criticism focused on the scale and expense of such projects rather than on whether they were a good idea. He questioned the fairness of using the labor of soldiers and commoners for temple construction, saying that this expenditure was "sucking people's blood."[6] In comparison, Sun Shi's memorial in 1010 puts forth a more sophisticated argument in taking issue with the emperor's indulgence in rituals. At this time the emperor was planning to perform the Sacrifice to Earth Queen (*houtudi qi* 后土地祇) at Fenyin 汾陰 (located in present-day Shanxi), northwest of the capital city, only two years after the *feng-shan* ritual. The main thrust of Sun's criticism was as follows:

> Doubtlessly, the commoners are masters of the spirits. Because of this the Former Kings first strove to benefit the commoners and afterwards turned their attention to the spirits. They made sacrificial offerings to report [about what they had done for the people] to the spirits.[7] ... In recent times the state's construction projects have gone on continuously. Water supplies dry up. Drought has occurred in many places. Nevertheless, [the state] wants to force people to labor in service to the spirits. Would the spirits be pleased by sacrificial offerings [of this kind]?[8]

Sun concurred with Wang Zeng as to the wastefulness of the ritual investment from a fiscal standpoint, but he went farther than Wang in arguing that "the commoners were the masters of the spirits," citing passages from the *Annals of Spring and Autumn*. In Sun's eyes, spirits operate according to the commoners' sentiment; therefore, the primary duty of a ruler is to take care of his subjects, and secondarily to make sacrificial rituals to report to the spirits about his accomplishments. Finally, Sun contends that the expending of the commoners' labor and financial resources in order to please the spirits turns the purpose of the ritual on its head.

---

6. CB 53.1612.

7. Yang Bojun, "Huangong liunian" 桓公六年 (The 6th year of Duke Huan), in *Chunqiu Zuozhuan zhu* 春秋左傳注 (Beijing: Zhonghua shuju, 1990), 111.

8. CB 74.1700.

Sun made a much more devastating attack on the ritual in a second memorial, delivered on the heels of the first. He recalled the origin of the Sacrifice to Earth Queen made by Emperor Wu of the Han (r. 141 BCE–87 BCE) in 113 BCE by arguing that a sacrificial ritual to Earth must be made after he performed the Suburban Sacrifice (*jiaosi* 郊祀) dedicated to Heaven, in accordance with the *yin-yang* theory.[9] Sun Shi, however, argued that according to the *Ritual of the Zhou* (*Zhouli* 周禮), the Suburban Sacrifices entailed offerings both to Heaven and to Earth, and that therefore there was no need to perform another ritual exclusively for the latter.[10] During the early Song prior to Zhenzong, the emperors personally performed the South Suburban Sacrifice both to Heaven and Earth every four years; therefore no independent sacrifice was made to Earth.[11] Sun Shi was so bold as to invalidate Sacrifice to Earth Queen, characterizing it a "sacrificial offering that was abolished long ago due to its violation of the canonical texts."[12] He pointed out that after Emperor Wu of the Han, subsequent emperors did not perform the ritual because it did not have any precedent in the classical ritual texts.

Sun Shi also expressed the concern that Emperor Zhenzong was taking a risk traveling to the north in order to perform the ritual in spite of the military instability of the region. Furthermore, he noted:

The *Spring and Autumn Annals* reads, "If the state is to flourish, [the ruler] listens to the people; if it is to perish, [he] listens to the spirits."[13]

---

9. In 110 BCE, he performed the *fengshan* ritual. Sima Qian, *The Grand Scribe's Records*, vol. 2: *The Basic Annals of Han China*, ed. William H. Nienhauser, Jr., tr. Tsai-fa Cheng et al. (Bloomington: Indiana University Press, 2002), 230 and 240–246; Michael Puett, *To Become a God: Cosmology, Sacrifice, and Self-divinization in Early China* (Cambridge, MA: Harvard University Asia Center, 2004), 307–314. For the history of the Suburban Sacrifice, see Howard J. Wechsler, *Offerings of Jade and Silk: Jade and Symbol in the Legitimation of the Tang Dynasty* (New Haven and London: Yale University Press, 1985), 107–122; Kojima Tsuyoshi, "Koshi seido no hensen" 郊祀制度の變遷, *Tōyō bunka kenkyūjo kiyō* 108 (1989): 123–219.

10. According to the *Ritual of the Zhou*, offering to Heaven was to be made in the southern suburbs at the time of the winter solstice, and to Earth in the northern suburbs at the time of the summer solstice. Wechsler, *Offerings of Jade and Silk*, 109.

11. Yamauchi Kōichi, "Hokusō jidai no kōshi" 北宋時代の郊祀, *Shigaku zasshi* 92, no. 1 (1983): 40–41.

12. CB 74.1701. Since the reign of Renzong, it had become a tradition that an emperor personally made the Suburban Sacrifice once every three years. Kōichi, "Hokusō jidai no kōshi," 43.

13. Yang, "Zhuanggong sanshiernian" 莊公三十二年 (The 32nd year of Duke Zhuang), in *Chunqiu Zuozhuan zhu*, 252.

> Therefore, this criticism is not [just] a silly idea of this foolish official [i.e., Sun Shi himself].[14]

Here, Sun decried the attention paid to the rhetoric of and practices related to the spirits in the realm of politics as evidence of a regime that was destined to fall.

In the same memorial, Sun made another important criticism, this concerning the nature of Heaven. When Emperor Zhenzong celebrated the Heavenly Text, he implied that it was Heaven that had sent the revelatory text. Yet he failed to clarify the nature of Heaven or *tian* 天, but rather used it as a generic term for the transcendental realm or being. In the Confucian tradition, it was generally understood that Heaven manifested its will through natural phenomena, based on the passage in the *Analects* (17.17): Confucius said, "How does Heaven come to speak? The four seasons operate by it, and all things are born from it. [Nevertheless] does Heaven speak?"[15] Sun Shi's bold criticism of the emperor in 1010 thus represented an orthodox position based on canonical scholarship: "I, though ignorant, have heard of the saying, 'How does Heaven come to speak?' How then did there come to be a text revealing the words of Heaven?"[16]

Although Sun Shi failed to persuade Zhenzong, as the latter performed the ritual in the following year, the phrase "How does Heaven come to speak?" was used rhetorically with some frequency by those critical of the emperor. When it was reported to Zhenzong that a soldier had attempted to damage a copy of the Heavenly Text, he wanted to punish the latter. However, Ma Zhijie 馬知節 (955–1019), the general in charge of the soldier's unit, refused to carry out Zhenzong's orders. Ma had been a consistent challenger of his superior, Wang Qinruo, Director of the Bureau of Military Affairs, with his belief that the state should invest more on increasing military strength than on venerating the Heavenly Text.[17] Ma argued, "High officials do not believe in the descent of the Heavenly Text because they personally have not heard the voice of Heaven. Isn't it all the more so for a soldier in training?" The emperor had no choice but to back down.[18]

---

14. Tian Kuang, *Rulin gongyi*, QSBJ, 1st series, 5: 95.

15. My translation.

16. CB 74.1699.

17. Later Ma Zhijie was discharged along with Wang Qinruo in 1014 because of the fights between the two in front of the emperor. Wang returned to the imperial court in 1015. Karl F. Olsson, "The Structure of Power under the Third Emperor of Sung China: The Shifting Balance After the Peace of Shan-Yuan" (PhD diss., University of Chicago, 1974), 191–193.

18. Tian Kuang, *Rulin gongyi*, QSBJ, 1st series, 5: 99.

Lu Zongdao 魯宗道 (966–1029), another official, elaborates upon Sun Shi's point:

> Heaven reveals [itself] by blessing the good and bringing disaster upon the evil. It neither speaks words nor demonstrates with strange signs. If the lord's governing follows these principles, then Heaven sends forth blessings as a reward; if he deviates from them, then *Heaven sends forth a supernatural event as a warning. Then again, how does Heaven's text come to be?* I am afraid that ill-intentioned ministers speak in absurdities in order to befuddle Your Majesty.[19] [italics added]

Here, Song scholar-officials recapitulated the arguments of the Old Text (*guwen* 古文) scholars of the Eastern Han (25–220 CE) when they rejected the Prophetic and Apocryphal Texts (*chenwei* 讖緯).[20] In fear of political maneuvers based on those texts, they argued that Heaven demonstrated its intention through natural phenomena, but not through unusual plants, strange signs, and revealed texts.

Some officials went so far as to declare that Heavenly auspiciousness would be found in healthy governance with a thriving agricultural economy and a formidable military capacity, not in strange signs, as seen in the following presentation of a court official to the throne:

> I wish Your Majesty would consider the supporting and promoting of loyal and good ministers as a public good and rebuke the ill-intentioned ministers, and consider support for the agricultural and military sectors and piling up the harvest in granaries as Heavenly auspiciousness. How can you be proud of auspiciousness in the form of unusual plants and trees?[21]

This criticism highlights that the government's priority lay in ritual performances to the detriment of issues of ordinary governance. Sun Shi also

---

19. CB 93.2142.

20. Jack L. Dull argues that the some scholars of the Old Text School to some extent embraced the ideas of the New Text School by adopting the notion that cosmic orders responded to moral and political order and by validating some apocryphal texts, such as the River Chart and the Luo Text. "A Historical Introduction," 388–399.

21. CB 101.2331. Another official, Cui Li 崔立 (979–1043), presented similar ideas: CB 93.2136; SSJBM 22.131.

challenged the cult of the deified Laozi, who was worshipped along with the Jade Emperor:

> It is unquestionable that Laozi is a saint. Therefore, even if he happens to actually send down his words, it is not absurd. ... Today, [however,] Lord Lao is presented on the top of a pavilion, tomorrow deep inside a mountain. High-ranking officials carry ritual gifts with which to greet him. ... They have falsely led people into heterodoxy [*zuodao* 左道], and caused political instability and done damage to the economy. The minds of the people are unsettled; [thus,] revolts thrive. Under these circumstances, is Lord Lao able to protect the imperial army? Can talismans ward off foreign invaders?[22]

Here Sun denied the divinity of Laozi, which was one of the fundamental premises of religious Daoism. After defining it as "heterodoxy," Sun warned that ritual performances associated with it would lack the efficacy to resolve military, economic, and social problems—and what was worse, such performances would aggravate these problems by wasting resources with frequent performances and by having false confidence in defense capacity.

During Zhenzong's reign, officials who took issue with the state's ritual programs focused their criticism primarily on the Daoist rituals that had been performed within the imperial court. They hewed to a more conservative line in seeking to prevent non-Confucian rituals from being frequently performed in the imperial court, and also to debunk the notion that Heaven's intention was revealed through unusual plants, strange signs, and revealed texts. They called for the emperor to pay more attention to practical matters rather than entreating the spirits via prayers and making offerings to the royal ancestors. However, their power was not strong enough to redirect the various projects of the emperor.

## Declaring the Primacy of the Canonical Rituals

Zhenzong died in 1022 and was survived by his wife, Empress Dowager Liu, and his son, the eleven-year-old Emperor Renzong. Empress Liu, as regent for the boy emperor, was careful to maintain Zhenzong's policies. She continued existing ritual programs and expanded building constructions for that purpose.[23] Significant shifts, however, did take place in the imperial court with

---

22. CB 93.2143. Sun Shi made a similar argument in 1013. CB 81.1850.

23. Patricia Ebrey, "Portrait Sculptures in Imperial Ancestral Rites in Song China," *T'oung Pao* 87, no. 1 (1997): 56–58.

respect to power relations among high officials. Those who had been in the minority during Zhenzong's reign gained power and came to constitute the majority, whereas the other party saw their power base erode. This change was epitomized by Grand Councilor Ding Wei's fall from grace in 1022, having been accused of conspiring to shift the burial vault to a geomantically forbidden location; he barely escaped the order of execution.[24] It was a dramatic turn of fate in that the person who requested Ding Wei's execution for his complicity in the Heavenly Text incident ended up facing his own execution; his head was put on public display in 1015.[25]

On the other hand, Wang Qinruo was reappointed as Grand Councilor in 1023, but he did not stay in that position for long, dying in 1025. Wang Zeng in 1025 replaced Wang Qinruo as Grand Councilor. It was his glorious return to power after demotion in 1017, having been incited by Wang Qinruo's attack for the latter's refusal to assume a post overseeing Daoist establishment.[26] Sun Shi, Vice Director of the Bureau of Judicial Administration (*xingbu shilang* 刑部侍郎), served as the Supervisor of the Academy of Ritual (*taichang liyuan* 判太常禮院) in 1027. Under his leadership, the Academy of Ritual became the central institution for the monitoring of various imperial rituals based on classical texts.[27]

Two of the major changes during Empress Liu's regency were her revival of the Complaint Review Office (*lijianyuan* 理檢院) in 1029 and her establishment of the Office of Remonstrance (*jianyuan* 諫院) as an independent institution in 1032.[28] These moves reflected her hope of gaining support in the form of political advice, having come from a humble background, courtesan-entertainer, without much of a personal political network.[29] The Complaint

---

24. Michael McGrath, "The Reigns of Jen-tsung (1022–1063) and Ying-tsung (1063–67)," in *The Cambridge History of China*, vol. 5, part 1: *The Sung Dynasty and Its Precursors, 907–1279*, eds. Denis Twitchett and Paul Jakov Smith (New York: Cambridge University Press, 2009), 280–281; John W. Chaffee, "The Rise and Regency of Empress Liu (969–1033)," *Journal of Sung-Yuan Studies* 31 (2002): 14. Ding Wei was very unpopular among the common people. They circulated a folk song and drew paintings through which they conveyed their wish that Ding resign as minister. Tian Kuang, *Rulin gongyi*, 110; CB 99.2293, 99.2296, and 105.2459; SSJBM 35.803.

25. Cahill, "Taoism at the Sung Court," 33.

26. CB 90.2078; Cahill, "Taoism at the Sung Court," 33.

27. CB 100.2320 and 119.2795. Zhenzong had established the Office of Ritual (*liyiyuan* 禮儀院) as a subordinate unit under the Academy of Ritual. Empress Liu, however, abolished it in 1023 after the office had criticized various rituals instituted by Zhenzong and had suggested that the size and frequency of such rituals be reduced. As a result, the Academy of Ritual absorbed the duties of the Office of Ritual.

28. CB 101.2585.

29. Yu Yunguo, *Xishuo Songchao* (Shanghai: Renmin chubanshe, 2004), 153–159; Chaffee, "The Rise and Regency," 1–25; Beverly Bossler, "Gender and Entertainment at the Song

Review Office had been created in 991 by Taizong to review "complaints by officials and commoners about official misconduct or major state policies."[30] Zhenzong, however, had shut down the office in 995, a move which caused some officials to say that he feared criticism.[31] During his reign, especially after the Shanyuan Alliance, memorials were restricted and screened before they reached the emperor. In fact, Zhenzong stopped reading memorials and relegated the authority of reading to Wang Dan.[32] In 1016 Zhenzong appointed six policy critiques, but their influence was limited.[33] Under Empress Liu's leadership, the newly established Office of Remonstrance had the responsibility of presenting memorials regarding various issues, including state policies, the emperor's manners, and officials' behavior. Early in the reign of Renzong, the Office of Remonstrance came to wield a great deal of influence, due to the absence of a powerful emperor.

As a result of the high profile of the Office of Remonstrance, many who served there quickly rose to power. One such example was Ouyang Xiu, who having held a post with the office at an early stage of his career, was able to accumulate enormous political power.[34] Sima Guang also expanded his power base quickly during his time as an officer of remonstrance. This institution encouraged a culture of criticism and freedom of speech among officials. The classical texts and historical precedents to which the officials referred functioned as a heuristic device that minimized the voice of the individual and strengthened their arguments. As an emperor, Renzong further fostered the culture of criticism with his willingness to entertain diverse opinions and criticism. As a result, his reign ushered in a new culture of discourse in which scholar-officials of varied ranks and regions engaged actively.

The increasing influence of scholar-officials during this period was partially attributed to Renzong's being largely free from his father's influence. By contrast, Zhenzong's devotion to Daoism might well have resulted from his father's

---

Court," in *Servants of the Dynasty: Palace Women in World History,*, ed. Anne Walthall (Berkeley: University of California Press, 2008), 271–273.

30. Charles O. Hucker, *A Dictionary of Official Titles in Imperial China* (Stanford, CA: Stanford University Press), 303.

31. CB 100.2321. Regarding the history of the institution, see Zhang Xiqing, *Songchao dianzhang zhidu* (Changchun: Jilin wenshi chubanshe, 2001), 39–40.

32. Olsson, "The Structure of Power," 69 and 149.

33. Olsson, "The Structure of Power," 128.

34. Xiao-bin Ji, *Politics and Conservatism in Northern Song China: The Career and Thought of Sima Guang (A.D. 1019–1086)* (Hong Kong: Chinese University Press, 2005), 103.

deep commitment to that religion. In addition, when Zhenzong assumed the throne he had to work with ministers who had come to power during his father's era. The education of the eleven-year-old boy-emperor Renzong was by contrast generally left to influential officials such as Sun Shi, who taught that the sole source of imperial legitimacy was Confucianism and that performing the canonical rituals was a key element of the maintenance of that legitimacy.[35] Han Qi 韓琦 (1008–1075) and Ouyang Xiu in particular figured significantly in the ending of the empress' regency, which allowed Renzong to assume the emperorship at the age of twenty-one. Under these circumstances, the inexperienced young emperor had no choice but to rely heavily upon his top advisors.

From the beginning of Renzong's reign, court officials launched harsher and more comprehensive attacks on the court's indulgence in nonclassical and non-Confucian ritual practice. Song Qi 宋祁 (998–1061) presented a memorial in 1037 that exemplifies a critical viewpoint on this issue. In it, he links serious governmental problems to the excessive numbers of personnel in three groups: Buddhist and Daoist clergy, government officers, and soldiers not at war.[36] He also defines the three "wastes" in government expenses, two of which are related to rituals.

> The first waste is [the setting up of] the ritual enclosure to perform the Purgation (*zhai* 齋) and the Ritual Offering (*jiao* 醮). There is no day on which such rituals do not take place. Some last for seven days, or a month, forty-nine days; each ritual has a primary name. With few breaks, all sorts of officials make numerous offerings such as wax, vegetables, oil, grain powder, wine, grain, money, and cotton. These are beyond calculation. In addition, those who preside over the rituals benefit by cheating; thus they revere the rituals of Daoism to the utmost. All the rituals have the themes of blessing the emperor for longevity, making offerings to deceased cultural heroes, and offering prayers for the well-being of the common people. Ministers dare not talk [about the problems of the state]. In my humble opinion, I understand that Your Majesty first makes offerings to Heaven and Earth, and the spirits in the Imperial Ancestral Shrine. Next, you should serve the gods of the land and agriculture, and the one hundred spirits. . . . Doubtless, the people cherish the state; and the state cherishes its people. Wealth does not come down

---

35. CB 103.2378 and 110.2564.

36. CB 125.2942.

from Heaven, but comes up from the earth. In the necessary tasks, [Your Majesty] does not employ ghosts but waits on people to perform them.[37]

In this memorial, Song Qi argues that overindulgence in the frequent performances of Daoist rituals has caused the state's financial problems. He identifies those rituals as nonclassical ones that cannot be held legitimately performed as state rituals. He lists the classical rituals in the order of proclaimed significance and asserts that they retain their ability to ensure the state's prosperity, and thus additional offerings to spirits not registered in the classical ritual system are unnecessary. At bottom, he disputes the efficacy of nonclassical rituals and in fact considers them sham.

Ouyang Xiu contended that what constituted proper rituals was not decided by the emperor, but rather by textual precedents. This idea was based on the understanding that the classical texts presented consistent ideas and regulations with regard to the various rituals and thus there was no room for alternative interpretations. Moved by the soundness of this argument, in the fifth month of 1035 Emperor Renzong decreed that the imperial rituals would follow the guidelines of the classical ritual practice or *dianli* 典禮, and that the Academy of Ritual would assess the legitimacy of rituals performed by the state.[38] With renewed emphasis on *dianli* came closer scrutiny of ritual texts, which resulted in the discovery of vague and contradictory regulations. Thus the government launched a project of making the texts consistent in 1037. Ouyang Xiu was in charge of the project and in 1065 published the text entitled *Newly Reformed Imperial Seasonal Rituals* (*Taichang yingeli* 太常因革禮).[39]

Supporters of the orthodox Confucian rituals emphasized the idea that the emperor would demonstrate his having been endowed with the Mandate of Heaven through the performance of those rituals. They contended that the nonclassical rituals could not do so, and even worse, might undermine his virtue.[40] Ouyang Xiu was relentless in his challenging of the emperor's performance of nonclassical rituals. In 1055, he presented the following memorial to the emperor:

From ancient times rulers have revered their ancestors and served the spirits. Each [of the rituals of this type] has a classical model. It is not necessary to construct [temples] on a grand scale in order to perform the classical rituals. . . . Your Majesty, rather than construct grand

---

37. CB 125.2942–2943.

38. CB 116.2730.

39. CB 120.2825.

40. CB 180.4365.

temples to serve the gods, you ought to be mindful of Heaven's warning and reflect and rectify [your conduct].[41]

Han Qi also advocated this position in opposing a plan to establish Daoist ritual enclosure in the Hall for Great Celebration (*daqing dian* 大慶殿), a place for the morning imperial audience. He argued that those Daoist rituals were not "regular seasonal rituals" (*changli* 常禮) registered in the classical ritual texts and thus were not legitimate. He urged the emperor to focus on the cultivation of virtue and being heedful of Heaven's warning instead of making offerings to the spirits at the Daoist ritual altars.[42]

The consensus reached by the emperor and the officials on the primacy of the classical rituals created a new dynamic between the emperor and officialdom. Whereas Zhenzong's personal choice had prevailed over the prescriptions of the classical texts, Renzong faced more difficulties when he wanted to get around the regulations of the classical ritual prescriptions.[43] This dynamic would greatly influence power relations between ruler and officialdom during his reign and those of subsequent emperors.

## *From the Royal Image Hall to the Imperial Ancestral Shrine*

As the foregoing discussion of legitimate imperial rituals shows, all the rituals initiated by Zhenzong could not be considered among their number. When Zhenzong institutionalized various rituals and festivals in order to celebrate the dynastic myth, he proclaimed them to be "eternal ceremonies." However, following his death the government took gradual steps to diminish the size and significance of the rituals he had initiated. This trend culminated with the shuttering in 1082 of all the Royal Image Halls, the centers for venerating the Sacred Ancestor, throughout the state except one in the Temple of Radiant Spirit. In so doing, officials reasserted the authority of the Imperial Ancestral Shrine, the venue for the most prestigious classical imperial death ritual.

---

41. CB 180.4361.

42. CB 120.2842–2843.

43. For example, the classical ritual texts specified that mourning clothes worn at a royal funeral should be taken off on the seventh day after the funeral. The geomantic system, on the other hand, prescribed another day. In 1007, the emperor chose to break with the classical ritual system, designating the thirteenth day following the funeral as the day when mourning clothes were to be taken off. CB 65.1453.

Under Wang Zeng's leadership, during Empress Liu's regency the rituals and festivals created by Zhenzong had already been reduced in size and frequency. As early as the third month of 1023 (the second year of Empress Liu's regency), the Office of Ritual (*liyiyuan* 禮儀院) began to recommend that the empress cease authorizing banquets throughout the state and limit them to the regions where the (Daoist) Ritual of Offering (*jiao* 醮) had recently been offered.[44] The government reduced the number of soldiers guarding the major temples and redeployed them with the army and elsewhere.[45] Following this action, it issued an edict abolishing the custom of presenting the Longevity Belt and the Thread of Continuing Life at the Celestial Ancestor Festival.[46] In the following year, 1024, it abolished the custom of lighting lanterns during the five major festivals.[47] In 1029, the government abolished the placement of government officers in major Daoist temples.[48] In 1041, the government announced that the prohibition of executions during major festival times would be limited to the day of the festival and not span multiple days before and afterwards.[49] It should be noted, though, that the reduction of the length and extent of festivals during Empress Liu's regency was for economic and practical reasons rather than out of concern about their legitimacy.

Zhenzong's ritual program still loomed large during Renzong's reign. In 1032, twenty years after the event, some people were still writing commemorative literary pieces on the appearance of the Heavenly Text.[50] The project of installing the portraits and sculptures of the late emperors continued across the state in the early years of Renzong's reign. Not only were new halls dedicated to the royal images built within existing temples, but images were installed in the Buddhist and Daoist halls as well, along with other sculptures.[51] Although there are no comprehensive records of liturgies that took place within the Royal Image Halls, it is reported that royal ancestral image

---

44. CB 100.2318. In 1059, Ouyang Xiu suggested that the custom of lighting lanterns during the Festivals of the Three Primes be abolished. He argued that when people were freezing to death, such a custom was a waste of fuel. CB 189.4547.

45. CB 100.2318.

46. CB 100.2323.

47. CB 102.2358; SS Benji 9, 9.179.

48. QSW 44: 949.176; SS Benji 9, 9.187.

49. CB 130.3084.

50. Li Lü 李履 (d.u.), "Ji Shengtu xu" 繼聖圖序, QSW 70: 1519.49.

51. For the records of one such installation, see CB 110.2555, 120.2832 and 174.4176; Liu Ban 劉攽 (1022–1088), "Hongqinggong sanshengdian fu" 鴻慶宮三聖殿賦, QSW 68:1484.230.

veneration rituals were performed in a variety of forms, depending upon location and occasion. The government enacted regulations concerning the burning of incense at the Royal Image Halls on the first month of each of the four seasons, as was done in connection with the rituals in the Imperial Ancestral Shrine.[52] Those who did not have a Royal Image Hall shrine in their house were to go to Buddhist temples and burn incense. In 1046, the government issued an edict specifying the particular rite to be performed in all Buddhist temples that had the emperors' images and in the Hall for Celestial Flourishing (*tianxing dian* 天興殿) at the Temple of Radiant Spirit.[53] It directed ritual officials to perform the rite of "praising the ascending and descending of [the Sacred Ancestor]," while the other officials were on the mat in the courtyard facing west. At the imperial palace in 1049, royal family members, high officials, and officers of remonstrance made a morning visit to the Royal Image Hall of Zhenzong, located within the Temple of Extensive Holiness (*guangsheng gong* 廣聖宮).[54] In 1055, in the Shrine of Longevity of Ten Thousand Years (*wanshou guan* 萬壽觀), Renzong placed a golden sculptural image of his father Zhenzong that cost 5,000 taels of gold, which bespoke his commitment to the cult of royal ancestral image veneration.[55] Within the hall, there had already been a golden image of the Sacred Ancestor and a silver image of the Supreme Thearch of August Heaven (*haotian shangdi* 昊天上帝), each of which weighed 5,000 taels.

Against the background of the continuing practice of the cult of the royal images, several events occurred that undermined the state support of the practice. In 1029, the Temple of Reflecting and Responding to the Realm of Jade Purity (*yuqing zhaoying gong* 玉清昭應宮), the most extravagant temple of its time, was almost completely destroyed by an accidental fire. Some officials interpreted the accident as a warning by Heaven that the ritual was invalid. The emperor agreed with this opinion and did not renovate the temple.[56] When another fire broke out at the Royal Image Hall at Nanjing in 1040, the

---

52. CB 331.7969.

53. CB 158.3823.

54. CB 167.4013.

55. The Shrine of Longevity of Ten Thousand Years was located within the Temple of Reflecting and Responding to the Realm of Jade Purity. It was the only building that survived the fire in 1029. CB 178.4304; Wang Yong, *Yanyi yimou lu*, rpt. with Wang Zhi, *Moji* (Beijing: Zhonghua shuju, 1997), 2.20

56. SSJBM 22.176; CB 108.2515; Hu Su 胡宿 (995–1067), "Yi Hongqinggong zai lun xiu huosi zou," 以鴻慶宮災論修火祠奏 QSW 22: 458.58.

government similarly did not rebuild it.[57] In another instance, the Shrine of the Souls' Gathering (*huiling guan* 會靈觀) burned down in 1053; the sculptures were moved elsewhere, and the shrine was not rebuilt.[58]

Fan Zhen's memorial of 1055 regarding the fire in the Royal Image Hall of Taizong at Bingzhou Prefect exemplifies scholar-officials' criticism of the ritual by making use of the accidental fires.

> I have heard that Bingzhou Prefect did not have a history of accidental fires. Not long after the construction of the Royal Image Hall started, somewhat surprisingly, an accidental fire broke out. Heaven's Will is speaking to Your Majesty in this fashion. Images of the royal ancestors should not be installed within the local temples. Recently I also heard that Bingzhou Prefect would again add more construction business. This construction work burdens people; it is not in accord with Heaven's Will. . . . If you make sure to remind the people about virtue, Your Majesty will fulfill your filial piety duty. How could it be compared with the building of a single Royal Image Hall?[59]

Fan Zhen here invoked a notion that Heaven's warning (*tianjie* 天戒) was delivered through natural disasters and astrological phenomena as its rebukes to human immorality, especially on the part of the ruler.[60] This idea was derived from the Correspondence Theory, an idea developed during the Western Han (206 BCE–24 CE) claiming that cosmic order and moral order responded to each other. Scholars of the Eastern Han accepted this notion as legitimate Confucian thought, while rejecting strange signs and texts as media for displaying Heaven's intention.[61] In this criticism, Fan Zhen adds a new element by stressing that the fundamental value of the cult of the royal image was to fulfill the emperor's filial piety duty, not bolster the loyalty of the people to the royal family. In valorizing the personal aspect of the ritual for the emperor, Fan dismisses all other uses of the cult of the royal images. He suggests that filial

---

57. CB 127.3013.

58. CB 174.4192.

59. CB 184.4365. A similar criticism was made in 1061 by an official who opposed the rebuilding of the Royal Image Hall within the Shrine of Longevity Star (*shouxing guan* 壽星觀). CB 195.4730.

60. Kojima Tsuyoshi, "Sōdai tenkenron no seiji shisō" 宋代天譴論の政治思想, *Tōyō bunka kenkyūjo kiyō* 107 (1988): 1–87.

61. Dull, "A Historical Introduction," 134 and 388–399.

piety was the concern of the emperor alone; the fulfillment of this duty need not occur publicly.

While participation in the royal ancestral cult continued to be mandatory for both the general populace and government officials, attacks on the cult's legitimacy became fiercer. Ouyang Xiu struck the fatal blow against the cult in 1058.[62] It was related to the *muqin zhai* 睦親宅 (the house of the close relatives of the royal family), which was used as a place of lodging for the royal kinsmen along with the *guangqin zhai* 廣親宅 (the house of the distant relatives of the royal family).[63] The *muqin zhai* was built in 1035 on the spot where the Temple of Reflecting and Responding to the Realm of Jade Purity had stood before it burned down.[64] Ouyang questions the need for establishing the Royal Image Hall within both places. He stated, "The Royal Image Hall is not appropriate for a private house. If one takes the *guangqin zhai* as an example and argues that the *muqin zhai* should also have the image hall, an inappropriate ritual will be perpetuated [, which should not have taken place to begin with]."[65] He found a precedent in a case from the Han dynasty in which national shrines in local areas were closed down.[66] Liu Chang 劉敞 (1019–1068) submitted a memorial to support Ouyang's argument.[67] As a result, the image hall at the *muqin zhai* was renovated for other purposes. The emperor, however, ordered that the one at the *guangqin zhai* be left intact, because it had been there for a long time.[68]

As this case provided the precedent that the Royal Image Hall was for the private use of the royal family, the construction of Royal Image Halls came to a halt in local areas. However, the Temple of Radiant Spirit continued to serve its originally intended purpose, as evidenced by the installation of a mural portrait of Renzong in a hall, accompanied by those of the high officials in 1065, two years after his death. Finally, in 1071 under the reign of

---

62. Yamauchi Kōichi, "Hokusō jidai no shingyoden to keireikū" 北宋時代の神禦殿と景靈宮, *Tōhō gakū* 70 (1985): 46–60.

63. Yamauchi Kōichi, "State Sacrifice and Daoism during the Northern Song," *Memoirs of the Research Department of Toyo Bunko* 58 (2000): 13.

64. SHY Dixi, 4.4 (QSW 44: 958.350); Hu Su, "Xiugai muqinzhai wuwangyuan shenyutang shangliangwen" 修蓋睦親宅吳王院神御堂上梁文, QSW 22: 470.263.

65. CB 187.4508.

66. Ban Gu, *Hanshu* (Beijing, Zhonghua shuju, 1962), 73.

67. Liu Chang, "Lun muqinzhai budang jian shenyudian shu" 論睦親宅不當建神御殿疏, QSW 59:1279.70.

68. CB 187.4508.

Emperor Shenzong 神宗 (r. 1048–1085), the Office of Ritual made the following announcement: "According to the canonical ritual, all marquises do not perform memorial services to honor [former] emperors, and public shrines should not be built in private homes. At the present time, royal family members have the [various] images of the former emperors, which is not the way to clearly honor and humbly venerate the legitimate succession (*zhengtong* 正統) of the imperial family."[69] Here, the Office of Ritual connects proper ritual performances with an abstract term, *zhengtong*, that has a broad connotation of "legitimate succession in a dynasty," "legitimate dynastic succession," and "political legitimacy."[70] From the time of this announcement, individuals and temples were not allowed to keep the sculptures and images of imperial ancestors.[71] Many sculptures and paintings of individual emperors in various locations were transferred to the Temple of Radiant Spirit, which necessitated the construction of eleven Royal Image Halls in the temple by 1082. At the ceremony of the consolidation held in that year, Emperor Shenzong expressed a great deal of emotion.[72] At that time, even wall paintings of late emperors hanging within temples and shrines were not available for public viewing, yet they were not destroyed out of fear of defaming the images.[73] Once all the local image halls were closed down, people went to the Temple of Radiant Spirit to burn incense on national memorial days.[74] After the consolidation, then, local veneration at the Royal Image Halls ceased.

During Renzong's reign, some officials urged that the ritual at the Imperial Ancestral Shrine (*taimiao* 太廟) be accorded its former degree of importance. Royal ancestral veneration offered here was one of the "great sacrificial rituals" (*dasi* 大祀) that were performed by emperors as the official state rituals prescribed in the Confucian classics.[75] Those officials thought that the emperor placed too much emphasis on the ritual of the Royal Image Hall at the expense of the ritual in the Imperial Ancestral Shrine. Although rituals at both places were meant

---

69. CB 225.5489.

70. Wechsler, *Offerings of Jade and Silk*, 14–16.

71. Zhou Hui (b. 1126), *Qingpo zazhi jiaozhu* 清波雜誌校注, annot. Liu Yongxiang (Beijing: Zhonghua shuju, 1994), 2.73.

72. For the details of the ritual of the consolidation, see Patricia Ebrey, "Portrait Sculptures," 42–43.

73. CB 348.8360.

74. CB 329.7940.

75. For the history of the ritual at this place and its political implications, see Wechsler, *Offerings of Jade and Silk*, 123–142.

for venerating royal ancestors, they operated differently. Rituals at the Imperial Ancestral Shrine were held in accordance with the liturgical calendar specified in the classical ritual texts, and participation in them was limited to court members. In the Imperial Ancestral Shrine, wooden spirit tablets, lacking any sort of image of a royal ancestor, were installed. In contrast, in the Royal Image Halls both portrait paintings and sculptures were installed, sometimes alongside those of Laozi and the Supreme Thearch of August Heaven (*haotian shangdi* 昊天上帝). In addition, the rituals at the Royal Image Halls were performed frequently at accessible locations, both within the palace and elsewhere, before their consolidation in the Temple of Radiant Spirit, and were open to general audiences even after the consolidation. Therefore, the Royal Image Halls accommodated the needs of ancestor veneration without the limitations of designated liturgical time and space as defined in the classical texts. Because the Royal Image Hall was an innovation of the time, its proponents attempted to enhance its legitimacy by naming it the Original Shrine (*yuanmiao* 原廟), echoing the Grand Shrine or Imperial Ancestral Shrine (*taimiao* 太廟), in addition to emulating the former's ritual.[76] This designation was intended to resonate with the precedent case recorded in the *History of Han* (*Hanshu* 漢書), according to which the Imperial Ancestral Shrines (*zongmiao* 宗廟) in local areas were called the National Shrine in Local Areas (*junguomiao* 郡國廟).[77]

Some officials took even stronger measures to diminish the significance of the ritual at the Royal Image Halls. Every year in the eleventh month, court officials of all levels gathered at the Department of State Affairs for a day of ritual fasting in preparation for the making of offerings at the Temple of Radiant Spirit. Two additional days of fasting followed, in advance of the Imperial Ancestral Shrine and the Suburban Sacrifice on subsequent days. In 1027, Grand Councilor Wang Zeng proposed that a single ritual of abstention would suffice for all three rituals, because the Daoist temples and shrines were all linked to the Suburban Sacrifice; the Temple of Radiant Spirit would be no exception.[78] His suggestion was finally adopted eight years later in 1035,[79] months after the imperial court announced that the classical imperial rituals would be the standards for orthopraxis. This suggestion was intended to reduce the prominence of the rituals at the Temple of Radiant Spirit, which

---

76. CB 73.1651.

77. Ouyang Xiu, "He hongqinggong chengfengan sansheng yurong biao" 賀鴻慶宮成奉安三聖御容表, QSW 31: 673.358; Yamauchi, "Hokusō jidai no kōshi," 46.

78. CB 105.2456.

79. CB 117.2753.

became subordinate to those of the Suburban Sacrifice. In 1038, a high official, Jia Changchao 賈昌朝 (997–1065), took another step to challenge the
prestige of the place by taking issue with the current sequence of the visita-
tion of the different places. As an alternative, he suggested that the emperor
make offerings at the Royal Image Hall after the Suburban Sacrifice, but prior
to visiting Buddhist and Daoist temples.[80] Jia's point was that it was proper
for the ritual at the Royal Image Hall to be the most prestigious one amongst
the nonclassical rituals, but that it should not overshadow any of the classical imperial rituals. In later times, the practice of visiting the Temple of
Radiant Spirit in the morning prior to performing the Suburban Sacrifice was
discontinued.[81]

The 1050s saw some officials advocate that renewed attention be paid to the
ritual at the Imperial Ancestral Shrine. The widespread flooding of 1056 led
Fan Zhen to present a memorial stating that the natural disaster was Heaven's
warning and meant to alert the emperor as to his negligence of the Imperial
Ancestral Shrine. He contended that the emperor had fulfilled all the requirements for preventing such a natural disaster by performing sacrificial rituals
and offering prayers in accordance with Heaven's will, with the exception of
the ritual at the Imperial Ancestral Shrine.[82] Other officials, such as Ouyang
Xiu, presented memorials that expressed the same concern.[83] One official, Wu
Kui 吳奎 (1011–1068), extended the argument to say that the emperor's neglecting to adopt a crown prince was proof that he did not take the matter of the
Imperial Ancestral Shrine seriously.[84]

Criticism of the rituals performed at the Royal Image Hall also worked to
erode the myth of the divine origin of the royal ancestors. The challenging of this
myth was a gradual process. The change of the name of the Hall of the Perfected's
Journey (*zhenyou dian* 眞游殿) spoke to the shift in the conception of the royal
ancestors. This hall was celebrated as the place where the Sacred Ancestor, a perfected being (*zhenren* 眞人), descended to earth. Later its name was changed to

---

80. Jia Changchao, "Qing huangdi chaomiao qian buxingye jinglinggong li zou"
請皇帝朝廟前不行謁景靈宮禮奏, QSW 23: 481.65.

81. Song Xiang 宋庠 (996–1066), "Wei nanjiao yu xiayuanjie geng buyu jinglinggong chao-
bei zougao shengzu neizhi biao," 爲南郊於下元節更不於景靈宮朝拜奏告聖祖內制表,
QSW 20: 426.358.

82. CB 182.4416.

83. CB 183.4424.

84. CB 183.4427. At this time, Emperor Renzong did not have a male heir, yet was reluctant to adopt one, which caused tension within the court. On this issue, see Ji, *Politics and
Conservatism*, 67–72.

the Hall for Sages' Gathering (*jisheng dian* 集聖殿) and then changed again to the Hall for Solemn Ritual (*suyi dian* 肅義殿) in 1033 (the second year of Renzong's direct governing).[85] The final name did not have any association with the Sacred Ancestor or Daoism.

It was not until 1072, however, during the reign of Emperor Shenzong, that sustained discussion concerning the veneration of the royal ancestors in the Imperial Ancestral Shrine took place. At that time, the imperial court was swarmed in conflicts caused by the implementation of the New Policies. Wang Jie 王介 (d. 1078), subeditor of the Imperial Archives, brought up the issue of the proper number of rooms honoring the former emperors in the Imperial Ancestral Shrine.[86] According to the classical ritual prescription, the proper number of rooms was seven, but at this time there were eight.[87] Heated debate centered on whether or not Xizu 僖祖, the great-great-grandfather of Taizu, was the first ancestor of the imperial family.[88] If not, the place of veneration of Xizu should be shifted to an annexed shrine. Wang Jie and his supporters declared, "The founding ancestor is Taizu. There is no other founding ancestor beyond him."[89] This statement in fact challenged the myth of the Sacred Ancestor. On the other hand, those who championed Xizu as the founding ancestor argued, "Although venerating Xizu in the Imperial Ancestral Shrine does not fit the [regulations of] the classical texts, its intention is not to disrespect ancestors. It would also be right to regulate ritual in accordance with the needs of the

---

85. CB 113.2644.

86. In ancient times, there were separate shrine buildings dedicated to individual emperors. However, since the Eastern Han, in a single building structure different rooms had been dedicated to individual emperors. Wechsler, *Offerings of Jade and Silk*, 126.

87. CB 236.5748–5750. This notion is based on the seven-generational liturgical scheme proposed by Zheng Xuan 鄭玄 (127–200 CE) in imitation of the Zhou ritual system. The three reputed dynastic founders were worshipped forever, while the remaining four would be dedicated to the present reigning emperor's most recent direct lineal ancestors. Robert P. Kramers, *K'ung tzu Chia-yü: The School Sayings of Confucius* (Leiden: E. J. Brill, 1950), 140, as cited in Keith N. Knapp, "Borrowing Legitimacy from the Dead: The Confucianization of Ancestral Worship," in *Early Chinese Religion, Part Two: The Period of Division (220–589 AD)*, eds. John Lagerwey and Lü Pengzhi, 2 vols. (Leiden: Brill, 2010), 1: 146.

88. CB 240. 5850. On the history on the number of shrines within the Imperial Ancestral Shrine, see Zeng Gong 曾鞏 (1019–1083), "Zongmiao" 宗廟, QSW 58: 1257.314. For the history of the ritual of the Imperial Ancestral Shrine, see Yamauchi Kōichi, "Hokusō jidai no taibyō" 北宋時代の太廟, *Jōchi shigaku* 35 (1990): 91–119.

89. CB 240.5850, 5856. This notion is based on Wang Su's 王肅 (195–256 CE) liturgical scheme that one shrine should be dedicated to the dynastic father and the remaining six should be dedicated to recent lineal ancestors. Kramers, *K'ung tzu*, 156, as cited in Knapp, "Borrowing Legitimacy,"146.

time."[90] They also emphasized the fact that Taizu himself had honored Xizu as the Emperor of Responsive Birth (*ganshengdi* 感生帝), or a celestial deity who begot a human emperor by pairing (*pei* 配) the former's tablet with the latter.[91]

In the wake of this controversy, Emperor Shenzong deferred to the opinion of Wang Anshi 王安石 (1021–1086), the most influential official of the time. Wang declared, "Not all sacrificial rituals to Heaven practiced in this dynasty are in line with the classical rituals. However, those practices neither compromise nor violate fundamental morality. [Given that,] there is no need to correct those current ritual practices, based on the classical texts."[92] Wang Anshi a supporter of stronger monarchical power, felt that there was no need to change the current practice against the emperor's will for the sake of observance of the classical rituals. In the end, Emperor Shenzong was able to dispense with the regulations of the classical rituals and keep Xizu as the first ancestor of the dynasty. Although the challengers did not carry the day, they were not only able to call into question the legitimacy of Xizu as the first dynastic ancestor, but also any royal ancestors of the dynasty beyond Taizu.[93]

The process recounted above illustrates that court officials were successful in challenging the Emperor Renzong's continuation of the cult of the Sacred Ancestor as a public ritual and in having it downgraded to the status of a private ritual of the royal family. The closing down of the Royal Image Halls in local areas and the restoration of the prestige of the Imperial Ancestral Shrine signaled a cultural shift at the Song imperial court. Some officials even challenged the status of the royal ancestors ritually constructed and called for orthopraxis based on the classical texts. In this process of confronting the emperors over their non-Confucian ritual practices, the challengers used the classical ritual prescriptions as the grounds for their arguments.

## *Counterbalancing Imperial Power through Criticism of the Royal Death Rituals*

The affirmation of the classical ritual texts as the sole source of legitimacy of various imperial and court rituals gave scholar-officials the authority they

---

90. CB 240.5855.

91. CB 240.5839; Yamauchi Kōichi, "Hokusō jidai no taibyō," 65.

92. CB 240.5861.

93. The tablet of Xizu was finally removed from the Imperial Ancestral Shrine during the Emperor Ningzong's era (1168–1224).

needed to criticize the death rituals of the royal family members. During the reign of Renzong, court officials gradually exercised their political intervention in the performance of death rituals held for royal family members. The complexity of the issue of funerary rituals stemmed in large part from the emperor's having multiple wives who were not of equal status. Their specific relations with the current emperor complicated the matter of defining their importance with regard to ritual procedures. Specifically, it was unclear how much honor should be shown to a particular wife and where her spirit tablet and image hall would be located. Although court officials during the reign of Renzong by and large agreed that that the criterion of the legitimacy of state rituals was the prescription in the classical ritual texts, conflicts among court officials came to the fore in the debates over interpretation of the texts.

Zhenzong's funeral in the main followed the guidelines of the classical ritual: his spirit tablet was installed within the Imperial Ancestral Shrine, and commoners were directed to wear white mourning clothes with no decoration.[94] Officials also followed the conventional custom of using geomancy, as per the *Book of Burial* (*Zangjing* 葬經), in selecting the site for the emperor's burial.[95] For his funeral, the Empress Liu did, however, incorporate certain elements that demonstrated a remarkable departure from tradition. She ordered that the original copy of the Heavenly Text be buried with Zhenzong.[96] A painted portrait of the emperor was carried in the funeral procession.[97] The empress ordered that the Buddhist death ritual be performed every seventh day after his death seven times at the Founding Sage Monastery (*qisheng yuan* 啟聖院), of which officers of the Bureau of Military Affairs (*shumi yuan* 樞密院) were in charge.[98] In addition, she had the Yongding Chan Monastery (*yongding chanyuan* 永定禪院) built for housing the caretakers of the emperor's grave. These arrangements demonstrated that the royal death rituals used multiple platforms drawn from different traditions for varied purposes.

Empress Liu was able to make these substantial modifications to imperial funeral because of the power she wielded. However, after the death of Empress Liu, objections by officials led to greater restrictions on modifications of the royal funeral ritual. In 1032, the first year after the end of the regency, court officials

---

94. SHY Li 29.18.

95. SHY Li 29.24. Some criticism of making use of geomancy in regard to the emperor's burial and funeral was recorded in Li 29.14.

96. CB 99.2297.

97. SHY Li 29.23.

98. SHY Li 29.20.

intervened in the realm of royal funerary rituals. At that time, Renzong had just learned that the courtier Lady Li, who served the Empress Liu, was none other than his birth mother. Because she had just passed away, the emperor wanted to hold a court funeral ritual honoring her status as the emperor's birth mother. This idea was clearly displeasing to Empress Liu, who objected to it adamantly.[99] The following year, the empress herself died. No longer bound by the empress's objections, Renzong bestowed the posthumous title of empress on his birth mother. However, this act, despite being one of filial piety, faced strong opposition from some officials. They argued that it was not possible for two legitimate empresses to exist simultaneously.[100]

Emperor Renzong installed his birth mother's portrait in the Hall for Abundant Filial Piety (*guangxiao dian* 廣孝殿) at the Temple of Radiant Spirit, and that of Empress Liu at a Buddhist temple, the Temple of Compassionate Filial Piety (*cixiao si* 慈孝寺), whose construction she had commissioned.[101] As the prestige of the Temple of Radiant Spirit far exceeded that of the other, Renzong in this fashion clearly demonstrated which of the two women he intended to exalt.[102] In 1033, Renzong commissioned a joint burial for both of them along with Zhenzong in the Yongding Mausoleum. The spirit tablets of both women were installed at the Shrine of Offering Compassion (*fengci miao* 奉慈廟). In 1045, Renzong transferred the spirit tablets of the two empresses to the Imperial Ancestral Shrine and placed his birthmother's tablet in its own room in the same hall where the Empress Liu's tablet was installed.[103] The spirit tablets of the two empresses were moved again, being placed in close proximity to the tablet of Zhenzong, though the tablet of Zhenzong's first wife was closest.[104] As this move violated the principle of one emperor's tablet paired to one empress' tablet, the officials were vocal in their criticism. Yet the officials were not able to force the emperor to follow their prescriptions. Renzong had by this time become powerful enough in his own right that the finding of a middle ground was necessary: in the end he was able to place his birthmother's tablet in the Imperial Ancestral Shrine.

---

99. CB 109.2577 and 10.2615.

100. CB 120.2610.

101. The primary purpose of building the Temple of Compassionate Filial Piety was to host Zhenzong's image. Ebrey, "Portrait Sculptures," 55.

102. CB 113.2640.

103. CB 157.3798.

104. CB 157.3803.

Nevertheless, the Academy of Ritual and some high-ranking officials did extend their influence in the course of Renzong's reign. In 1034, the Academy issued the strong recommendation that the emperor stop making seasonal offerings at the mausoleum of Zhenzong and his wives, because such offerings were not a part of the classical ritual.[105] In 1041, when the second son of Renzong died at the age of three, he made it known that he desired to perform a lavish funeral for his second son, which required five months of preparation. One measure of the extravagance was the emperor's wish to employ five thousand people in the funeral procession. Sun Mian 孫沔 (996–1066), officer of remonstrance, composed a memorial to the emperor expressing his objections to this on the basis of time constraints, expense, and security concerns. However, other officers did not dare present their objecting memorials to the emperor, knowing that the emperor's grief was keen, especially because he had lost his first son as well.[106] Three years later, in 1044, the emperor suffered the loss of his uncle, Prince Jing (荊王, 985–1044) who had been his father-figure after the death of Zhenzong at his young age. This time, Fan Zhongyan 范仲淹 (989–1052) quickly intervened in the emperor's move for holding a lavish burial with an application of geomantic theory, which would result in delaying the schedule determined by the classical ritual regulation. Fan suggested that limiting expenditures and following the classical ritual (*dianli* 典禮) would manifest the "identity" (正體; literally "correct body") of the state.[107] Ouyang Xiu largely seconded Fan's argument in his memorial to the emperor. He made the additional point that the moral offense of a lavish funeral was not only a waste of resources but would also damage the reputation of the deceased.[108] The emperor was swayed by their arguments.

The Academy of Ritual issued more and more regulations in the following years. In particular, it set limits on the lavishness of funerals on the part of wealthy families—which included royal families.[109] It also discouraged the use of geomancy in relation to funerals, a common practice among royal families, which resulted in some burials being delayed for many years. In 1062, the government

---

105. CB 114.2677.

106. CB 131.3103–3104.

107. CB 146.3532.

108. Ouyang Xiu, "Lun zang Jingwang zhazi" 論葬荊王劄子, *Ouyang xiu quanji* 歐陽修全集 (Beijing: Zhonghua shuju, 2001), 6 vols., 4:104.1585.

109. CB 228.5558–5559. For example, in 1054, it announced that state aid to the Imperial Consort Wencheng 溫成 would be reduced. Sun Bian 孫抃 (d. 1064), "Shang Renzong lun Wencheng huzang yi jiansun zhengli" 仁宗論溫成護葬宜減損正禮, QSW 22: 473.341.

announced that royal families could keep unburied corpses for no longer than five years; after that, burial was mandatory.[110] This trend of increasing regulation gradually diminished the freedom of royal families to manipulate the regulations of classical death rituals. By the end of his reign, the emperor himself was rarely able to override the decisions of the Academy of Ritual, and the authority of the classical ritual texts with regard to court rituals was much greater.

The intervention in and regulation of royal death rituals by some officials resulted in tension between the emperor and officialdom, and also exposed conflicts between factions within officialdom. The disputes that arose regarding the funeral ritual of Prince Pu poignantly illustrate this.[111] After the death of Renzong, his nephew, Yingzong 英宗 (r. 1064–1067), became emperor. Yingzong was brought to the court when he was four years old because Emperor Renzong did not have a male heir. Upon Renzong's death Yingzong was initially reluctant to assume the throne and fell ill as soon as he became emperor.[112] His lack of enthusiasm for ruling and his illness further undermined his status, already weak, as an adopted emperor. Grand Councilor Han Qi and Ouyang Xiu, the two most influential officials in that time, helped to shorten the regency of the Empress Dowager so that Yingzong's direct governance could begin sooner. They were the proponents of the Minor Reforms in 1043–1044, and were advocates of greater monarchical power.

In the fourth month of 1065, Yingzong raised the issue of the proper funeral ritual for his biological father, Prince Pu, in discussions with officials. This matter was linked to the following questions: (1) could an adopted son refer to his biological father as "parent" (qin 親)? (if not, Yingzong was required to refer to his biological father as "uncle"); and (2) could Prince Pu be elevated to the status of emperor (huangkao 皇考; literally, "imperial deceased father"), if he was recognized as the father of the current emperor? In that case, there would be two former emperors who had lived concurrently. The issue of how Prince Pu was to be referred to also involved the magnitude of the funeral and the length of the period for which Yingzong should mourn. A prince belonged to the first grade in official rank, and his spirit tablet would be installed in a family shrine. However, if Prince Pu were to become huangkao, his tablet

---

110. SS Li 27, 124.2912.

111. Detailed records of this debate are found in CB 205–208. Xiao-bin Ji has studied this debate, especially from the point of view of "distribution of power"; see Ji, *Politics and Conservatism*, 94–109.

112. On Yingzong's biographical background and illness, see Carney T. Fisher, "The Ritual Dispute of Sung Ying-tsung," *Papers on Far Eastern History* 36 (1987): 109–137.

could be legitimately installed in the Imperial Ancestral Shrine.[113] Out of filial piety, Emperor Yingzong wished to refer to Prince Pu as "imperial father" and establish a shrine in the capital city for him. He could not come to a decision himself, however.

After some discussion, several officials from the Bureau of Academicians and the Department of Secretariat rejected the emperor's idea. The majority agreed that the emperor should refer to his biological father as uncle because he had already been adopted by Renzong. They argued that a person could not have two fathers. They also believed that by associating with his biological father, the emperor would further undermine his own authority. Sima Guang, who was at an early stage of his career, led the opposition. He was also concerned that the influence of Han Qi and Ouyang Xiu would grow even stronger.[114] He emphasized the authority of the bureaucracy and of the classical texts, in his view the basis of imperial legitimacy. Sima specifically pointed to the "Records of Mourning Clothes" (*Sangfu ji* 喪服記) in the *Yili* 儀禮 (*Ceremonies and Rituals*), which reads: "An adopted son pays back his parents (*fumu* 父母)." It is not clear in this passage, however, whether "parents" specifies the biological or the adoptive father. For Sima, one could not have two fathers in terms of ritual obligations. Therefore he interpreted the male parent to be the adopted father only. He argued as follows:

> Your Majesty's not forgetting of the benefit [you received] from Prince Pu lies at the bottom of your heart, but not in the superficial and unsubstantial title [by which you refer to him.]. If a filial son loves his parents, then he should make offerings to them via the proper ritual. Recently, an improper ritual in which Prince Pu was referred to by an incorrect title has been performed and offerings made to him. How do these benefit Prince Pu?[115]

---

113. In that case, there would be two emperors of the same generation, which violated the classical ritual regulation. This aspect, however, was not a center of the debate, because the first two emperors of the Song were brothers, both of whom had already been installed in the Imperial Ancestral Shrine. This issue had been highly contested during the reign of Emperor Yuan of the Eastern Jin (r. 317–321), who was a cousin of the two previous emperors. He settled the matter by concluding that a succeeding emperor should treat the previous emperor as a previous generation in the ancestral shrine even if he was a brother. See Knapp, "Borrowing Legitimacy from the Dead," 160–165.

114. Ji, *Politics and Conservatism*, 101.

115. CB 207.5032.

Han Qi and Ouyang Xiu backed Yingzong as a means of increasing the emperor's political power. Ouyang brought up the precedent of Emperor Xuandi 宣帝 (74–49 BCE) of the Han dynasty. Xuandi had addressed his father as *qin* or parent, upon becoming emperor, and also built an imperial shrine for him in the capital city.[116] However, Ouyang's opponents discredited his use of the example of Emperor Xuan in this debate. They argued that Emperor Xuan had been the sole representative of the imperial lineage at that time, but that Prince Pu had his brother, the legitimate ruler Renzong.

Ouyang believed that the decision not to fulfill ritual obligations to one's biological father was based on an incorrect interpretation of a passage in the *Yili* 儀禮.[117] He also cited the *Periods of Five Clothing* (*Wufu nianyue* 五服年月), the state regulations promulgated in 1027,[118] which referred to adopted parents as *hou fumu* (後父母; literally, "later parents"), being differentiated from biological parents, *fumu*.[119] Therefore, he maintains, "According to the classical ritual laws, one should address his biological father as father and observe the 'three-year mourning' for his father's death."[120] He denounced those who did not perform the appropriate ritual for their biological fathers, saying that they were no better than beasts. In this dispute, Ouyang presented his theory of ritual, which focused on the tension between human nature and formal ritual. He understood that ritual articulated social expression of human nature endowed by Heaven (*tianxing* 天性), claiming, "The Sages established rituals based on human feelings (*renqing* 人情)."[121] For Ouyang, to call one's biological father "uncle" was contrary to human nature, and therefore went against the fundamental principle of ritual. In support of Ouyang, Sun Gu 孫固 (1016–1090) argued: "A ritual can be changed, but human nature endowed by Heaven cannot. Prince [Pu] can be legitimately called 'parent.'"[122]

Yingzong found himself at the center of strife among officials who split over the issue. Although the final decision rested with the emperor, he still

---

116. Building a shrine in the imperial city was the exclusive right of the emperor.

117. Ouyang Xiu, "Puyi, *juan er*" 濮議, 卷二, *Ouyang xiu quanji* 5:121.1858.

118. The state adopted Sun Shi's proposal to make the state regulations more accessible by revising the earlier version, the *Kaibao zhengli, wufu nianyue* 開寶正禮五服年月. CB 105.2453.

119. Ouyang Xiu, "Zhongshu qing jiguan zai yi jincheng zhazi" 中書請集官再議進呈劄子, *Ouyang xiu quanji* 5:122.1863–1864.

120. Ouyang, "Puyi, *juan er*" 濮議, 卷二, 5:121.1857.

121. Ouyang, "Wei hou huo wen, *xia*" 爲後或問, 下, 5:123.1873.

122. CB 207.5032.

needed to negotiate with the Empress Dowager. They reached a compromise by which the emperor could address Prince Pu as father but would not grant him the title of emperor. Yingzong announced shortly thereafter that there was no historical precedent for an emperor to address his biological father as "imperial uncle." He would thus call Pu "father." He also announced that he would build a shrine to Pu in the capital city, which was the exclusive privilege of a late emperor. With this edict, he considered the matter decided and warned dissidents that any further discussion of this issue would lead to punishment.[123] This threat notwithstanding, in 1066 three officers of remonstration reopened the issue by leveling harsh criticism at their opponents— Ouyang Xiu, Han Qi, and others. They accused Ouyang of "opening up a heterodox discussion and falsely presenting classical references." They also accused Han Qi of sticking to his initial erroneous position despite his knowledge of the classical ritual.[124] They called for the removal of both from office or they themselves would resign. They actually stopped coming to work and remained firm in their demand. Although the emperor asked them to return to work, they refused. The emperor, being unable to remove high officials like Han and Ouyang from office, had no alternative but to demote the three officers of remonstration.

This debate was the result of officialdom being split into two factions, one favoring greater power for the bureaucracy and the other favoring a more powerful monarch. Sima Guang and his followers, the former faction, made the case that ritual law took precedence over both human emotion and the emperor's personal opinion. By way of defending the prerogatives of the officials, Sima decried the emperor's punishment of the officers of remonstration as an attack on their freedom of speech.

For their part, the officials who sided with the emperor emphasized his sound judgment concerning ritual practice:[125]

The emperor said to Wen Yanbo 文彦博 (1006–1097), "Ritual is neither what heaven sends down nor what the earth produces. It is derived from human feelings. Ritual officials habitually stick to the old tradition of Confucianism and disregard the common laws established by the emperors of recent times. Their argument does not help me

---

123. CB 207.5043.

124. CB 207.5023–5024.

125. Regarding the history of the imperial *mingtang* ritual, see James T. C. Liu, "The Sung Emperors and the Ming-t'ang or Hall of Enlightenment," in *Études Song: In Memoriam Étienne Balazs*, Série II, ed. Françoise Aubin (Paris: Mouton, 1973), 45–57.

demonstrate filial piety and assure the well-being of people." Yanbo said, "Only Your Majesty's sagehood attains ritual's clarity, and is able to comprehend the emotional aspect of ritual and assimilate changes to the ritual. This cannot be done by ministers."[126]

The point here made by the emperor is that he is not bound by the classical ritual laws, and moreover could be a role model for his subjects. He was contrasting ritual law with monarchical power, bureaucratic structure with the emperor. Wen responded that ritual could be changed, and it was the emperor who had the power to define "ritual" and put it into practice. A statement made by Sun Bian 孫抃 (996–1064) sums up the argument for monarchical power: "The imperial court's laws are Your Majesty's laws, and Your Majesty's laws are none other than the Laws of Our Founders (*zuzong zhifa* 祖宗之法)."[127]

The debate over the ritual status of Prince Pu demonstrated how power relations had changed as a result of such debates.[128] Sima's faction rose to great prominence among the officials, although this faction appeared to have suffered a defeat, insofar as some members were demoted. By drawing upon the authority of the classical text and the power of the bureaucracy, they were able to check substantially the two greatest powers of the time: the emperor and the two most influential officials. The tensions brought to the fore by this debate were not resolved, and became even more pronounced during the era of New Policies (1069–1076) (which will be discussed in the following two chapters of this book). Those scholar-officials who advocated a return to Confucian rituals as prescribed in the classical texts gradually expanded their influence, using various methods to promote Confucianism as the shared values and moral core of society.

## *Shifting Discourse: Proper Funeral Ritual Practice for Officials*

The court officials' efforts to define the legitimate imperial death rituals gave rise to debates about what constituted proper protocol for funeral rituals and mourning for officials themselves. The reign of Renzong saw a sharp increase

---

126. The context of this discussion was the relevance of the current ritual practice of the *mingtang* 明堂, in light of the classical ritual tradition that took place in 1050. CB 168.4037–4038.

127. CB 179.4339.

128. Xiao-bin Ji acknowledges that Sima and the officers of remonstration gained prestige as a result of the controversy, despite their demotion. However, he contends that Yingzong was the victor in the end. Ji's conclusion grows out of his basic premise that the Song emperors took advantage of factional strife to increase their political power by positioning themselves as the mediators of disputes. However, in this particular controversy Yingzong did not take

in the number of new regulations related to those rituals promulgated by the government, where state officers were concerned. In 1029, the government issued *The Ordinances of Funerals and Burials* (*Sangzang ling* 喪葬令), which specified procedures and spending limits in accordance with the deceased's official rank.[129] There was a significant public component in death rituals, especially as mourners had to abstain from various specified social activities, including their jobs, by wearing mourning garments. As the state enacted criminal laws aimed at state officers regarding their observance of funeral rituals and mourning, more heated discussion on the subject—and thus extensive study of the classical texts—followed.

One of the most sensitive issues of the time was the observation of the "three-year mourning" (*sannian sang* 三年喪) period, which in actuality lasted twenty-seven months after the death of a parent.[130] "Three-year mourning" refers to various forms of ritual, including funeral, burial, mourning, and obsequies to be performed for one's parents. After the Western Han court adopted Confucianism as the state's ideology, civil officers were required to take a leave of absence in order to fulfill the mourning duty. Since then, scholarly debates around the "three-year mourning" had tended to focus on exactly how officials should observe it, what obligations should be applied to cases that the classics failed to mention, and to what extent flexibility could be allowed by reflecting current circumstances and human feelings.[131] Following the tradition of previous dynasties, the Song state also required that officers resign from their posts and return to their hometowns after the death of their parents. However, some officers did not return home, fearing the permanent loss of their posts, especially when their hometowns were far away from where they lived.[132] In

---

the lead in the initiating and shaping of the debate. Rather, he found himself on the defensive and was forced to abandon much of his plan in the face of opposition. Ji, *Politics and Conservatism*, 100–109.

129. Zhongguo shehui kexueyuan, Lishi yanjiusuo, annot., *Tianyige cang Mingchaoben Tianshengling jiaozheng: Fu Tangling fuyuan yanjiu* 天一閣藏明鈔本天聖令校証: 附唐令復原研究 (Beijing: Zhonghua shuju, 2006); CB 118.2798, 140.3361, 167.4025–4026 and 217.5275; SS Li 27, 124.2909.

130. For debates on the length of the period, see footnote 1 in "Introduction."

131. See Mu-chou Poo, "Ideas Concerning Death and Burial in Pre-Han and Han China," *Asia Major* 3, 3rd series, no. 2 (1990): 25–62; Miranda Brown, *The Politics of Mourning in Early China* (Albany: State University of New York Press, 2012); Masakazu Fujikawa, *Gishin jidai ni okeru mofuku rei no kenkyû* 魏晉時代おける喪服禮の研究 (Tokyo: Keibunsha, 1961); Norman Kutcher, *Mourning in Late Imperial China: Filial Piety and the State* (New York: Cambridge University Press, 1999), 1–20.

132. Wang Yong, *Yanyi yimou lu*, 1.9.

1021, toward the end of Zhenzong's reign, responding to a memorial, the state issued an edict declaring that officers who did not wear mourning garments during their "three-year mourning" period would be punished.[133] It was more likely Empress Liu who made that decision, because she had been the de facto ruler since Zhenzong fell ill in 1019.[134] As a result, the state transformed the observance of the "three-year mourning" from a moral responsibility into a legal obligation.

This policy was the cause of controversy for years to come. One of the serious questions that arose during Renzong's reign was whether all officers should have their salaries paid during the mourning period, or whether there should be distinctions according to rank. In particular, military officers who were at war were not allowed to return home to fulfill their mourning obligation. This policy was directly related to military concerns, but also reflected the fact that military officers were less privileged than civil officers of equivalent rank.[135] The unfair treatment of military officers in this regard was brought up at court as early as 1030.[136] Nevertheless, it was not until 1041 that the emperor made an adjustment by allowing military officers at the rank of deputy commissioner of the Three Offices and above outside of the border areas to go on leave while continuing to draw their salaries.[137] Officers below this rank who were not on duty at the border were permitted to go on leave as well, though without being paid. Both civil and military officers of this rank and above who were on duty in border areas could request one month of vacation after a parent's death. In 1043, the Academy of Ritual weighed in on this matter, arguing that distinctions of office or military rank should not factor into the granting of the mourning period:

> The Academy of Ritual discussed the issue as follows: "According to the *Records of Rituals* (*Liji* 禮記), 'In the case of a parent's funeral and mourning, there is no [distinction between] noble and commoner: the ritual should be the same.' The text also says, 'The observation of the 'three-year mourning' is the ultimate demonstration of humanity.' [Thus] we request that distinctions not be made between civil and

---

133. CB 97.2242.

134. Chaffee, "The Rise and Regency," 1–25.

135. CB 263.6450.

136. CB 130.2535

137. CB 134.3195.

military officers, or between the ranks; all should have [the same period for] public hearing to end mourning."[138]

The emperor, however, did not defer to the Academy in this regard, on the grounds that military officers came from a variety of social strata. His decision implied that the "three-year mourning" was the exclusive prerogative of civil officers and members of the royal families, and many military officers did not share their social standing. Against this background, in 1045 a military commander, Tian Kuang 田況 (1005–1063), changed the emperor's mind. He took a leave of absence from his work at a border station in order to observe his mourning period. Despite having declined the first invitation, he was recalled to work a second time. After resuming his work, he had an audience with the emperor on the pretext of reporting about the security situation at the border. Because he was sobbing while making the request to allow him to complete the "three-year mourning", the emperor was touched and allowed him to do so. The tradition of military commanders completing the "three-year mourning" began with this case in 1045.[139]

Whether or not an official would draw a salary during the mourning period was also a matter of contention. In 1044, the government enacted the policy that officials at the rank of deputy commissioner of the Three Offices and above would receive salary during their mourning periods. This policy also included military officers of equivalent rank who were not on duty at the border.[140] However, it excluded all officers of lower rank. A memorial presented by Liu Chang 劉敞 (1019–1068) in 1054 gave voice to the sentiment among officials that all government officers, regardless of their rank and type of post, should be subject to the same obligations and benefits:

> Your minister humbly observes that, in the old system, officials of deputy commissioner of the Three Offices and above in rank, as well as the envoys of equivalent ranks, regardless of their rank, all [were to] remove their mourning garments officially (*gongchu* 公除) on the one hundredth day after their parents' funeral service. . . . *Your minister humbly requests that the "three-year mourning" be applied to the whole society . . .* At the present time, the government stops paying salaries of officials during the mourning period as soon as they take a leave of duty. That

---

138. SS Li 28, 125.2923; CB 142.3398.

139. CB 157.3796.

140. CB 177.4286.

is too harsh treatment for them. Why are those who practice the proper ritual treated worse than those exiled officers? Your minister sees that those observing the mourning period are too poor to buy food. They beg for food. Their appearance hurts the filial heart. It is not because they have the appearance of commoners or live in a vulgar lifestyle [but because they are poor]. Your minister thinks that all the civil officials of the Hanlin Academy and the Department of Secretariat and various military personnel at the rank of commissioner and above should be paid their full salaries during the "three-year mourning." In addition, court officials and envoys of equivalent rank should be paid half of their salary. In this way the imperial court will be noted for its adherence to proper ritual practice and for being guided by an abundance of [Confucian] wisdom. . . .Your Majesty has kindly commanded all officials close to you to observe the "three-year mourning" without worrying about salary. They can fulfill the obligations of mourning [expected of] human beings and manifest a high degree of humanity and benevolence. However, [other] officials who have regular audiences at the imperial court and officers of equivalent rank do not [have the privilege of] taking advantage of that command. In your minister's opinion, although officers have different titles, they serve the same lord. It is not appropriate to have such distinctions among them.[141] [italics added]

The "three-year mourning" was only required of civil officers at this time; this memorial reflects the conviction of many scholar-officials that the duty should be extended to all levels of society as a normative expression of filial piety. At the same time, this memorial is critical of the emperor's favoritism in his support of mourning officials and requests a fair policy concerning officers being paid while in mourning. In response, the government in 1059 issued the edict that military officers were allowed 100 days' vacation with salary following the death of their parents. The edict also stated that those military officers who wished to observe the "three-year mourning" were permitted to do so, but it was not required. This policy reflected the aforementioned case of Tian Kuang. As for salary, there was no change from the previous policy: royal family members would be paid their full salaries while in mourning.[142] In the long process of defining the state's policies on this issue, the emperors tended to favor lessening the mourning requirements for efficient governance, especially in case of military urgency,

---

141. CB 177.4285–4286.

142. CB 190.4592.

whereas scholar-officials wished to extend the full-length obligations to more people and to have paid salaries during the period.[143]

The government also laid out more concrete administrative procedures for officials with regard to funerals and mourning. Officers were required to report the scheduling of their parent's funeral in order to request their "withdrawal from office" (*jieguan* 解管).[144] In the very beginning of the Song dynasty (994), the government enacted the regulation that officials were prohibited from attending public functions until one hundred days had elapsed following the funeral of a parent. The Bureau of Censorate (*yushitai* 御史臺) had jurisdiction over this matter and was also to be notified that the period of restriction from public activity had ended.[145] In 1024, the second year of Renzong's reign, the government instituted the following protocol for officials with posts in the capital city and at the imperial court who had completed the mourning period: they were to report to the Bureau of Censorate and then proceed to the court prior to resuming work.[146] If an official failed to report prior to resuming work, he was to be fired. However, the law allowed for some exceptions. If the government needed an official for a particular post before the mourning period was over, it would invite that official to work. This invitation was called *qifu* (起復) or "recall for work."[147] Such an invitation from the government was generally considered an honor, because it indicated one's significance as an official. A recalled officer could decline this invitation on the grounds that he was bound by the duty of filial piety.[148] If an official had no alternative but to work during a period of mourning in order to support his family, he could ask that special permission be granted for him to work. For instance, in 1024 Du Qi 杜杞 (1005–1050) wrote a letter making such a request. He explained that

---

143. This tendency continued during the Ming, and became more drastic under the Manchu rulers of the Qing dynasty. Kutcher, *Mourning in Late Imperial China*, 61–67 and 104–152.

144. Besides this extensive period, in 1024 the government allowed two days' vacation for mourning someone other than one's parents. SHY Li 14.15. One could also request a special vacation in order to return home and see to the maintenance of the family grave. See Li Shu 李淑 (fl. 1027), "Qi jia ji sao fufen zou" 乞假祭掃父墳奏, QSW 28:597.238.

145. SS Li 28, 125.2922.

146. QSW 44: 944.63. However, from 1070 onward they did not need to report to the office in order to make an appearance at court. CB 217.5275.

147. SS Li 28, 125.2924.

148. For an example of a letter declining this invitation, see CB 260.6335; Fu Bi 富弼 (1004–1083), "Ci qifu biao" 辭起復表, QSW 28: 599.263. As for official letters either granting or declining such requests written by Su Song 蘇頌 in his official capacity, see QSW 60:1309.194–196.

his grandmother had died leaving no sons, only daughters-in-laws and seven grandchildren, of whom he was the eldest.[149]

An ongoing matter of concern was which rituals an official was eligible to attend during the mourning period. By definition, mourning and funerals were categorized as "inauspicious rituals" (*xiongli* 凶禮), during which participants should wear inauspicious clothes; furthermore, officials in mourning were to refrain from attending auspicious events. In an effort to present a clear stance on this issue in 1018, the government enacted a regulation that prohibited both civil and military officers from attending banquets during the mourning period.[150] Going further, the government issued an edict in 1027 specifying that those who had left a parent's funeral unfinished were not eligible to participate in the ritual of the Imperial Ancestral Shrine. It noted in particular that those who had officially reported they had taken off their mourning clothes (*gongchu* 公除) but had not yet performed the burial ritual (due to problems with selecting the date for the burial in accordance with geomancy) would be barred from the ceremony.[151] Much discussion ensued in the wake of this latter edict.

Having promulgated these laws on mourning conduct, the government was active in enforcing them. In 1035, the Academy of Ritual examined the case of an official who attended the ritual of the Imperial Ancestral Shrine before completing the burial of a parent. It was the academy's recommendation that the offender receive fifty lashes and his attendants thirty, based on a regulation from the early Tang dynasty. In 1047, Shao Bi 邵必, an officer of ritual, presented a memorial asking that more detailed regulations be provided for the case of the Suburban Sacrifice and various rituals at the Temple of Radiant Spirit, as well as for that of people recalled to work during their mourning periods. Shao Bi requested that mourners be granted special permission to attend the rituals or be able to send a substitute. His suggestion was accepted and became a government regulation.[152] In 1044, Song Qi proposed a policy that mourners during the "three-year mourning" should

---

149. Du Qi 杜杞 (1005–1050), "Wen sangfu zou" 問喪服奏, QSW 30: 638.75 (SHY Li 36.6). For another case, see CB 172.4129.

150. CB 94.2172.

151. CB 105.2449; SHY 36.15.

152. SS Li 28, 125.2925; CB 161.3894. The entire body of the memorial is available in Shao Bi, "Qi jiaomiao xingli chenliao ju fumu sangzhe bing buxu fu zou" 乞郊廟行禮臣寮居父母喪者並不許赴奏, QSW 29:67.169.

not sit in state exams.[153] Although this proposal was enacted for less than a year, it is likely that it became a social norm to demonstrate candidate's moral qualifications.[154]

Growing concerns about funeral and mourning practice voiced by officials prompted the Academy of Ritual to clarify how the laws were to be interpreted in complicated cases. For example, some people withdrew from office to mourn the death of their remarried mothers, which led to a debate about the propriety of doing so. The *Book of Ritual* does not specify a son's mourning duty for a remarried mother after her husband's death. Yet it defines a case for a divorced mother: a male heir should not wear mourning garment for her, but other sons should wear it for one year.[155] The distinction was drawn between a divorced mother and a remarried mother, on the grounds that the former was thought to have wronged her husband, the latter not. Nevertheless, some scholars during the Jin Dynasty (265–420 CE) challenged this ritual code as some complicated cases emerged. There were sons who were compelled to take care of their mothers' death rituals because there was no one else to do so, and a divorced mother who returned to her ex-husband's house to live with her son after the ex-husband's death. After serious scholarly debates, the Jin State (266–420 CE) prescribed "mourning at heart" (*xinsang* 心喪) for remarried or divorced mothers, which was adopted by the Tang state's regulations.[156]

The Song state followed the previous dynasties' regulations regarding this issue in the *Periods of Five Clothing* (*Wufu nianyue* 五服年月) promulgated in 1027: in the case of the mourning of a divorced or remarried mother, the male heir of the family should not wear mourning clothes, but rather was to practice "mourning at heart." [157] The theoretical basis for not requiring the public mourning of a remarried mother was that her position was the same as that of

---

153. John W. Chaffe, *The Thorny Gates of Learning in Sung China: A Social History of Examinations* (Albany: State University of New York Press, 1995), 54.

154. There is a record during the Ming that a candidate left the examination scene upon hearing of his father's death. Kutcher, *Mourning in Late Imperial China*, 63. During the Qing, exam takers were required to demonstrate that they were not in the status of mourning for a parent. Richard J. Smith, *The Qing Dynasty and Traditional Chinese Culture* (Lanham, MD: Rowman & Littlefield, 2015), 116.

155. Yiqun Zhou, "The Status of Mothers in the Early Chinese Mourning System," *T'oung Pao* 99, nos. 1–3 (2013): 16–18.

156. Masakazu Fujikawa, *Gishin jidai ni okeru mofuku rei no kenkyû* 魏晉時代おける喪服禮の研究 (Tokyo: Keibunsha, 1961), 162; Ya-ju Cheng, *Qinggan yu zhidu: WeiJin shidai de muzi guanxi* 情感與制度: 魏晉時代的母子關係 (Taipei: Guoli Taiwan daxue chuban weiyuanhui, 2001), 85–91 and 99–114.

157. SS Li 28, 125.2927.

a divorced mother, neither of whom had any legitimate status within her ex-husband's family.[158] This view suggests that the practice of mourning was not just about expressing filial piety, but rather more about affirming the family lineage. An official who practiced "mourning at heart" could participate in any auspicious activities; he could also fulfill the requirements of public mourning while holding his position, if he so desired. The requirement not to wear mourning garments was limited to a male heir of the family; other sons and daughters could wear them if they desired to do so. Some officials continued to mourn the passing of their remarried mothers by temporarily resigning their positions. Amid heated debates that lasted for years, a scholar brought attention to a ritual code of the Tang Dynasty prescribing the wearing of mourning garments for "three years" for divorced or remarried mothers. Due to the disagreements between the texts, the government in 1035 amended the regulation so that an official had to report having "withdraw[n] from office," but could practice "mourning at heart" without wearing mourning clothes in the case of the death of a divorced or remarried mother.[159]

The ritual requirement for a son of a concubine was also ambiguous. In legal terms, he was a son of a legitimate wife, though not of his biological mother. Early in 1016, the government specified that he should not wear mourning clothes for his biological mother if his adoptive mother was alive. On the other hand, if his elder half-brother was alive and his father was dead, he should observe the "three-year mourning" for his biological mother.[160] In this latter case, the son of a concubine was not a legitimate heir of the family anyway, and there was no reason for him to be under his adoptive mother's care after his father's death.

The number of legal cases involving an individual's failure to follow funeral ritual protocol increased during Renzong's reign, and even more so during the reign of Shenzong. Many allegations were made, especially in cases where family relations were complicated but the prescriptions of the classical ritual texts were vague. Local government offices and the Academy of Ritual at the central government usually functioned as the courtroom where ritual violations were tried, a process that involved a great deal of interpretation of the classical texts. In one instance, an officer accused of failing to demonstrate filial piety in this way defended himself by saying that he did not know about his father's death

---

158. Liu Ban 劉攽, "Lun chumu jimu jia fu yu Wang Jiefu" 論出母繼母嫁服與王介甫, QSW 69:1503.173.

159. SS Li 28, 125.2928–2929.

160. CB 86.1966–7.

while serving his office away from his hometown. However, his father's death was public knowledge. Even if he actually did not know about his father's death, it indicated he had not tried to contact his father for "three years." For this reason, the judgment was that he was unfilial, and consequently was fired from his position.[161] There was a case where someone stole the corpse of his remarried mother in order to bury her along with his deceased father. The verdict was that the act was derived from filial piety, although it was illegal. He was released.[162] In 1045, a governor's wife reported to the authorities that her husband had attended a theatrical show featuring female entertainers during the mourning period for his father's death. He was demoted to a military position.[163] In 1037, the central government addressed whether one could live in a dwelling separate from one's grandparents after a parent's funeral. The answer was that one could, if there was no issue of dividing property. But if the parent's burial had not been held at the request of grandparents, one could not live separately. If the waiting period for the burial was very lengthy, this should be reported to the government office so that the office could keep the money for a future burial day.[164] This new edict announced in 1037 showed that legal cases concerning funerals and burial were also related to the distribution of family property among the surviving family members.

The observance of the funeral ritual and mourning had become the quintessential test of a person's morality. The key points were attending the funerals of friends and showing respect to the families of the deceased, in addition to proper conduct in mourning one's parent's death.[165] Funeral and mourning observance as a primary moral characterization of officials led to fierce political disputes in the era of New Policies, during which the officialdom was split over the public policies. In 1071, just after Wang Anshi had been designated to implement the policies, he informed the emperor that he could not implement the New Policies unless Sima Guang stayed away from the imperial court. Sima chose to leave the court. Later that year, Wang and Sima clashed again concerning the case of Li Ding 李定 (1028–1087), Wang's protégé. Officials in Sima's faction brought legal proceedings against Li Ding for his failure to

---

161. CB 176.4270. For similar examples, see CB 157.3808, 159.3840–3841, 239.5807, 268.6572, and 280.6859.

162. CB 120.2828.

163. CB 154.3747.

164. CB 120.2820.

165. CB 106.2468.

perform both the funeral and mourning rituals for his birth mother, despite his taking leave of absence upon learning of her death. Li Ding defended himself by saying his father did not confirm that she was his birth mother when asked about the truth. Li, however, knew that she was his birth mother, which was public knowledge. According to him, without his father's acknowledgement he was not able to carry out his mourning obligations. After a series of public disputes within the court, Wang Anshi was able to successfully defend Li Ding. As a result, Li escaped punishment; those who had accused him were fired.[166] In 1072, Wang Zishao 王子韶 was accused of not conducting burials for his parents' death along with other misbehavior, such as using flattery for personal gain. With Wang Anshi's confirmation of the charge, the emperor fired Wang Zishao.[167] Later, in 1084, Wang Anli 王安禮 (1034–1095), the younger brother of Wang Anshi, was charged for his unethical lifestyle, which involved practicing geomancy, conducting funerals without the proper respect, and holding banquets with courtesans.[168]

In the wake of increasing concerns over funerary rituals, the central government defined specific regulations on various mourning and funeral matters for government officers, based on the interpretations of the Confucian classical texts. As a result, death rituals were no longer just a matter of individual moral obligation; they were subject to close legal scrutiny by the state. The increasing number of allegations concerning funeral rituals and observation of the mourning period in turn demanded more specific regulations to be defined.

## *Promoting the Confucian Funeral and Mourning*

Establishing funeral and mourning rituals as a legal obligation for government officers promoted the infusion of Song society with Confucian ethics and rituals. Scholar-officials, during the reigns of Renzong and Shenzong in particular, strongly emphasized that the state should make death rituals a priority. Nevertheless, Confucian death ritual practice exacted a high price from those performing them, monetarily and otherwise, especially when one took a leave of absence without pay for twenty-seven months for mourning.

---

166. CB, 215.5231–5232, 216.5259, 219. 5326 and 232.5631–5632; SS Li 28, 125.2929.

167. CB 239. 5807. Su Shi wrote a memorial to revoke the decision. Su Shi, "Zai lun Wang Zishao zhazi" 再論王子韶劄子, QSW 95:2070.186.

168. CB 347.8329.

Becoming cognizant of the burden involved, the government provided assistance with funeral and burial as a part of the state welfare system.

One way the state did so was by sponsoring funerals of high officials and royal family members as a regular program under the name of *chizang* 敕葬 or "imperial burial." In such cases, the state arranged for a doctor to visit ill officials, and the patients had to take the medication prescribed by that doctor. In 1028, the government decided to grant a fixed amount of money per funeral, because it could not afford to absorb the entire cost. Despite government aid, many families found that funerals still cost more than they could afford. For this reason, many chose not to perform the *chizang*, in order to reduce the expense of the funeral. The government became aware of this problem and in 1074 modified the regulations, so that it was an option rather than a requirement.[169]

Because the funeral and burial were so costly, some government officers—new officers especially—were not able to afford them. Records exist from the reign of Zhenzong of special support for particularly poor officers, and many more cases are recorded from Renzong's reign.[170] Such support was based on individual need and merit, rather than through an institutionalized program. In 1043, Fan Zhonyan proposed that the state sponsor poor government officers by letting them use public land for burials.[171] Although his proposed reform was not adopted, the proposal itself revealed that burial was a serious concern among officers. During the New Policies era (1069–1076), people could borrow money for funerals, up to a maximum of 2,000 copper coins, from the government without paying interest.[172]

Many commoners were simply not able to meet Confucian ritual requirements. The Confucian canon itself does not hold commoners to its ritual norms, as indicated in the following passage in the *Records of Rituals*: "Rituals do not go down to the commoners."[173] Given that, many officials at the local government level established public graveyards for the poor. The central government instituted a program of mass burial and memorial service as a part

---

169. Ye Mengde, *Shilin yanyu* 石林燕語 (Beijing: Zhonghua shuju, 1984), 5.67; CB 105.2461; SS Li 27, 124.2908.

170. CB 43.916, 83.1888 and 266.6523.

171. CB 143.3438–3439.

172. CB 297.7217.

173. Sun Xidan, ed., *Liji jijie* 禮記集解, "Quli, *shang*" 曲禮,上 (Beijing: Zhonghua shuju, 1989), 4.81. Kong Yingda 孔穎達 (574–648) of the Tang dynasty commented that this was because commoners were not capable of meeting all the material needs.

of disaster relief, which will be discussed in Chapter 5. Local governments also rewarded commoners who demonstrated extraordinary acts of abiding by Confucian ritual norms. Examples of these funeral "virtuosi" include a man who lived in a hut near the grave of his parents, another who slept inside the tomb of his mother for thirty-six months, and a third who carried his father's corpse home from the battlefield for a proper burial, risking his own life, out of intense grief. Examples of two such "virtuosi" are given below:[174]

> [In] Henan province, a commoner, Zhou Jinneng, mourned his parents by living in a hut near the grave. He sold firewood to make money in order to make morning and evening offerings. The local government talked about him [to a higher office], and granted him twenty-four bolts of silk and ten bushels of rice.[175]

> In Lingxuan, a commoner, Chen Xuan, held his mother's funeral. Once he completed the burial, he did not close the door of the tomb, and drew paintings on the wall of the entryway inside the tomb. At night, he lay down leaning on the coffin. He lived there for thirty-six months. Thereupon he closed the door. The width of the tomb was thirty-three meters. His wife, Mrs. Gao was also filial. In an announcement, the local government granted him grain and cotton cloth.[176]

Although local governments did not have a particular program rewarding this type of conduct, virtuous acts were reported to them. Such people were intended to become role models, inspiring changes in mourning behavior on the part of the many who were negligent in their funeral duty.[177]

Seeking to promote the adoption of Confucian death ritual practice from the top to the bottom of society, the state installed various programs that were tailored to the needs of different social strata. More systematic assistance was granted to high officials who deserved rituals on a grander scale, and special forms of aid were given to individual officers when approved. In particular, the state's recognition of commoner funeral "virtuosi" testified that funerals and

---

174. Death due to the grief of mourning, CB 114.2671; living inside a tomb for thirty-six months, CB 157.3811; son carrying father's corpse from battlefield, CB 192.4652.

175. CB 133.3162.

176. CB 342.8220.

177. CB 335.8073.

mourning had become one of the most visible avenues for the active dissemination of Confucian values at the local level.

## *Conclusion*

During the mid–Northern Song era, spanning the reigns of Renzong, Yingzong, and Shenzong, a gradual revival of Confucian death rituals took place. Scholar-officials endeavored to minimize Daoist influence on rituals at the imperial court and to establish the classical ritual as the highest priority concerning ritual affairs in the court. Defining textual authority as such laid the groundwork for court officials to criticize the emperor's neglect of the strict ritual prescriptions. In addition, when ritual prescriptions were not clear, high-ranking officials and ritual officers were able to provide interpretations well suited to their arguments, and saw their influence at the imperial court expand. Recurrent sanctions against death rituals conducted for royal family members caused additional power to flow to the bureaucracy during the Northern Song era.

Later on, when the officialdom was split by factional strife, those who advocated increasing the power of the bureaucracy at the expense of the monarch took the lead in deploying the classical ritual laws as a means to compel compliance by the emperor and also to attack officials of the opposing faction. Mid–Northern Song discourse on funerals gradually expanded into the legal and practical domains, to the extent that funeral ritual and mourning performance became the focal point for the demonstration of morality among scholar-officials. The government employed a double-edged strategy of regulating and encouraging proper funerary practice. This process helped scholar-officials call attention to the "classical ritual laws" and impose a Confucian way of life, initially among the educated elites and later among the general populace.

3
___

# *Ordering Society through Confucian Rituals*

DURING THE REIGN of the Song emperor Renzong 仁宗 (r. 1022–1063), traditional Confucian death rituals (*sangzang li* 喪葬禮) were significantly revived, and "three-year mourning" became a legal obligation for civil officers.[1] However, non-Confucian and noncanonical ritual practices, Buddhist rituals in particular, prevailed in all social strata, including prominent scholar-officials and royal families.[2] Moreover, the government employed Buddhist monks to carry out state-sponsored mass burials and death rituals.[3] Financial concerns also came into play. The economic disparities of the time were especially manifest in funeral practices: wealthy people, merchants in particular, performed "lavish burials," whereas many of the poor turned to cremation or water burial due to lack of resources. In order to rein in overconsumption in funeral and burial practices, the government promulgated the *Ordinances of*

---

1. CB 97.2242.

2. Song Sanping, "Songdai de fenan yu fengjian jiazu 宋代的墳庵與封建家族," *Zhongguo shehui jingji yanjiu* 52, no. 1 (1995): 40–47; Chikusa Masaaki, "Sōdai bunji kō 宋代墳寺考," *Toyo gakuho* 61 (1979/80): 35–66; Bai Wengu 白文固, "Songdai de gongdesi he fensi 宋代的功德寺和墳寺," *Qinghai shehui kexue*, no. 5 (2000): 76–80; Patricia Ebrey, "Education through Ritual: Efforts to Formulate Family Rituals During the Sung Period," in *Neo-Confucian Education: The Formative Stage*, eds. John W. Chaffee and William Theodore de Bary (Berkeley: University of California Press, 1989), 281; "Cremation in Song China," *American Historical Review* 95, no. 2 (1990): 406–428; Edward L. Davids, *Society and the Supernatural in Song China* (Honolulu: University of Hawaii Press, 2001), 180; Zhu Ruixi, "Songdai de sangzang xisu 宋代的喪葬習俗," *Xueshu yuekan*, no. 2 (1997): 69–74.

3. Mark Robert Halperin, "Buddhist Temples, War Dead, and the Song Imperial Court," *Asia Major* 12, 3rd series, no. 2 (1999): 71–99; CB 166.3985, 239.5807, 253.6297, 297.7231, 297.7233, and 297.7234.

*Funerals and Burials* (*Sangzang ling* 喪葬令) in 1029, which specified spending limits in accordance with the deceased's official rank.[4] The ordinance also set forth regulations concerning the burial of low-ranking officers—the fifth, sixth, and seventh ranks—about whom there was no particular guidance given in the *Record of Rituals* (*Liji* 禮記), a collection of pre-Han to late-Han texts that eventually entered the Confucian canon and received intense commentary and disputation among scholar-officials. Nonetheless, the ordinance seems to have failed to change people's funeral and burial practices, judging from many archaeological reports.[5]

While some scholar-officials considered the above-mentioned practices acceptable, Sima Guang 司馬光 (1019–1086) and other strict ritualists viewed non-Confucian funeral rituals as indicators of decadence in Chinese culture and advocated a return to classical Confucian death rituals as orthopraxis.[6] Yet there was no single authoritative text that the families of *shidafu* 士大夫, scholar-officials, could consult,[7] and so each family followed its own traditions. This impelled Sima to author the *Shuyi* 書儀 (*Letters and Rituals*), a type of manual for both formal epistolary writing and domestic rites. It was the most

---

4. Zhongguo shehui kexueyuan, Lishi yanjiusuo, annot., *Tianyige cang Mingchaoben Tianshengling jiaozheng: Fu Tangling fuyuan yanjiu* 天一閣藏明鈔本天聖令校証: 附唐令復原研究 (Beijing: Zhonghua shuju, 2006); CB 118.2798, 140.3361, 167.4025–4026 and 217.5275; SS Li 27, 124.2909.

5. Dieter Kuhn, *A Place for the Dead: An Archaeological Documentary on Graves and Tombs of the Song Dynasty (960–1279)* (Heidelberg: Forum, 1996).

6. On the life of Sima Guang, see Kida Tomo, *Shiba Kō to sono jidai* 司馬光とその時代 (Tokyo: Hakutei sha, 1994); Gu Kuixiang, *Sima Guang* (Harbin: Heilongjiang Renmin chubanshe, 1985). For a systematic study of Sima's thinking, see Demerie Paula Faitler, "Confucian Historiography and the Thought of Ssu-ma Kuang" (PhD diss., University of Michigan, 1991); Anthony William Sariti, "Monarchy, Bureaucracy, and Absolutism in the Political Thought of Ssu-Ma Kuang," *Journal of Asian Studies* 32, no. 1 (1971): 53–76. For a recent delineation of the political history of the mid–Northern Song dynasty via Sima Guang's thought and career, see Xiao-bin Ji, *Politics and Conservatism in Northern Song China: The Career and Thought of Sima Guang (A.D. 1019–1086)* (Hong Kong: Chinese University Press, 2005). For a study comparing Wang Anshi and Sima Guang, see Peter Bol, *This Culture of Ours: Intellectual Transition in T'ang and Sung China* (Stanford, CA: Stanford University Press, 1992), 212–253, and "Government, Society, and State: On the Political Visions of Ssu-Ma Kuang and Wang An-shih," in *Ordering the World: Approaches to State and Society in Sung China*, eds. Robert Hymes and Conrad Schirokauer (Berkeley: University of California Press, 1993), 128–192; Paul J. Smith, "Shen-Tsung's Reign and the New Policies of Wang An-Shih, 1067–1085," in *The Cambridge History of China*, vol. 5, part 1: *The Sung Dynasty and its Precursors, 907–1279*, eds. Denis Twitchett and Paul J. Smith (New York: Cambridge University Press, 2009), 347–483.

7. According to Patricia Ebrey, composing a ritual manual for one's family came into vogue in the late Tang and belonged within a genre known as *shuyi* 書儀, that is, "letters and rituals." Patricia Ebrey, *Confucianism and Family Rituals in Imperial China: A Social History of Writing about Rites* (Princeton, NJ: Princeton University Press, 1991), 39–40.

comprehensive manual of this kind to appear during the Northern Song era and became the single most important reference book for Zhu Xi's 朱熹 (1130–1200) *Family Ritual* (*Jiali* 家禮).[8] Six of the *Shuyi*'s ten chapters address the matters of funeral, mourning, burial ritual, and memorial services, underscoring each one's particular significance.[9] The content indicates that the *Shuyi*'s assumed readers were mainly of the *shidafu* group, more broadly, but also—to a much lesser extent—commoners.

Sima Guang's *Shuyi* was a product of an era when debates over sacrificial rites, funerals, and memorial services reached their zenith. It was written during Sima's stay in Anyang from 1071 to 1084; he had withdrawn from the imperial court, as had many of his sympathizers who were critical of the New Policies (*xinfa* 新法) engineered by Wang Anshi 王安石 (1021–1086). The text of the *Shuyi* provides us with clues for solving questions about the role the discourse and practice of funeral ritual played in the rise of Confucian revivalism among scholar-officials and their family members; in particular, how scholar-officials' visions of politics and society were connected to their understanding of rituals. This chapter builds on a study of Sima's conception of ritual; it explains how Sima, in writing, negotiated with the authority of Confucian ritual canons whenever he adjusted regulations to meet the needs of his Confucian contemporaries. A deep analysis of the text reveals his standards and rationales for endorsing or condemning certain contemporary ritual practices. Here, particular attention is devoted to the issue of how the Confucian notion of transcendence and the spirit world factored into Sima's condemnation of certain ritual practices, and how this condemnation was linked to his overall vision of a correct society and how it could be realized through ritual reform.

## *Sima Guang's Ritual Theory: Ritual for Hierarchical Social Order*

Sima Guang entered into various ritual discourses at the court and quickly rose to become a leading voice in favor of ritual reform for government and society.[10] His

---

8. Ebrey, *Confucianism and Family Rituals in Imperial China*, 104–109.

9. The "letters" section (j. 1) deals with the proper forms of memorials and private letters in accordance with the status of and relationship between correspondents. The "ritual" section covers capping (j. 2), marriage (j. 3), and funerary rituals (j. 7–10). For a discussion of weddings in the *Shuyi*, see Christian de Pee, *The Writing of Weddings in Middle-Period China: Text and Ritual Practice in the Eighth through the Fourteenth Centuries* (Albany: State University of New York Press, 2007), 55–64.

10. Carney T. Fisher, "The Ritual Dispute of Sung Ying-tsung," *Papers on Far Eastern History* 36 (1987): 109–137; Ji, *Politics and Conservatism*, 94–109.

conception of ritual crystallized early in his career, during the period 1049–1053, when he received a post in the Academy of Ritual (*taichang liyuan* 太常禮院). He was employed as an officer of remonstrance to the emperor from 1061 to 1065, during which time he was actively involved with ritual affairs at court. In 1066, he began his large historiographical project, which would become a principal resource for studies of Chinese history through to the present day, namely the great work titled *Zizhi tongjian* 資治通鑑 (*Comprehensive Mirror for Aid in Governance*); he expounded it to the emperor in person until his retreat from the court in 1070 due to conflicts with Wang Anshi.[11]

Sima's ideas on ritual can be best understood by locating them in a social context and by comparison with Wang Anshi's thought and politics. Wang identified a major economic problem that confronted the state, one for which he held rich landowners, large merchants, and moneylenders, who monopolized the grain trade and the private banking business, responsible.[12] Wang accepted that the desire for luxurious lifestyle was a natural human disposition; the crucial task for the government was to prevent the rich from making money inappropriately rather than to regulate their consumption patterns.[13] He propounded a comprehensive policy that was named "New Policies"; through them the government engaged in the grain trade and lent money to benefit the poor, while taking action to prevent the rich from abusing their power.[14] Lacking pragmatic alternatives to Wang's policies, Sima placed less emphasis on the role of government within society; rather, he focused on moral reform within the bureaucracy. By reforming ritual, Sima thought people's desires would be transformed and, in turn, society would become ordered.[15] We might conceive how ritual could serve such a role in part by discussing some of the

---

11. In 1068, he was appointed as the director of the newly established Office of Expenditure Reduction (*caijianju* 裁減局), which was soon abolished due to its failure to present measures for solutions other than pointing out problems. Peter J. Golas, "The Sung Fiscal Administration," in *The Cambridge History of China Volume*, vol. 5, part 2: *Sung China, 960–1279*, eds. John W. Chaffee and Denis Twitchett (Cambridge, UK: Cambridge University Press, 2015), 150.

12. In fact, however, many families of officials were rich landowners who were active in the grain trade and money lending. On ostentatious consumption by the wealthy in the Song era, see Christian de Pee, "Purchase on Power: Imperial Space and Commercial Space in Song-Dynasty Kaifeng, 960–1127," *Journal of the Economic and Social History of the Orient* 53, no. 1 (2010): 149–184.

13. Wang Anshi, "Shang Renzong huangdi yanshi shu" 上仁宗皇帝言事書, in *Wang Linchuan ji* 王臨川集, 39.85–86 and "*Feili zhi li*" 非禮之禮, 67.51–52.

14. Bol, *This Culture of Ours*, 246–250.

15. Bol, *This Culture of Ours*, 219 and 250–251.

semantic underpinnings of the concept of "ritual" as understood in China's earlier periods, as well as by Sima.

The Shang dynasty (c.1600–1046 BCE) had developed ritual practice in the context of *zongfa* 宗法—a social organizing system in which kinships (*zu* 祖) were traced and observed hierarchically. In various rituals passed down in writings, this was expressed by, for example, the robes worn by participants that distinguished their status and rank within the social system.[16] After the disintegration of the *zongfa* system, Confucius (551–479 BCE) redefined the concept of *li* 禮 by taking it as the universal ground in which individuals acted morally.[17] Confucius's concept of *li* encompasses propriety, etiquette, and ritual practice. He regarded *li* as one of the cardinal virtues; it formed an inner quality of virtue (*de* 德) that was to be linked with an outer quality, namely, ritual practice. *Li* was the thread of continuity between social relationships and one's relationship to Heaven. Later, Xunzi 荀子 (ca. 310–218 BCE) argued that rituals served the ethical function of moderating human desires and the social function of clarifying the hierarchical order by their positing of distinctions (*fen* 分) amongst people.[18] At the same time, in Xunzi's understanding, since rituals had become the sole criterion of moral and social behavior among the *shi* group (the administrative officers), they had become an end in and of themselves.

During the Northern Song, as scholarly debates and legal disputes came to center on various imperial rituals and the funerals of state officials at the imperial court, scholars also developed theories of ritual. Zhang Zai 張載 (1020–1077) was the preeminent exponent of this conception of ritual as a cosmic-moral principle that ought be manifest in individuals. According to Zhang's understanding, the concept of *li* 理, meaning "principle" or "pattern," permeated that of *li* 禮 (ritual); thus, ritual could be seen as possessing a metaphysical basis and acting at different levels of human life.

> In general, ritual is principle (*li* 理). It must be this: to study principle
> to its utter end; if so, then ritual is what enacts the [moral] meanings [of

---

16. Yongping Liu, *Origins of Chinese Law: Penal and Administrative Law in its Early Development* (Hong Kong: Oxford University Press, 1998), 19–86.

17. Liu, *Origins of Chinese Law*, 87–110.

18. "Li lun" sect. in *Xunzi* 荀子 (Taipei: Taiwan shangwu yinshuguan, 1969), 105–126; Yuri Pines, "Disputers of the Li: Breakthroughs in the Concept of Ritual in Preimperial China," *Asia Major* 13, 3rd series, no. 1 (2000): 35–40; Kurtis Hagen, "Xunzi and the Nature of Confucian Ritual," *Journal of American Academy of Religion* 71, no. 2 (2003): 371–403.

principle]. If one understands principle, one can institute ritual. In this case, then, ritual emerges from principle subsequently.[19]

Sima Guang was less metaphysical, in that he placed ritual in the position of a broad base for social actions. His conception is laid out clearly in his opening comment in the *Zizhi tongjian*:

> Your minister Guang says, "Your minister has heard that, among the Son of Heaven's responsibilities, none is greater than ritual (*li*); in ritual none is greater than social roles (*fen* 分); in social roles nothing is greater than [their corresponding] titles (*ming* 名). What is ritual? It is the guiding principle (*jigang* 紀綱) [of public order]. What are social roles? They are [the rank of] ruler and minister. What are titles? They are duke (*gong* 公), marquis (*hou* 侯), councilor (*qing* 卿), and high official (*dafu* 大夫)."[20]

Here, Sima takes ritual, or *li*, as *jigang*, the guidelines for public order that set forth the roles of individuals within social institutions. This understanding echoes Xunzi's theory of ritual, which conceptualizes the double role of *li* as the basis of social hierarchy and as an ethical imperative.

In another passage of *Zizhi tongjian*, Sima specifies the social functions of rituals:

> Ritual's application in things and affairs is indeed great! When ritual is applied to the body, both one's movement and stillness have guidance, and all actions are perfected. When it is applied to the family, then there are distinctions between men and women, and the nine ranks of clan are in harmony. When it is used for villages, the old and the young have ethics, and vulgar customs will become refined. When it is used for the state, the ruler and ministers have hierarchical order, and governing will be perfected. When it is used for the whole society, all marquises will obey [the ruler]; and the guidelines of public order (*jigang*) will be upheld.[21]

---

19. Zhang Zhai, *Zhang Zai ji* 張載集 (Beijing: Zhonghua shuju, 1978), 326–327.

20. Sima Guang, *Zizhi tongjian* 資治通鑑 (Beijing: Zhonghua shuju, 1981), 1.2.

21. Sima, *Zizhi tongjian* 資治通鑑, 11.375.

Sima perceives social relations as the sum of the complementary relations of individuals within the hierarchy.[22] The universal principle of ritual as establishing hierarchical divisions become applied to familial and social relations, and to the state; society in turn would function as a unified whole. In essence, Sima defined ritual as the preeminent mechanism for achieving a hierarchical and thus harmonious social order.

Sima's use of the term "ritual" operated on two levels of meaning: concrete action and abstract principle. Ritual as concrete action primarily served as a means to express and cultivate virtues within social activities. Ritual as abstract principle operated as ethical imperative and the guidelines for public order based on which individuals responded to given situations ritually. Therefore ritual as abstract principle both embraced and transcended concrete ritual actions by presenting itself as the conceptual basis for the former. Sima believed that ritual as principle was unchanging, although the regulations for its situational application did allow for modification. Ritual as principle is thus universal and can be applied to everyone, whereas ritual as concrete action draws hierarchical divisions among social members. Sima emphasized that these dual aspects of ritual are both unifying and dividing, and are thus the means by which a society can achieve a hierarchical social order in the form of an organic unity in which each part knows and performs its function. For Sima, the classical ritual system of the Zhou dynasty best manifested these dual aspects. However, he was not advocating for a return to an ancient system; his goal was to reinstate ritual practice as the foundation of the social and political system of his day.

Sima and other like-minded scholar-officials attacked vernacular religious practices of their day under the rubric of "popular customs" (*fengsu* 風俗) and "unsanctioned ritual" (literally 'nonritual rituals,' *feili zhi li* 非禮之禮). In general, prescribed rites in the classical texts were called *li*, but those without authoritative textual sources were called *su* 俗 or 'customs.' Sima used the word *su* with connotations of crudeness and challenged the validity of such acts because of this lack of canonical warrant. In his "Discussion of Notes on Contemporary Customs" (*Lun fengsu zhazi* 論風俗劄子), Sima was concerned that some scholar-officials were not following Confucian practice to the letter, and moreover were continuing to perform rituals associated with Buddhism or Daoism: two notable examples were Wang Anshi and Su Shi

---

22. "[T]he high commands the lowly, as heart moves hands and legs, and as root controls branch and leaf. The lowly serves the high, as hands and legs guard the heart, and as branches and leaves rely on the main root. Be that as it may, afterwards the top and the bottom rely on each other, and the state is governed in peace." Sima, *Zizhi tongjian* 資治通鑑, 1.2.

蘇軾 (1037–1101). Sima, for his part, referred to officials such as Wang as "vulgar Confucians" (*suru* 俗儒).[23]

Whereas Sima Guang was Wang Anshi's political critic, Wang was critical of Sima's ritual theory. Wang thought that the economic, social, and political realms were the foundation of human life, and that ritual helped to sustain them.[24] He therefore viewed ritual practices as one of components of culture and society, but not the mainstay. Wang identified two major trends in the political thought of the time: one sought to revive the "classical ritual law system," and the other was intent on reforming Song society according to the New Policies. He accused those who supported the revival of the "classical ritual law system" of "not doing anything [for society]" and, if anything, "cheating" while in government office.[25] He was unstinting in his criticism of them for "championing the ancient ritual laws because they alone could follow them."[26] The essence of this charge was that the complexity of the classical ritual laws allotted special privileges to those who had intertextual exegetical skills. Along with his ideas of social reform, Wang thought that ritual as well could be changed for the better. He did not think that current society needed to conform to the "old ritual system," because everything in the world had naturally changed. For him, trying to reinstate the old system in contemporary times went against the current of "adaptation to circumstances" (*quanshi* 權時).[27] Thus, he viewed Sima's theory of ritual as an obstacle to his comprehensive social and economic reform program.

Sima and Wang also had different understandings of "custom," or *su* 俗, with respect to its semantic field and the method for its transformation. In response to ritualists, Wang wrote essays titled "*Fengsu*" and "*Feili zhi li*." In "Fengsu" he used the concept of *su* as a neutral term, translatable as "prevalent contemporary practice." He included both cultural customs and social customs, and focused more on the latter in terms of reform.[28] He said, "[The current social] customs do not care about loyalty [*zhong* 忠] and trustworthiness [*xin* 信]. People's lack of sense of shame is very extreme."[29] He thought

---

23. The word *suru* 俗儒 appears in CB 346.4866 and 357.8533; Sima, *Zizhi tongjian*, 27.881.

24. Wang Anshi, "Liyue lun 禮樂論," in *Wang Linchuan ji*, 66.42; Bol, *This Culture*, 228.

25. CB 224.54.

26. CB 224.54.

27. CB 224.54.

28. Wang, *Wang Linchuan ji*, 69.74.

29. CB 243.5921.

that promoting "positive social customs" was one of the responsibilities of the government and believed his reform policies would do just that.[30] He therefore criticized his opponents for taking the ancient ritual laws as the standard by which to judge contemporary customs.[31]

Sima Guang consistently advocated correct rituals based on the classics—for emperors and for scholar-officials. Whereas Sima wrote numerous memorials that criticized emperors' nonclassical practices, Wang wrote various prayers to be used in Buddhist and Daoist rituals offered on behalf of royal family members.[32] Wang believed that reformation of the society could be achieved through the implementation of his well-known new policies, not through ritual reform. He did not hold that canonical ritual texts should be the standards for judging the worth of contemporary ritual practices, and therefore the government could facilitate Buddhist and Daoist rituals simply to address practically people's important needs. Sima, on the other hand, promoted Confucian rituals as the mainstay of governance, through which both the moral lives of individuals and the public order would be reformed.

## Negotiating with Canonical Authority and Contemporary Practices

Reflecting his vision of establishing the social order through ritual, Sima Guang wrote a manual of ritual practices, the *Shuyi*, which was intended for his own family and those of fellow scholar-officials. Given that he was a fervent advocate of the "classical rituals," how did he incorporate the latter in this new ritual text? To what extent did the *Shuyi* allow for flexibility in applying classical ritual prescriptions in an effort to make them suitable in the contemporary context?

In seeking to reestablish "correct" or orthodox ritual, Sima consulted texts of unquestioned authority. Three early compilations—the *Liji* (see above), the *Zhouli* 周禮 (*Rituals of Zhou*), and the *Yili* 儀禮 (*Ceremonies and Rituals*)—were considered to be the authoritative writings on ritual, and authorship in all

---

30. *Xu zizhi tongjian changbian* reads, "Wang spoke to the emperor: 'If Your Majesty would like to foster virtue necessary for governing, he will need to follow the social and cultural changes and obtain the desired customs or *fengsu*. If today's absurd customs are not transformed thoroughly, I'm afraid that the virtue necessary for governing will not be developed.'" CB 242.5894. See also CB 215.5232 and 250.6135.

31. Wang, "Menxi" 悶習, in *Wang Linchuan ji*, 69.75–76; CB 249.5855.

32. These are collected in *j*. 45 and 65 in *Wang Linchuan ji*.

cases was attributed to Confucius.[33] Patricia Ebrey sums up how the authority of the classics was generally conceived: they were "created by human sages who understood the principles of heaven and earth, including the social and psychological needs of people."[34] In addition, Sima drew on another major primary source that was compiled for and during the Tang dynasty, namely, the *Kaiyuan li* 開元禮 (*Rituals of the Kaiyuan Reign-period*). This imperial ritual code of the Tang issued in 732 was an outcome of a concerted academic endeavor of the court to present a systematic manual for all of its ritual programs, based on centuries of Confucian texts and commentaries.[35]

Sima used the *Yili* as his primary source for the *Shuyi*, because it contained individual chapters prescribing the funeral and mourning ritual procedures for ordinary administrative officers—the *shi*.[36] It would appear, based on the descriptions in the *Liji*, during ancient Zhou times the word 大夫 referred to officials of the second grade and *shi* to the third, fourth, and fifth grades.[37] During the Northern Song, *shidafu* came to connote a social group, civil bureaucrats and their family members who were familiar with Confucian teachings.[38] Therefore, by taking all *shidafu* together, Sima prescribed the requirements for the lowest rank set forth in the *Yili*. Because the economic position of the *shidafu* varied widely—from rich landowners to poor low-ranking officer—Sima simplified the material requirements of the classical texts in order to soften the demands of ritual performances, including financial burdens. In addition, some particular ritual matters from the classics were

---

33. Tang dynasty scholars in the seventh and eighth centuries accorded unchallengeable prestige to these three compilations by citing them for their new canons of imperial ritual. See David McMullen, "The Ritual Code of the Tang," in *Rituals of Royalty: Power and Ceremonial in Traditional Societies,* eds. David Cannadine and Simon Price (Cambridge and New York: Cambridge University Press, 1987), 182; Michael Nylan, "A Problematic Model: The Han 'Orthodox Synthesis' Then and Now," in *Imagining Boundaries,* eds. Kai-wing Chow, On-Cho Ng, et al. (Albany: State University of New York Press, 1999), 17–56; Kai-Wing Chow, "Between Canonicity and Heterodoxy: Hermeneutical Moments of the Great Learning (Ta-hsueh)," in *Imagining Boundaries,* eds. Kai-wing Chow, On-Cho Ng, et al. (Albany: State University of New York Press, 1999), 147–164.

34. Patricia Ebrey, "The Liturgies for Sacrifices to Ancestors in Successive Versions of the Family Rituals," in *Ritual and Scripture in Chinese Popular Religion,* ed. David Johnson (Berkeley, CA: Publications of the Chinese Popular Culture Project, 1995), 10.

35. McMullen, "Ritual Code of the Tang," 184.

36. These sections are *j.* 12, 13, and 14: "*Shisangli*" 士喪禮, "*Jixi*" 既夕, "*Shiyuli*" 士虞禮.

37. The "Wangzhi" 王制 section of the *Liji* specifies that *dafu* are subdivided into *qingdafu* 卿大夫 and *xiadafu* 下大夫; *shi* are subdivided into *shangshi* 上士, *zhongshi* 中士, and *xiashi* 下士.

38. For the transformation of the *shi*, see Bol, *This Culture of Ours,* 32–36 and 48–75.

no longer available due to vast cultural shifts. This part of my argument will be discussed in detail later on.

Certain scholars who lived earlier in the Song had established that the *Yili* and the *Liji*, while in some sense timeless, incorporated the customs of their own times and that inconsistencies and contradictions now existed among both the various ritual topics and the numerous scholarly opinions lodged in the classics.[39] Sima therefore sought to establish an approach to rituals in ways that which acknowledged the authority of the classics and met contemporary needs. He organized the *Shuyi* by giving a specific heading to a rite via its order as found in the *Yili* and the *Liji*. Under each heading, Sima first composed the prescriptions for the rite based on directions stated in the two classical texts, also borrowing their archaic language as a way of establishing the textual authority of his own *Shuyi*. Second, under these prescriptions he inserted his commentary using the vernacular language. He often introduced regulations found in the *Kaiyuan li* and other texts in order to compare the vaunted classical prescriptions with later practices.

[heading] Changing Clothes

[prescription] All must remove ornaments from their clothes,
[commentary] This refers to embroidery, red or purple colors, gold, jade,beads, and feathers.

[prescription] and wear clean and plain clothes.
[commentary] *According to the Kaiyuanli,* immediately after a death, men are to change into white clothing and no longer bind their hair. Women are to change into blue, unhemmed clothing. . . . *These days,* people usually do not change clothes and their hair looks especially bad. *Therefore, follow the Kaiyuanli.* However, if one is not able to manage white and blue unhemmed clothing immediately after death, then just remove the ornaments from clothing. . . . [C]ommoners do not change their ordinary clothes. . . . *Contemporary custom* has many taboos. Some people have their hair on the left for the father's funeral; on the right for the mother's funeral: on the left back for the uncle's: and on the right back for the mother-in law's. *None of this is in accordance with proper ritual procedure.*[40] [italics added]

---

39. Song scholars tackled these problems. In the beginning of the dynasty, when Taizu commissioned the *Sanli tu* 三禮圖, scholars debated whether to revise the regulations in the canonical texts. SSJBM 8.41.

40. Sima Guang, *Sima shi shuyi* 司馬氏書儀, vol. 35 of Congshu jicheng edn. (Changsha: Shangwu yinshuguan, 1935–1937; hereafter *Shuyi*), 5.49.

Using this double-edged style of exegesis, Sima Guang effected authority: he at once endorsed and condemned contemporary customs. By referring to the canonical texts and adopting their linguistic style, he intended his own text to deliver a certain canonical authority. Yet he applied canonical prescriptions selectively to contemporary situations, because he knew it was impractical to condemn contemporary custom solely due to the absence of canonical warrant.[41]

## Condemning and Endorsing Contemporary Ritual Practices

Through his editing and writing commentaries on ritual texts, Sima Guang was naturally merging the voice of traditional authority with his own authorial (or editorial) voice. It would be safe to say that he sought to convince readers that these two were one and the same. It is crucial for our analysis to distinguish the original ideas found in the ritual classics from those added or altered by Sima. This will aid us in developing an understanding of what he found problematic in the ritual practices of his time, what relationship those practices had with the practices given in the classical texts, and which people were the main targets of his criticism.

The purpose of the Confucian funeral ritual prescribed in the *Shuyi* was to begin the process by which the deceased depart this world, take their journey to an unspecified other world (which will be discussed later in this chapter), and return to bless their descendants.[42] This parallels the process of segregating the family from society and later reintegrating it. The ritual was comprised of five main stages, spanning either twenty-five months or twenty-seven months, and each stage consisted of several subsets of rites. The five stages were:

1. *Preparation for mourning* (segregation of the family; preparation for the soul's departure): When death is approaching, the family starts their ritual. Immediately after death, they perform the rite of "soul-calling," which

---

41. Although Sima did not in any extreme way demand punctilious observance of classical ritual prescriptions, he was at least more sympathetic to strict observance than to looseness. In 1085, Fan Zuyu 范祖禹 (1041–1098) proposed obliging people in the palace to wear mourning garments for "three years" after the emperor's death, arguing that it was prescribed in the classical ritual laws. This plan was not approved due to its impracticality. Although Sima did not agree with Fan, he defended Fan's position against other critics. CB 359.8593–8594 and 359.8607.

42. Laurence G. Thompson, *Chinese Religion: An Introduction* (Belmont, CA: Dickenson, 1969), 47–52.

exhorts the deceased to come back to life. If there is no return, they are assured that the death was final. The family determines who is to be the presiding mourner (*sangzhu* 喪主), and chooses a funeral director (*husang* 護喪) from among the family. Family members change clothes and write letters to inform others of the death, and in the meantime take care of the corpse.

2. *Mourning and condolence period* (receiving guests; the soul is on its journey). The family members accept the condolences of visitors and ritually dress the corpse. They abstain from food and drink and wear the proper mourning clothes in accordance with their relation to the deceased.

3. *Preparation for burial* (practical preparation for the burial). In order to find a fitting burial spot, a hired liturgist (*zhishi zhe* 執事者) undertakes divination. The family worships the god of the earth, who is in charge of the grave site, and they excavate the vault. They prepare the funeral items in advance.

4. *Burial* (procession to the grave and burial; the soul's integration into the other world). The funeral procession leaves the house with the coffin and burial goods. When the procession arrives at the grave site, they make the tomb inscription tablet and wail. The rite of sacrifice follows burial. The next day, the family makes the first offering to the deceased.

5. *Extended mourning period and closure* (the family's segregation from and reintegration into society; the soul's return to the family as an ancestor). A year after the death, the family members make the small sacrifice for auspiciousness (*xiaoxiang* 小祥) to the deceased and change into auspicious clothes. The liturgist places the ancestral offering board (*cipan* 祠版) for the deceased. In the twenty-fifth month after the death, the grand sacrifice for auspiciousness (*daxiang* 大祥) is made. The family clears away the soul seat from the house and other funerary items, selects a convenient day in the second month after the *daxiang*, and performs the peace sacrifice before returning to ordinary life.[43]

The participants whose roles were specified in Sima's *Shuyi* were the families, relatives, guests, servants, and ritual specialists. The presiding mourner

---

43. Sima noted that the *Liji* describes the length of the "three-year-mourning" as twenty-five months; he has the peace sacrifice come in the same month as the grand sacrifice for auspiciousness. However, he noted that the government's ordinance specified twenty-seven months, which followed the commentary of Zheng Xuan 鄭玄 (127–200 CE). Without presenting his own exegetical judgment, Sima commented that one could not violate the Song state's ordinance; *Shuyi*, 9.99 and 9.102; "Lilun," in *Xunzi* (Taipei: Taiwan shangwu yinshuguan, 1969), 122; Guolong Lai, "The Diagram of the Mourning System from Mawangdui," *Early China* 28 (2008): 57–59.

was typically the eldest son of the deceased, or, if required, the son of the eldest son. He assumed the central role in the funeral process, which included receiving the mourning guests. The funeral director was typically a relative who saw to practical matters, such as sending letters and collecting donations. A liturgist was hired to oversee the sacrifices, which included divinations, reading of prayers, and libations. Among those who might be hired for the procession to the burial site were exorcists (*fangxiang* 方相) and bearers of the funeral items. The female members of the family were often segregated from the male members by occupying designated places or by following gender-specific liturgical sequences. Servants did not participate in the ritual proper, but did perform certain manual tasks, such as the washing and dressing of the corpse.

Many of the ritual elements described above were seen as having been the practice before and after Confucius's time. What, then, were the standards that Sima Guang had in mind when he either endorsed or condemned contemporary practices? In order to understand how he classified ritual elements and used this classification to endorse and condemn, I borrow (but modify) analytical terms proposed by Roy Rappaport in *Ritual and Religion in the Making of Humanity* as a heuristic device for analyzing the *Shuyi*: (i) central messages of the tradition; (ii) canonical liturgical order; (iii) indexical rites that transmit the central messages and/or canonical liturgical order; (iv) nonindexical rites that do not convey any meaning or message in and of themselves, but simply regulate behavior in certain ways by following the canonical liturgical order; and (v) rites with messages that are often at odds with the central messages of the tradition.[44]

The central messages of the tradition are its core doctrine, which is implied in the many ritual elements and also which justifies performance.[45] Therefore, participating in the ritual itself denotes a ritual agent's adherence to the tradition's central message. One of these messages in the Confucian tradition is "cultivation of virtue," and ritual is a locus where such virtues are manifested.[46] By performing death rituals, a ritual agent makes known that he or

---

44. Rappaport proposed two primary categories: "self-referential messages" and "canonical messages." He explained that "self-referential messages" informed the current status of the ritual participant. Canonical messages, on the other hand, were encoded in "canonical liturgical order" and transmitted by "indexical messages" in liturgy. Although Rappaport noted in passing that not all rites were indexical, he did not include the categories (iv) and (v), listed above, in his discussion. Roy Rappaport, *Ritual and Religion in the Making of Humanity* (Cambridge and New York: Cambridge University Press, 1999), 52–105.

45. I have modified Rappaport's term "canonical messages" to "central message of a tradition." Rappaport, *Ritual and Religion in the Making of Humanity*, 54.

46. Recent discussions on the relation between *ren* 仁 (humanity, or an all-encompassing ethical ideal) and *li* (ritual) include Kwong-Loi Shun, "*Jen* and *Li* in the *Analects*," *Philosophy*

she is a moral subject who fulfills the duty of filial piety, the foremost virtue and duty. Confucian tradition regards filial piety as a universal virtue, because all human beings are children of their parents. It is why the death ritual is seen as a cardinal duty: one's body is the gift of one's parents, and taking care of the remains of a parent is a way of showing gratitude. It also derives from the belief that the status of the deceased in the spirit world is, to a large degree, dependent upon how descendants treat their remains; if maltreated, the spirit will likely become a wandering ghost.

The canonical liturgical order, consisting of the proper sequencing of individual rites, was transmitted through the authoritative texts. Because the Confucian canonical texts were meant to be reference books, with discrepancies and gaps among texts and within a text, it was possible that ritual agents could streamline a given ritual by omitting a particular rite, yet maintain the overall sequence. Although Sima was flexible in prescribing particular ritual elements within a given sequence, he was, in my view, taking great caution to preserve the order and formalism of the ritual as prescribed in the canonical texts. He maintained that formalism, despite its supraindividual character, was a means through which a ritual agent's interior qualities could be ritually manifested.[47]

The canonical liturgical order in the Confucian canonical texts includes hierarchical differentiations in accordance with official rank of the deceased, in the material requirements, the duration of the mourning period, and the forms of rites and gestures of the participants. Taken together with the central message, this aspect of the ritual constitutes a key liturgical agenda of the tradition: Confucian values are universal, yet their ritual expressions are differentiated according to the official rank of the ritual agent. Sima Guang propounded this liturgical agenda in his theory of ritual, as discussed earlier—ritual upholds the hierarchical social order. The ancient classic *Liji* is extremely clear about how distinctions should be made in rites for each of three distinct groups: rulers, high officials (*dafu*), and low officers (*shi*). Taking *shidafu* as one social group, the *Shuyi* specifies a hierarchical differentiation with regard to clothing, the style of tomb, the size of the tomb inscription tablet, and the number of burial items.[48]

---

*East & West* 43. no. 3 (1993): 457–479, and Chenyang Li, "*Li* as Cultural Grammar: On the Relation between *Li* and *Ren* in Confucius' *Analects*," *Philosophy East & West* 57, no. 3 (2007): 311–329.

47. This idea is clearly expressed in his criticism of pretentious wailing in front of other people. *Shuyi*, 5.57.

48. See, in order, *Shuyi* 6.66–69, 7.79, 7.81, and 7.80.

The indexical rites are intended to transmit the central messages of the tradition and canonical liturgical order. Sima allowed any one of them to be altered so long as it fulfilled its purpose. For example, he prescribed that the "soul cloth" (*hunbo* 魂帛) be put on the seat of a chair near the dead body in order to let the spirit in after the death. He then offered a detailed commentary as to why he prescribed this item rather than the *zhong* 重, the spirit seat made of a wooden structure, which was prescribed in the canonical texts.[49] His explanation of its meaning and function through extensive textual references indicates that his contemporaries were not familiar with the material item:

> According to the *Ordinances of Funerals and Burials*, in all cases of *zhong* 重, for [the funeral of] the first-rank official one uses six tripod cauldrons 鼎 [to be hung on three horizontal poles]: for the fifth rank and above, one uses four cauldrons [on two horizontal poles]: for the sixth rank and below one uses two cauldrons [on one horizontal pole].[50] *Nevertheless, officers [shi] and commoners do not know of the use of the cauldron. They all use the "soul cloth," which also follows the principle of serving the spirit.*[51] [italics added]

Here, Sima references the state's ordinances pertinent to an item, but does not advocate that they be enforced rigidly. As most scholar-officials and commoners did not know of the cauldron, he endorsed their customary use of a substitute item—the "soul cloth," which served the same purpose. In the same spirit, he sometimes adjusted material requirements so that poor people could uphold the central messages of the tradition. For example, concerning mourning clothes, he states: "But commoners and those who cannot afford the requirements of the mourning clothes can follow the current custom."[52] If a person was unable to afford a coffin for a deceased family member, Sima endorsed, citing a passage in the *Liji*, an economical form of burial that

---

49. For an image of the *zhong* with horizontal poles on which to hang cauldrons, see Nie Chongyi 聶崇義, *Sanlitu jizhu* 三禮圖集注, in *Yingyin Wenyuangge Siku quanshu*, vol. 129, 17.27–28. For the description of *zhong*, see Sun Xidan 孫希旦, ed., *Liji jijie* 禮記集解, "Tangong, *xia*" 檀弓,下 (Beijing: Zhonghua shuju, 1989), 10.254; K. E. Brashier, "Text and Ritual in Early Chinese Stele," in *Text and Ritual in Early China*, ed. Martin Kern (Seattle: University of Washington Press, 2005), 268–270.

50. *The Ordinances of Funerals and Burials* prescribes this regulation. *Tianyige cang Mingchaoben Tianshengling jiaozheng* (cited fn. 4, above), 353.

51. *Shuyi*, 5.54.

52. *Shuyi*, 6.69.

consisted simply of placing the wrapped corpse in a pit.[53] Clearly, he was advocating leniency toward those who desired the proper rituals but were unable to meet the canonical requirements. Although later scholars, such as Zhu Xi, found Sima's prescriptions too complicated, Sima's own idea was to simplify the canonical regulations.

Concerning rich mourners, Sima saw that some exceeded the limits determined by their status, limits derived either from Confucian ritual laws or the state's ordinances. In particular, he railed against "lavish burials" that were popular among the wealthy, whether merchants, large landowners, or well-to-do officials:

[Commentary:] In ancient times, only the Son of Heaven was able to have a passageway [into the subterranean vaulted tomb] and all the rest lowered the coffin directly into the grave pit. These days some people often make a passageway; it is against ritual [regulations].[54]

[Commentary:] According to the *Ordinances of Funerals and Burials*, the first rank's grave is eighteen feet in depth; each rank below reduces the depth by two feet ... the sixth rank and below cannot be deeper than eight feet, and people of the fifth rank and above can have a tomb inscription tablet. ... For all mourning and burials, *those who cannot afford the ritual requirements can follow the lower rank's requirements.* People of lower rank, regardless of their wealth, cannot follow the requirements above their rank. . . .[55] [italics added]

Sima Guang based his case against such practices on two points: first, they violated the Song state's sumptuary regulations, and second, luxurious tombs would tempt grave robbers, which would bring harm to the deceased.[56] Regarding the first point, he cited the *Ordinances of Funerals and Burials*: "People of lower rank, regardless of their wealth, cannot follow the requirements above their rank."[57] He condemned the tendency to upgrade one's social status in the ritual setting by making use of one's wealth. Sima recognized the violators' intent in his criticism: "It was unfair and selfish that

---

53. Sun, *Liji jijie*, "Tangong, *xia*," 278.

54. *Shuyi*, 7.79.

55. *Shuyi*, 7.80.

56. *Shuyi*, 7.80.

57. *Tianyige cang Mingchaoben Tianshengling jiaozheng: Fu Tangling fuyuan yanjiu*, 358.

the rich would be richer in the other world."[58] However, he avoided discussion of the validity of such an assumption by limiting the issue to the realms of practicality and ritual stipulation.

The nonindexical elements of a rite do not have significance in and of themselves, but guidelines for them are specified in the canonical texts. In the *Shuyi*, we see that such elements are concerned with materials for treating the dead body, mourner's hairstyles, funeral items, and where in the house the dead body could be placed.[59] Sima expressed considerable flexibility here, because many materials used in antiquity were no longer available or were very hard to come by. In many cases, he recommended simplification of ritual prescriptions or replacement of traditional materials with those that were currently available. For example, he reaffirmed that the amount of the contribution could not be regulated, because it was contingent upon the donor's financial situation:

> [Commentary:] Therefore, in ancient times there were rites for offering condolences that used a variety of items. An offering of pearl and jade was called *han* 含; clothes and blanket for the deceased were called *sui* 襚; cart and horse were called *feng* 賵; [and] material goods and money were called *fu* 賻. All of these items for the deceased's dressing and burial were means to aid the household with the funeral. These days, people bring facsimile paper money, which becomes ash [with the ritual burning]. This is merely wasteful. How does this benefit the bereaved household? Gold, cloth, money, and grain are acceptable as donations; their amount is dependent upon the financial situation of the donor.[60]

Contributions to express condolences were virtuous acts that served the purpose of relieving the family's financial burden. Here, he reemphasized that the amount of the contribution could not be regulated, because it was contingent upon the donor's financial situation. His project of simplifying the prescriptions of classical texts was mainly applied to nonindexical elements.

Rites with messages at odds with the central messages of the tradition are also present in the canons. They reflect the customs of the time when the canons were created and which became embarrassing to later Confucians on

---

58. Sima Guang, "*Zanglun,*" in *Sima Wengong wenji* 司馬溫公文集 (Shanghai: Shangwu yinshu guan, 1937), 13.299–301.

59. See, respectively, *Shuyi*, 5.50, 49.7, and 5.50.

60. *Shuyi*, 5.55–56; Sima, "*Xu fu li*" 序賻禮," in *Sima Wengong wenji*, 11.270.

philosophical grounds. For example, the rites of soul-calling,[61] the worship of the god of the earth,[62] and the employing of the exorcists during the procession[63] all grew out of a belief in the spirit world, about which Confucius did not wish to engage discussion. Though the above-mentioned three rites had been practiced since antiquity, the Confucian tradition did not develop concrete and articulated narratives regarding what the deceased, gods, and baleful spirits did in association with those practices. Sima, who did not engage with metaphysical issues, endorsed these practices without elaboration.

Sima reserved his harshest criticism for practices that did not have canonical warrant and were contrary to the central message of Confucianism. These were contemporary customs that can be categorized as follows: (1) noncanonical forms of rite interpolated into classical Confucian funeral practice; (2) the partial use of another kind of ritual, such as leaving the dead body in a Buddhist temple; and (3) a completely different set of rituals, such as cremation.[64] Examples of noncanonical forms of ritual were the placing of a painted portrait of the deceased behind the "soul cloth" (*hunbo* 魂帛) and decorating the soul cloth:

> Some popular customs employ a cap, hat, clothes, and shoes to decorate the cloth as if it were a living person. Its excellence becomes vulgarity,

---

61. *Shuyi*, 5. 47. The origins of the soul-calling rite are often assumed to have had roots in shamanistic practices of ancient southern China. The custom is indeed recorded in *Songs of Chu* 楚辭, presumably written, or collected, by Qu Yuan 屈原 (4th c. BCE). It is also endorsed both in the *Yili* and the *Liji*. See David Hawkes, tr., *Ch'u Tz'u: The Songs of the South: An Ancient Chinese Anthology* (Boston: Beacon Press, 1962), 104–105 and 110; Ying-shih Yü, "'O Soul, Come Back!' A Study in the Changing Conceptions of the Soul and Afterlife in Pre-Buddhist China," *Harvard Journal of Asiatic Studies* 47, no. 2 (1987): 363–395.

62. *Shuyi*, 7.77. This rite was meant to apologize to the god of the burial spot for invading his territory. It appeared in the *Kaiyuan li*, which means it was later incorporated into the Confucian ritual. Anna Isim, "Status Symbol and Insurance Policy: Song Land Deeds for the Afterlife," in *Burial in Song China*, ed. Dieter Kuhn (Heidelberg: Forum, 1994), 311. Also see Terry Kleeman, "Land Contracts and Related Documents," in *Chūgoku no Shūkyō, Shisō to Kagaku* 中国の宗教,思想と科学 [*Religion, Thought and Science in China*], ed. Makio Ryōkai Hakushi Shōju Kinen Ronshū Kankōkai 牧尾良海博士頌寿記念論集 (Tokyo: Kokusho Kankōkai, 1984), 12.

63. *Shuyi*, 8.89. The exorcists *were* presumably employed to clear the road to the burial spot of unwanted spirits and evil influences. SS Li 27, 124.2909–2910. For a Song scholar's discussion on the legitimacy of employing exorcists at funerals, see Patricia Ebrey, *Chu Hsi's Family Rituals: A Twelfth-century Chinese Manual for the Performance of Cappings, Weddings, Funerals, and Ancestral Rites* (Princeton, NJ: Princeton University Press, 1991), 115.

64. Although Song emperor Taizu (r. 960–976) prohibited cremation, people continued to practice it anyway. In Renzong's era, the state reversed its previous regulations and endorsed

which should not be followed. Another current custom is to place a portrait of the deceased behind the cloth. It is all right to use a portrait of a man that was drawn during his lifetime. However, needless to say this is not the case for a woman. While she was alive, she lived in a secluded women's quarter. When she went out, she traveled by curtained carriage, her face veiled. After her death, how can one allow a painter to enter her secluded chamber?[65]

Essentially, Sima Guang objected to any show of the deceased's corporeality as if he or she were alive. In this same vein, he also criticized dirges, often sung by hired entertainers who drummed loudly, for the purpose of "entertaining a corpse."[66] This practice contrasted sharply with neo-Confucian thought, which contended that the substance of the spirit was dispersed after death. Sima followed this idea when he attacked the Buddhist idea of punishment in hell, arguing that the dead, having no substance, experienced no bodily pain. Finally, he condemned the burning of facsimile paper money, intended as a payment to the gods on behalf of the deceased's well-being.[67] It was widely practiced to the extent that people brought it as a donation, and the government granted facsimile paper money to officials' funerals.[68] Although Sima was aware that this custom was based on belief in the spirit world, he avoided any explicit discussion of the belief itself, choosing to ground his criticism in practical concerns.

---

cremation, because land was scarce and the population was dense, hence land burial was not possible in all cases. SS Li 28, 125.2918–2919.

65. *Shuyi*, 5.54.

66. *Shuyi*, 6.65. In 984, the government concluded that dirges and theatrical performance in front of the soul-seat was damaging to culture and humanity, and declared them criminal. Those who hired dirge singers would be jailed and forbidden to take state examinations; SS 125.2917–2918.

67. *Shuyi* 5.55–56. The ritual of burning facsimile paper money was traced back to the Han imperial family. Emperor Xuanzong of the Tang included it as a part of imperial sacrifice, and its origins were often ascribed to him. During the Tang, emperors bestowed facsimile burial money to officials. Hou Chinglang argues that from the Sui dynasty on, this ritual became popular among people of all social strata. Hou Chinglang, *Monnaies d'offrande et la notion de trésorerie dans la religion chinoise* (Paris: College de France, Institut des Hautes Etudes Chinoises, 1975), 9, 14, and 17. See Anna Seidel, "Buying One's Way to Heaven: The Celestial Treasury in Chinese Religions," *History of Religions* 17, no. 3–4 (1978): 419–431. During the Northern Song, the practice was used quite widely, from palace royals to commoners. Sima Guang records Confucian skepticism about this ritual.

68. SS Li 27, 124.2908.

The incorporation of Buddhist practices into funeral rituals was clearly beyond the boundary of canonical warrant. Sima was especially disapproving of scholar-officials who used Buddhist temples for the temporary storage of corpses, even after performing Confucian funeral rituals. To do so was popular, as some wanted to wait for an auspicious burial time and others were unable to afford an immediate funeral.[69] Sima also brought up the problem of having Buddhist monks preside over death rituals after the Confucian one had been performed.[70] Cremation was often the first step, according to Buddhist tradition, and services were held every seventh day until the forty-ninth day after death in order to accumulate merit for the deceased. Sima argued that these practices violated Confucian norms in numerous ways. First of all, cremation was not a proper treatment for a dead body. Second, in many cases Buddhist practitioners placed sutras inside the tomb and built pagodas as a part of the process of accumulating merit for the deceased:

[Commentary:] It is the current custom that [many people] believe in the misleading words of Buddhism. Right after death, seven times on every seventh day, on the hundredth day, on the first and the second anniversary of the death, and on the day of the removal of mourning clothes, they provide food for the monks and hold memorial services. Some perform the Great Water-Land Purgation, copy Buddhist sutras, cast sculptures, and build pagodas and temples. They say that these rituals will obliterate the outrageous sins of the deceased. [Not only that, but] the deceased will be reborn in heaven and enjoy all kinds of pleasures. Those who do not perform these rituals will certainly enter hell, be sliced, roasted, pounded, and ground up, experiencing eternal waves of suffering . . . In addition, what Buddhists call heaven and hell is a strategy to encourage goodness and punish evil. But unless one dispenses this [reward and punishment] fairly, how can even ghosts be governed? For this reason, the Tang dynasty prefect of Luzhou, Li Dan 李丹 wrote to his younger sister as follows: *"If heaven does not exist, that is all. If it does, then virtuous people will ascend there. If hell does not exist, that is all. If it does, then morally inferior people will enter it."*[71] [italics added]

---

69. *Shuyi*, 7.75–76.

70. *Shuyi*, 6.63 and 7.76.

71. *Shuyi*, 5.54–55.

In this passage, Sima's criticism of various Buddhist death rituals points out the wrong notion—that the mourners' ritual performance could actually influence the ultimate situation of the deceased's afterlife. By citing Li Dan, Sima neither confirms nor negates the existence of heaven and hell, and, furthermore, he highlights their ability, merely as concepts, to steer people to moral action while alive: if they do not exist, then as to one's life "that is all"; but if they do exist, then it is only moral persons who will enter heaven. Here, Sima also shows an attitude of agnosticism—typical in Confucian writings—whereby no definite position is taken on the existence of heaven and hell. A key Confucian precedent is the following passage in the *Analects* (7.21): "The Master never talked of wonders, feats of strength, disorders of nature, or spirits."[72]

In short, Sima, without engaging arguments on Buddhist notions of heaven and hell, has emphasized that heaven and hell were conceptual tools for encouraging moral actions. While leaving the possibility of heaven's existence, he has indicated that the moral actions of the deceased, not the death rituals offered for the deceased, should be the basis for one's situation in a world-beyond, if it exists. Sima's criticism of Buddhism in general and of Buddhist death rituals in particular, especially the Water-Land Purgation, was linked to his criticism of the government's facilitation of those rituals for both private and public services.[73] The government granted tax exemptions to certain temples, recognizing that they had taken up the task of tending family graves and of holding memorial services for various high officials and members of royal families.[74] Sima showed his distaste for this in his memorials to the emperor that criticized the throne's desire to build a Buddhist temple near Renzong's tomb so that monks could care for it. Sima's criticism was in line with certain scholar-officials' efforts to suppress the custom of entrusting graves to Buddhist temples. To supplant the practice, Sima promoted the ancient custom of building a family shrine (*jiamiao* 家廟), which had been revived during Renzong's reign.[75]

---

72. *The Analects of Confucius*, tr. Arthur Waley (New York: Vintage, 1989), 120.

73. For Sima's broad-based criticism of Buddhism and Daoism, see "Yan Yongzhaoling jiansi zhazi" 言永昭陵建寺劄子, in *Sima Wengong wenji*, 4.78 and "*Chizhuang*" 斥莊, 14.316; CB 192.4778.

74. Chikusa, "Sōdai funji ko," 35–66; Bai, "Songdai de gongdesi he fensi," 76–80.

75. In 1041, the government issued an edict regulating the building of family shrines in accordance with official rank. SS Li 28, 125.2917–2918; CB 169.4070–4071. See Chikusa, "Sōdai funji ko," 49–50. On the later development of this practice, see Timothy Brook, "Funerary Ritual and the Building of Lineage in Late Imperial China," *Harvard Journal of Asiatic Studies* 49, no. 2 (1989): 465–495.

For Sima, ritual practice amounted to an embodiment of moral and social principles, and it should fit one's place in the social order. He espoused flexibility in terms of the material fulfillment of ritual requirements when resources were limited, as long as the ritual expressed the universal virtue of filial piety. However, he was sharply critical of the rich for their excessive expenditures in death rituals, on the grounds that they were going beyond what was permitted for their official rank. Finally, he reserved his harshest condemnation for non-Confucian death rituals, especially those presumed to influence the deceased's well-being positively in the imagined world-beyond, which in turn challenged his notion of ritual as having an end in and of itself.

## *Problems with the Spirit World and the World-Beyond*

Sima Guang recognized that ritual practices that violated Confucian regulations derived from the practitioner's belief in the spirit world and the world-beyond. Yet some Confucian ritual practices did imply the existence of the spirit world; how did he make the distinction between valid and invalid ritual? Even more fundamentally, how did he discuss topics about which the Confucian tradition maintained a deliberate silence? How did Sima deal with certain Confucian ritual practices, such as divination, that were at odds with his conception of ritual but were endorsed in the Confucian liturgical tradition?

Although, as mentioned above, the mainstream Confucian tradition tended to abstain from discussion of the spirit world and the world-beyond, its rituals implied their existence. Examples in the *Shuyi*, which gathers from the appropriate classics the proper ritual program in proper order, of the implication of the existence of the spirit world and spirits are the following: (1) the soul-calling rite,[76] which was an attempt to bring back the soul to this world before it takes off on its final journey; (2) condolences and mourning,[77] whereby the deceased is not yet treated as a spirit before his or her integration into the other world; (3) the rite of sending away the coffin,[78] being a report to the ancestors that the coffin will be removed from the house and go toward the grave; (4) worship of the god of the earth,[79] which informs the deity that the corpse will be buried;

---

76. *Shuyi*, 5.47.

77. *Shuyi*, 5.55–58 and 6.61–66, respectively.

78. *Shuyi*, 8.88–89.

79. *Shuyi*, 8.91.

and (5) installation of the ancestral offering board (*cipan* 祠版) after burial:[80] the deceased joins the ancestors and can bless descendants. In the above rites, which mark off the soul's transition, the spirit world is implied as the background, and spiritual beings such as ancestors and the god of the earth are addressed as recipients of offerings.

Despite the apparent presence of the notion of the spirit world in the Confucian death rituals, the tradition failed to offer a systematic and coherent concept of the spirit world, partly due to the eclectic nature of the canonical rituals themselves. Thus, two different ideas of the soul after death are present in Sima Guang's *Shuyi*. One is that the connection between the soul and the body ends with death, and the former disperses with no substance retained. The other suggests that the soul embarks on a journey to the other world and later becomes present in the sacrifice through the medium of the ancestral offering board:[81]

> The deceased's body and spirit are separate. The deceased's body enters the earth, then decays and disappears along with wood, stone, and so forth. The spirit (*shen* 神) floats like wind and fire. We do not know about it.[82]

> Your body returns to the earth, and your spirit (*shen*) returns to the [ancestor] hall. The ancestral offering board having been made ready, I humbly request that your revered soul (*ling* 靈) abandon the old [body] and follow the new [ancestral offering board], depending on this, relying on this.[83]

The first quotation—from one of Sima's vernacular commentaries—reflects a Song scholar's understanding of what happens to the spirit after death; this was later fully articulated in a popular line of thinking called the Learning of the Way (*daoxue* 道學).[84] The metaphor of wind and fire is applied to the

---

80. *Shuyi*, 8.93–98.

81. The ancestral offering board is a simpler version of the spirit tablet (*shenzhu* 神主). Sima comments that, according to Zheng Xuan, the spirit tablet is not used by *qing* 卿, *dafu* 大夫, and *shi* 士; therefore, he prescribes the ancestral offering board for *shidafu* that is used by his contemporaries. *Shuyi*, 7.81.

82. *Shuyi*, 5.54.

83. *Shuyi*, 8.92.

84. Daniel K. Gardner, "Ghost and Spirit in the Sung Neo-Confucian World: Chu Hsi on Kuei-Shen," *Journal of the American Oriental Society* 115, no. 4 (1995): 598–611.

spirit (*shen* 神) because it has an immateriality akin to that of the *qi* 氣 of the deceased, which dispersed completely. Sima derived the second quotation from the liturgical address that occurs when the liturgist installs the ancestral offering board in the ancestral hall and calls upon the spirit to be present in the board after shedding its physical body. In this way, the ritual context of ancestor veneration assumes that the spirit is present in the ancestral offering board. The soul's journey to the other world in the soul-calling rite, by contrast, relied on another kind of imagination—one that asserts a dwelling place for the soul in the other world.

Thanks to Confucius' decision to remove the spirit world from his discourse, this kind of conceptual incoherence remained implicit but unproblematized in the classical texts and by Confucian thinkers.[85] There was also no notion of communication between spirits and ritual participants, which we see in the *Analects*:

> Of the saying, "The word sacrifice is like the word 'present'; one should sacrifice to a spirit as though that spirit was present," the Master said. "If I am not present at the sacrifice, it is as though there were no sacrifice."[86]

The words "as though" inform us that Confucius did not really make an issue of whether or not the spirits were present at the sacrifice. Rather, he emphasized that by assuming their presence, practitioners were able to take the ritual seriously. In this context, the spirit world has syntactic value, which systematizes rites and renders them meaningful.[87] This conception of the spirit world was linked to Confucius's idea of Heaven as the source of ethics, but not something to be known or defined. Whereas Confucians tended to confine transcendence within the limits of syntactic value only, "heterodox" practices

---

85. Whether or not the soul had knowledge was an issue Confucius avoided. Later, Xunzi would take up the issue, arguing that the dead did not have any knowledge at all, and that the funeral was held to console the mourners; sect. "Lilun," in Xunzi, 105–126; see also sect. "Discourse on Ritual," in *Xunzi: The Complete Text*, tr. Eric L. Hutton (Princeton, NJ: Princeton University Press, 2014), 206–216; Paul Goldin, "The Consciousness of the Dead as a Philosophical Problem in Ancient China," ed. R. A. H. King, *The Good Life and Conceptions of Life in Early China and Graeco-Roman Antiquity* (Berlin: De Gruyter, 2015), 59–92.

86. *The Analects of Confucius*, 97.

87. I am borrowing the term "syntactic value" from Steven Collins, *Nirvana and Other Buddhist Felicities* (New York: Cambridge University Press, 1998), 116–117. He argues that nirvana has a latent syntactic value that organizes the other doctrines within Buddhism via its location at the symbolic center.

presented other notions of the spirit world and the world-beyond. Many narrative imaginations were filling in the blanks concerning Heaven or the world-beyond that Confucian discourse had left. The rituals that Sima condemned were expressions of such narrative imaginations. However, just as Confucius left Heaven and the spirit world to the realm of the unspoken, so did Sima.

Sima's abstaining from engagement with the issue of the spirit world and the world-beyond was well illustrated in his treatment of the widespread practice of geomancy, or *fengshui* 風水. Geomancy is a form of divination, itself a general term referring to rituals that consult spirits or other supernatural means to inquire about future affairs. For predicting future affairs, tortoise and milfoil divination (*bushi* 卜筮) had been practiced before Confucius' time and continued long after his death. On the other hand, for siting buildings there was geomancy, various forms of which had been applied since very early times in Chinese civilization; a relatively more unified scheme of cosmic-terrestrial and other coordinations appeared only beginning in the Han dynasty (206 BCE–220 CE). It was used especially for siting graves, under the assumption that the appropriate location would positively affect the descendants of the tomb occupant.[88]

During the Song, continuing its long tradition, *fengshui* was employed for selecting the proper time and place of burial. The need for geomantic verification was partly the reason that large numbers of unburied corpses were kept in Buddhist temples for years and even decades.[89] Royal families, in particular, often employed geomancy to discover the most suitable gravesites. For example, in an earlier era the mother of Taizu (r. 960–976) specified in her will that her body should be buried in an auspicious place so that her descendants would flourish.[90] Sima Guang added his voice to those of other scholar-officials who opposed geomancy for both practical and metaphysical reasons, as seen in his essay, "Discussion of Burials" ["Zanglun" 葬論]. He declared, "Wealth and lifespan have nothing to do with geomantic burial practice, but with Heaven's will."[91] By this statement, he debunked the belief that applying

---

88. Ole Bruun, *An Introduction to Feng Shui* (New York: Cambridge University Press, 2008), 19–23.

89. For example, when empress Wencheng died in 1054, her burial was held along with those of her grandparents and parents, because their burials had been delayed for many decades. CB 177.4287.

90. "Sangzang bu" 喪葬部, in Chen Menglei 陳夢雷 and Jiang Tingxi 蔣廷錫, eds., *Gujin tushu jicheng* 古今圖書集成 (Shanghai: Tushu jicheng yinshuju, 1884), 709.20.

91. Sima, "Zanglun," in *Sima Wengong wenji*, 13.300. Wang Yucheng's 王禹偁 essay "Wufuxianhou lun" 五富先後論 presented the same idea; in *Xiaoxu ji* 小畜集 (Taipei: Taiwan shangwu yinshuguan, 1963), 9.61.

geomantic techniques would affect the wealth and lifespan of the descendants; he declared that Heaven was the ultimate agent of determining human fate. He also discussed this issue in the *Shuyi*:

> The current custom is to believe in the explanations of burial specialists [*zangshi* 葬師]. Having already selected a year, month, date, and hour, burial specialists also select a mountain-and-water configuration [for a burial spot]. They believe that geomancy affects many aspects of the lives of descendants, including "wealth or poverty," "social status and intelligence," and "longevity or premature death." The reliance on geomancy at the present time is far beyond what is reasonable . . . Furthermore, *geomancers* (*yinyangjia* 陰陽家) *claim that the year, month, date, and hour of birth are sufficient to determine one's fate for a lifetime* . . . [If this is the case,] [h]ow can one alter it through burial practice? These two explanations contradict each other; but people believe in both. Their falsity has serious consequences. If indeed a burial could result in either harm or a blessing for people, for the sake of descendants, how can one bear to allow one's parent's body to smell, decay, and be exposed without being buried, for the sake of one's selfish interests? This is the worst case of violating ritual and being harmful to moral principle.[92] [italics added]

The above statements cover many issues. First, the belief that one can alter one's fate is at odds with the fundamental concept of Confucianism, namely, the commandment of Heaven (*tianming* 天命). The semantics of *ming* incorporate both fate and commandment. By this double meaning, the concept of *tianming* invites individuals to accept their life-situations, and yet to fulfill their mission by using one's talents and morality endowed by Heaven.[93] However, the concept of fate in geomancy does not include a sense of fulfilling one's mission by positing that people are able to control fate, to some extent, by acting upon the spirit world or cosmic flow. This belief is diametrically opposed to Sima's notion that ritual has an end in itself and the spirit world has, as mentioned, the syntactic value of organizing ritual and grounding morality. In addition, geomancy inverts the relation between the descendants and the deceased. In Confucian thought, it was the descendants' moral obligation to

---

92. *Shuyi*, 7.75.

93. Ding Weixiang, "Destiny and Heavenly Ordinances: Two Perspectives on the Relationship between Heaven and Human Beings," Frontiers of *Philosophy in China* 4, no. 1 (2009): 13–37.

help the deceased transit to the realm of the spirit world through the proper treatment of his or her remains. As Sima sees it, geomancy is performed for the benefit of descendants, often at the cost of mistreatment of the deceased's remains, a wholly undesirable outcome from the standpoint of filial piety.

Although Sima Guang condemned geomancy, he faced difficulty in abolishing divination, the techniques of which were given a place in the *Kaiyuan li*. Because divination had been an enduring practice within the Confucian burial tradition, having been endorsed in the text of the *Yili,* Sima Guang's strategy was to allow it partially. He said that there was no need to undertake divination for selecting the year, month, day, and time for burial, yet he did permit divining for the burial place.[94] In so doing, he removed the possibility of violating the ritual regulations relating to the mourning period as well as other negative impacts on the corpse. In maintaining this stance, Sima was very caustic toward a plan to use geomancy to select a spot for an imperial mausoleum, because it delayed the burial.[95] Though he did eventually endorse divination for determining the burial spot by adopting a pragmatic viewpoint, he disapproved of the notion that burial siting would influence the lives of descendants:

> The *Classic of Filial Piety* says, "Conduct divination in order to select the grave plot, and lay the dead body there in peace." As the text specifies, the purpose of divination for the grave plot is to distinguish its auspiciousness and inauspiciousness. *It is not like current geomancers' inspecting of hillocks, and wind and water terrain . . .* Naturally, the heart of the filial son is worried about the grave's depth and distance: if it is shallow, then it might be dug up by people; if it is deep, then it is moist and the corpse will decay quickly. Therefore, [one should] certainly select a place where soil is abundant and the water table is low, and bury the corpse.[96] [italics added]

Sima here states that the purpose of divination for selecting burial plots differs from that of contemporary practices in geomancy. His cursory

---

94. However, in the case of divination for the small and grand sacrifices for auspiciousness (*xiaoxiang* 小祥 and *daxiang* 大祥), it was used to select a day within the regulated month: "If the first ten days' period turns out to be inauspiciousness, try the second ten days' period; if it is inauspiciousness as well, select one auspicious day among the last ten days' period." *Shuyi,* 9.99.

95. Sima, "Yan shanling zedi zhazi" 言山陵擇地劄子, in *Sima Wengong wenji,* 4.78.

96. *Shuyi,* 7.75.

justification of burial site divination, without any further clarification of what the spirits do during the selection process, resonates with the Confucian silence about the world of spirits. In expressing his approval of divination, Sima merely attempts to invert the notion of geomancy by saying that the purpose of selecting a good burial place was derived from filial piety. In this case a person is concerned with the state of the corpse, not with his or her own well-being.[97]

Sima Guang hewed closely to the Confucian prescript of not speaking about the affairs of the spirit world and the world-beyond even in his criticism of noncanonical rituals. While there was a fine line between geomancy and divination in terms of their ideas and practices, there was a huge difference in their status of canonical warrant. The use of geomancy that lacked canonical grounding he saw as a moral failing, in that descendants sought blessings for themselves through burial practice. However, Sima reluctantly endorsed divination as having originated in the customs of the past and become a part of canonical ritual. He reinterpreted their meanings by divesting the magical effects from such customs and investing them with Confucian values.

## Conclusion

Sima Guang believed in the moral reformation of society through the dissemination of Confucian ritual norms. In writing the *Shuyi*, he endeavored to simultaneously revive the ideas of the Confucian ritual canons and adjust their requirements in order to meet contemporary needs. Sima maintained that rituals were the locus in which the hierarchical social order should be manifested according to official rank. He condemned non-Confucian and noncanonical ritual practices, such as various Buddhist death rituals, lavish burials, and geomancy. He especially objected to the extravagant burials performed by wealthy people, because he believed that the wealthy imagined a world-beyond where the status of the deceased could be improved by their material investments in ritual performance. From a rigorous Confucian point of view, these practices dismissed moral aspects from transcendence and from ritual, and made ritual primarily a means to wish fulfillment. His conception of ritual testifies to his vision of a fundamentally hierarchical society in which official rank is (and must be) the basis. It was one element of his effort to remind people of their place in the hierarchy, a place built on official rank, not wealth.

---

97. He makes a similar argument in his explanation of soul-calling, commenting that it was practiced out of the filial son's wish that the soul would come back. He dismisses the possibility that this ritual could result in the deceased's actual resuscitation.

*4*

# Social Imaginaries and Politics in the Narratives on the World-beyond and the Supernatural

MANY RELIGIOUS RITUALS imply social imaginaries in the world-beyond and supernatural agents as backgrounds of making those rituals meaningful. In the popular narratives of eleventh-century China, many people perceived that the world of the living was connected to the world-beyond and the supernatural, as evidenced by eyewitness accounts of hell, being summoned to the underworld tribunal, and encounters with ghosts. Traditionally, these types of narratives appeared in examples of the independent literary genre of *zhiguai* 志怪, tales of the anomalies that recorded strange encounters with nonhuman or spiritual beings and paranormal events spurred by the spirit world, and tended to pay little attention to the issues of the social world.[1] Many stories of the Song period put a different spin on this genre of literature by addressing sociopolitical issues in which the distinctions between the social and the imaginary worlds were often blurred.[2] Those stories are collected in the *biji* 筆記, or miscellaneous writings, in which authors recorded what they heard and experienced in their daily lives, including rumors and gossips about nationally

---

1. For a concise introduction of this genre of literature, see Robert Campany, "Tales of Strange Events," in *Early Medieval China: A Sourcebook*, ed. Wendy Swartz, Robert Campany, Yang Lu, and Jessey J. C. Choo (New York: Columbia University Press, 2014), 576–578.

2. Sarah M. Allen argues that in the tales of the late eighth and early ninth centuries, the writers found ways to blur the boundaries between the two worlds. See *Shifting Stories: History, Gossip, and Lore in Narratives from Tang Dynasty China* (Cambridge, MA: Harvard Asia Center, 2014), 163.

renowned figures' paranormal experiences.[3] Eleventh-century authors or recorders of those stories came from a wide range of backgrounds, including notable scholar-officials, Buddhist monks, and local administrative officers. The new accessibility of woodblock prints contributed to the wide circulation of multiple copies of individual writings that have survived into the present.

Previous scholarship on the tales of anomaly tends to focus on identifying their moral and religious nature and interpreting people's perception of the world-beyond and the supernatural others.[4] Shifting the focus of study, this chapter will engage the following inquiries. First, how did eleventh-century popular narratives of the world-beyond and the supernatural convey political criticism, especially in the highly polarized climate generated by the New Policies and its aftermath? Second, how did ordinary and under-privileged people use those narratives in ways that challenged the current political authority or the privileged people who evaded the scrutiny of the state's judicial system? Third, how did Confucian discourses engage such a powerful presence of the social imaginaries of the spirit world in popular narratives, given the tradition's explicit rejection of participating in such discourse?

## Wang Anshi in Hell

By the eleventh century, the notion of hell was quite familiar to most Chinese people, due to the outpouring of old and new accounts of people who claimed to have seen it. Most narratives on hell in China take the form of hearsay rather than of a first-person account. Previous studies on the Song literature on this topic tend to highlight retribution as an overriding theme in this

---

3. Sarah M. Allen studies two different types of tales developed in the eighth and ninth centuries: rumors about national figures concerning their political careers, and tales about anomaly encounters. Some popular narratives of the Song period merged these two types of tales by including nationally renowned figures' encounters with the supernatural and their life after death in the other world. See her *Shifting Stories: History, Gossip, and Lore in Narratives from Tang Dynasty China*.

4. Robert Campany researches this genre, spanning the period from the Han dynasty to the Six Dynasties, in his *Strange Writing: Anomaly Accounts in Early Medieval China* (Albany: State University of New York Press, 1996). He argues that such writings delineate a cosmography that connects the human world with the supernatural world by means of a single thread of moral law. Glen Dudbridge studies the eighth-century narratives of this genre by analyzing surviving pieces collected in the *Guangyi zhi* in his *Religious Experience and Lay Society in T'ang China: A Reading of Tai Fu's Kuang-i chi* (Cambridge: Cambridge University Press, 1995). A vast number of stories were circulated during the twelfth century and were collected in the *Yijian zhi*; see Alister D. Inglis, *Hong Mai's Record of the Listener and Its Song Dynasty Context* (Albany: State University of New York Press, 2006).

period.[5] Following that line of thinking, this chapter will focus more specifically on how some of those narratives conveyed strong social and political criticism targeting high-profile figures, something rarely seen in earlier literature. Attention will be given to a series of narratives about Wang Anshi's (1021–1086) presence in hell, found in numerous collections of different authorship that have received very little scholarly attention. As a Grand Councilor, Wang engineered the New Policies, which had a tremendous impact on social and political spheres in the 1070s. By locating those stories in the social and political contexts of the post-New Policies era, I will address why narratives in the form of rumor, especially concerning souls' whereabouts in the world-beyond, served as an effective channel to advance the political interests of certain groups of people.

Chinese imaginaries of the underworld had been evolving long before Buddhist accounts of the underworld tribunals and the hell emerged in the seventh century.[6] The Chinese word, *diyu* 地獄, translated as "hell" literally means the underworld prison, because early Chinese people imagined that the deceased would enter the netherworld located beneath the earth's surface. Therefore, the soul suffering in the hell was called "criminal" or *zuiren* 罪人. Popular narratives of the eleventh century paint a picture of many prison cells managed by infernal bureaucrats specializing in different kinds of torture, such as boiling and amputation.

Accounts of the world-beyond usually took the form of reports of people who had near-death experiences. By the eleventh century, a conventional narrative structure and themes in the experiences of life after death had already been established. Typical cases involving near-death experiences arise from being mistakenly called to death,[7] being summoned as a witness at a tribunal for the deceased, and indictment by the deceased. Some people are sent back to the world of the living as a reward for good deeds or religiously meritorious acts. Their experiences have a common structure. When they fall sick, underworld magistrates visit and take them to the underworld. They sometimes cross a

---

5. Inglis, *Hong Mai's Record*, 69–88; Hsien-huei Liao, "Encountering Evil: Ghosts and Demonic Forces in the Lives of the Song Elite," *Journal of Song–Yuan Studies* 37 (2007): 95–104.

6. Yuri Pines, "History as a Guide to the Netherworld: Rethinking the *Chunqiu Shiyu*," *Journal of Chinese Religions* 31 (2003): 101–126; Laurence G. Thompson, "On the Prehistory of Hell in China," *Journal of Chinese Religions* 17 (1989): 27–41; Stephen Teiser, *The Scripture on the Ten Kings and the Making of Hell in Medieval Chinese Buddhism* (Honolulu: University of Hawaii Press, 1994).

7. Zhu Yu, *Pingzhou ketan* 萍洲可談, QSBJ, 2nd series, 6:153–154.

bridge or simply walk for a while before arriving at a palace.[8] Magistrates and officials of the underworld bureaucracy are often the recently deceased, who can recognize newcomers to that world. All the deceased are supposed to go through at least one courtroom before they have a placement for their future. In the Buddhist narratives, the ten kings of the underworld are in charge of the courts[9]; in the Daoist narratives, the *siming panguan* 司命判官 or Judge of Commissioning Destiny. If they successfully resolve the matter that caused their premature death, they are sent back to the world of the living. Some of them have the chance to take a look at hell before their departure. The road to the exit to this world is either over a bridge or through a river. At the moment they leave the underworld, they wake up from their near-deaths.

Although pre-eleventh-century stories employing this topic typically do not feature politically influential people or convey sociopolitical criticism, an exceptional story is found in a document in the Dunhuang cave about Emperor Taizong of the Tang dynasty. In the story, the emperor encountered an underworld magistrate, a former low-ranking officer during his reign, who accused the emperor of fratricide.[10] A happy ending is facilitated by the emperor's successful negotiation with a promise to evangelize his subjects to Buddhism after his return to life. In contrast, some of the eleventh-century narratives about previously powerful people highlight their dreadfully grim fates in the underworld. An account reports that someone saw Tang dynasty figures, including the notorious Empress Wu (r. 690–705), cruel jail officers, and evil ministers, being held in separate prisons in hell. Their crimes were too grave for them to have any prospects for release; they were condemned to suffer eternal punishment.[11] This account attempts to make an exception to the notion of universal salvation of all souls, a popular concept advocated in Buddhist and Daoist rituals.[12]

---

8. Su Shi, "Chen Yu bei mingli wuzui" 陳昱被冥吏誤追, in *Dongpo zhilin* 東坡志林, QSBJ, 1st series, 3.60.

9. Teiser, *The Scripture on the Ten Kings*.

10. Arthur Waley, *Ballads and Stories from Tun-huang: An Anthology* (London: G. Allen & Unwin, 1960), 164–188.

11. Liu Fu, "Congzheng yanshou" 從政延壽, in *Qingsuo gaoyi* 青瑣高議, buyi 补遗, QSBJ, 3rd series, 4:266.

12. Stephen F. Teiser, *The Ghost Festival in Medieval China* (Princeton, NJ: Princeton University Press, 1996); Mihwa Choi, "Materializing Salvation: A Liturgical Program and Its Agenda," *Journal of Daoist Studies* 6 (2013): 29–57.

Some renowned scholars were also eager to record hearsay accounts when they found that their messages conveyed social criticism. Su Shi 蘇軾 (1037–1101), a celebrated scholar and a practitioner of Buddhism, heard from the father of a man who was resuscitated from a near-death experience. His son allegedly saw a group of monks from the region suffering in hell with their yellow-haired bodies in cangues for their stealing of donations and food offerings.[13] Su Zhe 蘇轍 (1039–1112), younger brother of Su Shi, also recorded what he heard from a Daoist practitioner who claimed that he often visited the hell located underneath Tai Mountain. He said that he had seen many monks and magistrates there who had transgressed precepts and embezzled public property, respectively.[14] The Daoist practitioner told him, "Had you seen them, you might have not wanted to be a state official." Su Zhe, an official himself, recorded his warning of how hard it was for a state official to escape punishment in hell.

One of the most striking cases in point with respect to public criticism of high-profile figures is found in a series of stories about Wang Anshi. Wang faced severe opposition within officialdom led by a group of scholar-officials, many of whom chose to retire from the political domain mainly due to political conflicts with Wang and his clique. Wang's program was also critically received by the general populace, especially because of the state's harsh treatment of people in the process of implementing the policies. Even after his death in 1085, the imperial court continued to be entangled with severe conflicts over the issue of rescinding or reinstating the programs that Wang had initiated.[15] Formal accusations against members of the oppositional group often resulted in many people being exiled and demoted. In this environment, court officials were held accountable for their words, expressed in various forms, regarding public policies and political theories, because the opposition seized upon them as the bases for allegations.

Wang Anshi's family tragedy, his splendid career notwithstanding, provided ample fodder for gossip. Wei Tai 魏泰 (11th–12 cent.) in the *Dongxuan bilu* 東軒筆錄 (*Essays from an Eastern Balcony*) summarized the story about Wang Pang 王雱 (1044–1076), the only son of Wang Anshi who survived to

---

13. Su Shi, "Lishi zi zaisheng shuo mingjian shi" 李氏子再生說冥間事, in *Dongpo zhilin*, 9:2.54–55.

14. Su Zhe, "Zhao Sheng xiashu er you zhidao" 趙生挾術而又知道, in *Su Huangmen Longchuan lüe zhi* 蘇黃門龍川略志, Congshu jicheng chubian, vol. 3887, 2.7.

15. Ari Daniel Levine, *Divided by a Common Language: Factional Conflict in Late Northern Song China* (Honolulu: University of Hawaii Press, 2008), 99–180.

maturity.[16] According to the story, Pang doubted he was the father of his infant son, due to the lack of resemblance between them. As Pang was planning to kill the infant, he died due to stress. Wang Anshi knew that Pang had lost his mind at this point in his life and believed in the innocence of his daughter-in-law. Thereupon Wang Anshi arranged her remarriage to his son-in-law as a way of resolving the conflict. On the other hand, Wang Anshi criticized the widow of Hou Shuxian 侯叔獻 (1023–1076), his protégé, for her lack of propriety, which resulted in her being sent back to her natal family. Wei Tai, the storyteller, included a phrase that was circulating in the capital city: "Wang married off his daughter-in-law while his son was alive; Hou divorced his wife after his death." This anecdote was recorded in many other essay collections of different authorship, attesting to its wide circulation.[17] As Wang Pang himself died following the death of his infant son, Wang Anshi became heirless. A wildly imaginative story was circulated concerning Wang's grave misfortune, the termination of his lineage.

In a story in the *Tieweishan congtan* 鐵圍山叢談 (*Collection of Conversations of the Iron Enclosed Mountain* [i.e., Cakravada]), someone answered the question as to why Wang Anshi was heirless: "He was a wild badger in the celestial world in his previous life. How could he have an heir?"[18] The story took place in the Shrine of Sweet Spring (*liquan guan* 醴泉觀), where the popular deity Zhenwu 眞武 or Perfected Warrior was installed. It was one of the most prestigious and luxurious shrines of the time, which was attested by Emperor Renzong's visit in order to pray for rain.[19] In his poem "The Shrine of Sweet Spring," Wang Anshi portrayed the shrine as appearing to be a heavenly paradise that had been relocated in the lower human world. In the story, when Wang made an offering to the deity, the former asked Wang, "Aren't you a 'son of badger'?" Li Shining 李士寧 (fl. 11th) happened to see this scene without Wang noticing him. Li Shining knew that Wang's childhood nickname was

---

16. Wei Tai, *Dongxuan bilu* 東軒筆錄, QSBJ, 2nd series, 8:7.51.

17. Zhang Shizheng, *Juanyou zalu* 倦遊雜錄, rpr. with Yang Yi, *Yangwengong Tanyuan* 楊文公談苑 (Shanghai: Shanghai guji chubanshe, 1993), 15; Kong Pingzhong, *Tanyuan* 談苑, QSBJ, 2nd series, 5:1.301; Don J. Wyatt, "Bonds of Certain Consequence: The Personal Responses to Concubinage of Wang Anshi and Sima Guang," in *Presence and Presentation: Women in the Chinese Literati Tradition.* ed. Sherry J. Mou (New York: St. Martin's Press), 232–233.

18. Cai Tao, *Tieweishan congtan* 鐵圍山叢談 (Beijing: Zhonghua shuju, 1991), 4.72.

19. Shao Bo, *Shaoshi wenjian houlu* 邵氏聞見後錄, QSBJ, 4th series, 6:1.7. For a brief history of this shrine in association with Zhenwu worship, see Shin-yi Chao, *Daoist Rituals, State Religion, and Popular Practices: Zhenwu Worship from Song to Ming (960—1644)* (London and New York: Routledge, 2011), 32–32.

"Little Badger." Pretending to be the deity, Li said to Wang, "You left from the celestial world for over twenty-four years and became a councilor."[20] This story was intended to denigrate Wang as originally being nonhuman in order to explain the reason for his causing problems in the Song state.

Yet who was Li Shining, someone perceived as being capable of throwing such bold remarks at Wang? Sima Guang portrays Li Shining as follows: Li "used paranormal activities to befuddle people. Many high officials and influential people admired him. Among them especially Wang Anshi trusted and admired him."[21] Li's close ties to Wang Anshi were evidenced by Wang's two poems dedicated to Li.[22] Li Shining was exiled, having been charged with treason for his alleged secret prophecy that a certain royal family member would become emperor, which was carefully orchestrated by Wang's opponents.[23] The politically charged allegation against him reveals the politics surrounding Li. Given that, it is less likely that the above conversation between Wang Anshi and Li Shining (pretending to be the deity) took place. Rather, it was more likely that people used Wang's dedication to the deity and his intimate relationship with Li Shining as literary devices to disgrace him effectively.

Rumors about Wang Anshi's family took on a more serious tone following Wang Pang's death. In one story, Wang Anshi himself sees a vision of his son wearing a metal cangue like a prisoner convicted of grave felonies. Thereupon Wang converts his residential place into a Buddhist temple and makes offerings for the sake of his son's salvation.[24] Another version presents more detailed accounts in a believable tone:

One day Wang Anshi and [his nephew-in-law] Ye Tao 葉濤 [1050–1110] were sitting in a government office at Jiang Mountain. A low-ranking military officer had an audience. Wang asked him why he had come. After requesting the withdrawal of the surrounding people, he told the following story. "Last night in my dream I entered the underworld.

---

20. The original text gives twenty-four years. Yet a note within the text indicates that some other versions of the story specify the lapse of time as twelve years. Considering Wang's tenure as the grand councilor, "twelve years" better fits his biography.

21. Sima Guang, *Sushui jiwen* 涑水記聞, QSBJ, 1st series, 7:16.207–208.

22. Wang Anshi, "Ji Li Shining xiansheng" 寄李士寧先生, *Wang linchuan ji* (Shanghai: Shangwu yinshuguan, 1933), 13.92; "Zeng Li Shining daoren" 贈李士寧道人, *Wang linchuan ji* (Shanghai: Shangwu yinshuguan, 1933), 25.80.

23. Wang Zhi, *Moji* 默記, QSBJ, 4th series, 3:134, 157–158.

24. Shao Bowen, *Shaoshi wenjian lu* 邵氏聞見錄 (Beijing: Zhonghua shuju, 1997), 11.121.

I saw the Edict Attendant [i.e., Wang Pang] in horrible pain wearing a metal cangue. He asked me to tell Your Honor [about his situation], hoping that there might be something to be done to save him. I was afraid that Your Honor would not believe my account and be hesitant to do something about it. He said, 'Tell my father that I am now imprisoned and tortured here. It is because of the matter that he and I discussed at a certain time in a such-and-such place.'" Having been reminded of that matter, Wang felt extremely distraught and remorseful. [Now,] Wang Anshi is already dead. A military man who died after falling behind the group was resuscitated. He said, "Both Wang Anshi and his son were wearing metal cangues [in the underworld prison]. I personally asked them what kind of crime brought them there. They said they ended up there because they discussed the reinstitution of cruel corporal punishment." *So, his story and the previously mentioned military officer's dream roughly coincide. Today's scholar-officials more or less know these stories.* [italics added][25]

This version of the story provides concrete information on the location and the social setting where the alleged conversation took place. It may have evolved from the previously mentioned story about Wang Pang's imprisonment, but it emphasizes that the Wangs themselves as policy makers suffer the very kind of punishment that they had wished to inflict upon others. At the end of the story, the recorder puts it into the context of another version of the story in order to highlight the agreement of their core narratives. He also inserts a comment that the source of the story is now commonly known by the scholar-officials of the time. Another version of the story, recorded in the *Sungong tanpu* 孫公談圃 (*Honorable Sun's Garden of Conversations*), allots an even more grim fate to Wang Pang:

Zhang Jing 張靖 said, "A year before his fatal illness, Wang Anshi was at Jinling [present-day Nanjing]. [One day,] During the daytime he saw a man entering his room and bowing twice. He was none other than a deceased magistrate who had been dead for a long time. Wang was startled and asked him the reason for his visit. The magistrate said, 'Having received Your Honor's benevolence, I came here on the Edict Attendant's [i.e., Wang Pang's] behalf.' Wang despondently asked him if Pang was doing all right. The magistrate said, 'As of today, the verdict

---

25. Fang Shao, *Bozhai bian* 泊宅編, j. zhong 中, QSBJ, 2nd series, 8:226.

has yet to be made. If you would like to be present in the tribunal, you could enter the makeshift office on a certain evening. Please make sure not to cry out in fear. You can take one person with you whom you trust.' So Wang did. Soon he saw a man in a purple gown with a wide belt. He took a table and had a seat. He was none other than that deceased magistrate. Several prison guards put a cangue on a criminal and then entered the place through a big door. The criminal's body was all bound with shackles. He dragged his aching legs and stood on the courtyard. He shed blood on the ground. His moaning sounded very painful. He was none other than Pang. Pang said, 'Inform me about the verdict as early as possible.' After a while, he vanished. Wang Anshi almost cried out, but blocked his mouth with his fingers. The following year, Wang Anshi also died." *Zhang Jing's students know this story in details.* [Italics added][26]

This story, presumably originating with Zhang Jing, presents a reversal of status. The then low-ranking officer, wearing "a purple gown with a wide belt," represents the underworld's authority to judge the son of someone who had once been, after the emperor, the most powerful person in the state. This story also fills in the gap in the previously mentioned narratives by linking Wang Anshi's shock and his fatal illness.

A follow-up story is recorded under the title of "Wang Anshi Entered Hell" in the *Mantang suibi* 漫堂随筆 (*Mantang's Jottings*). The story presents the actual names of the people and their relationship: originator, reporter, and respondent.

Chen Zhao 沈昭, Chen Xi's 沈錫 son, related that Guo Quan 郭權 was a relative of his wife. Quan became a Secretariat Court Gentleman. In the beginning of the Chongning period [1103–1106], he died but was later resuscitated. [After resuscitation,] Quan said, "An affair in the underworld is truly sad. In the area of hell entitled the Department of Corrections, there is a nobleman in a cangue. His white beard is as full as that of Liu Chen 劉忱 [fl. 11th cent.]." Why didn't Quan want to identify the man as Wang Anshi? Cai Bian's 蔡卞 [1048–1117] wife is Wang's daughter. She ordered someone to ask whether or not Quan had ever met Wang before [in order to know if he was able to recognize him in the hell]. Quan answered, "No. Nonetheless, make good offerings of

---

26. Sun Sheng, *Sungong tanpu* 孫公談圃, j. zhong 中, QSBJ, 2nd series, 1:153–154.

the Buddhist Ritual of Merit." Anshi is none other than Chen Xi's uncle on his mother's side.[27]

The recorder traces a rather complicated network of people to clarify the origin of the story, which gives it credibility. Chen Zhao, cousin of Wang Anshi, heard about the experiences of Guo Quan, a relative of his wife. It was more likely that Chen transmitted the story to Wang's daughter. Clearly, here Guo intended to evade taking responsibility for confirming Wang's incarceration but merely hinted at Wang's well-known semblance to Liu Chen because of their distinctive full beards. Wang's daughter could not afford to dismiss this simple allusion, because she was already familiar with the widespread rumor about Wang's wretched fate in hell.

As seen in the reaction of Wang Anshi's daughter, the stories were meant to pose a warning and to invoke fear in people who might be associated with the implied theme. Because experiences in the world-beyond were basically unverifiable, an alleged originator of the account was relieved of the burden of proof. It was even more convenient for a recorder to treat such stories as ones he had heard from someone else while inserting his own comments about them. In this era, when the effects of the New Policies were still a national political concern, reports on the Wangs' fate could strongly influence the evaluation of the policies. Thus, certain literati utilized the social imaginary of hell as a convenient and effective tool for advancing their agenda of punishing their political opponents and condemning their policies in a way that was not possible with other literary genres.

## *Han Qi's Glory in Heaven*

Traditionally, rewards of the deceased had rarely taken on political overtones, mostly because this notion itself had evolved out of Buddhist and Daoist traditions. The most popular reward for souls in eleventh-century narratives was an extension of lifespan: because of the deceased's extraordinary moral or religious actions, she or he would be returned to the world of the living. A better reward in the Daoist imaginary was that the deceased become a god or an immortal in the celestial bureaucracy. Eyewitness accounts of such cases were scarce. Nevertheless, there is one from 1076, a year after the death of Han Qi 韓琦 (1008–1075) and the closing year of the era of the New Policies.

---

27. Wu Jian, "Mantang suibi" 漫堂隨笔, in *Shuofu* 說郛, ed. Tao Zongyi (Shanghai: Shanghai shangwu, 1927), 64.9.

Han Qi engineered the Minor Reforms (1043–1045) and later vehemently opposed the New Policies. The genesis of the popular story about Han Qi (aka Han Weigong 韓魏公, or Honorable Wei of Han) is found in the following narrative. The internal date of the event is the birthday of the emperor, the fifth month of 1076. Two high-profile figures had died recently: Han Qi in the previous year, and Hou Shuxian a few months prior:

In 1076, on the birthday of His Majesty, the Office of Entertainment staged a memorial opera. It was the time that Hou Shuxian, an official of irrigation, had just died. The actor Ding Xianjian played a Daoist master who was good at disembodying his spirit. There was [also] a Buddhist monk whose expertise was in entering into a meditational trance. Someone asked the Daoist master what his disembodied spirit saw. He answered, "Recently my spirit went to the highest heaven and saw a man wrapped in gold and purple. Upon a close look at him, it turned out that he was none other than the Grand Councilor Han of the state. He was holding an item. I discreetly inquired about that item of a man standing by me. He said, "Han Qi dedicated the Painting of Eternal Prosperity of the Imperial Family to the state." The Buddhist monk said, "Recently in my meditational trance, I went to hell. I saw a man to the side in the hall of King Yama, wearing clothes with a crimson fish pendant. Once I got a close look at him, I realized that he was none other than the Directorate of Waterways, Minister of Works Hou [Shuxian]. He was holding an object in his hand. I secretly asked people around me. They said, 'It is the Dedicated Map of Shallow Water in the Naihe 奈河 [i.e., a river in hell], and it is his desire not to open the waterways.' It was the time when Shuxian developed an irrigation system, and was rewarded for the project. Nevertheless, people suffered because of it. That's why the actor said those words."[28]

Han Qi was rewarded in heaven for his painting intended to promote the state's prosperity, whereas Hou Shuxian was punished for his blueprints of the irrigation project. Hou Shuxian devoted his professional career to an irrigation project as a part of the New Policies. Earlier in the year 1076, the emperor had heard a report about massive casualties of workers during the project of

---

28. Peng Cheng, "Xianxiang zaju" 獻香雜劇, in *Xu Moke hui xi* 續墨客揮犀, rpr. with Zhao Lingzhi, *Houqing lu,* and *Moke huixi* (Beijing: Zhonghua shuju, 2002), 5.470–471; Zhang Shizheng, "Jiaofang zaju" 教坊雜劇, in *Juanyou zalu,* 59.

rebuilding a canal.[29] Although the emperor did not believe this rumor, he sent investigators to probe the matter. When Hou was taken by a fatal illness later, the emperor declined to send a doctor for his care on the pretext that the distance was too great.[30] Against this background, the play presented political criticism of his irrigation project as one which supposedly benefited farmers, but actually did them a great deal of harm, which was a talking point in the barrage of criticism of the project by Wang's opponents, led by Sima Guang.[31] It is noteworthy that the opera was performed on the birthday of Emperor Shenzong, to whom the painting and the map by the two deceased officials were likely to be presented. Furthermore, the agency producing the opera was the Office of Entertainment, a governmental institution. The high political stakes would not have gone unnoticed by Wang Anshi, yet he was not capable of responding to it. Five months later, Wang Anshi was placed in retirement, which marked the coda of the era of New Policies (1069–1076).

How does Han Qi fare in the celestial world? A story introduced in the *Qingsuo gaoyi* 青瑣高議 (Exalted Discourses on Forbidden Topics) takes up this question in a relatively long and detailed narrative:

[Synopsis:] Sun Mian 孫勉 [fl.11th cent.] was in charge of rebuilding a levee of a city. In the process of carrying this out, he intentionally killed a huge turtle. One day a magistrate visited him and informed him. "You have killed a turtle. As of today you are indicted for that incident. Therefore we summon you to probe that matter." Mian walked with him about twenty-four miles until he saw a grandiose palace portal. It was the palace of the Perfected in the Purple Bureau, where Honorable Wei of Han resided. He recalled that Honorable Wei of Han had granted him a favor of giving him a broom; thus, he could ask him to help him out this time. Mian bowed to him and said, "I have been indebted to Your Honor for receiving protection in the past." He continued to explain the situations that led him to this predicament. Honorable Wei brought a yellow note and read, "Turtle is not same as human beings. Turtle lives over a hundred years. Moreover, its lineage continues for five hundred generations. It is as precious as human beings." Mian said, "Demolishing turtle holes as part of refurbishing the levee is my duty." Based on this defense Mian was released. A lad in

---

29. CB 274.6702–6703.

30. CB 273.6692–6693.

31. CB 263.6423–6425; Sima Guang, *Sushui jiwen*, QSBJ, 1st series, 7.192–199.

jade green clothes sent Mian to his home. When the lad called Mian's name, he woke up.[32]

This story has the backdrop of a Daoist imaginary, in which the Perfected presides over the tribunal. It features the conventional theme that even a nonhuman being can file a suit against human beings. What is novel in this story is that Han Qi has become the Perfected in the Purple Bureau, the first stop for a deceased soul. The story does not question whether or not Han Qi deserves such a prestigious position, which indicates that his posthumous reputation by this time is very likely unchallenged.

Zhang Shizheng 張師正 (b. 1016) also includes this story entitled "Supervising the Rebuilding Levee of Daming Prefect" in the *Kuoyi zhi* 括異志 (*A Collection of Anomaly Tales*).[33] The author relates that he heard this story from Liu Xili 劉襄禮, Minister of Court. He notes that the refurbishing work took place in 1076, a year after Han Qi's death. It adds information that the note the Perfected Han Qi consulted with was "The Guidelines of the Highest Clarity" (上清格), a Daoist text. Ye Mengde 葉夢得 (1077–1148), who showed a great interest in writing stories on the supernatural, also commented on this widely known anecdote in the *Bishu luhua* 避暑錄話 (*Records of Conversations in Summer Vacation*):

There are many extant stories about a military man who supervised refurbishing work of the levee of the Yellow River during the Yuanfeng Reign [1078–1085]. He shot and killed a turtle during the work. Not long after [the incident], the man died but was resuscitated. He related that the turtle had filed suit [against him] in the underworld. The man defended himself as best he could, saying that the turtle's allotted lifespan was an obstacle to his rebuilding work; therefore for the sake of his duty he had to kill it. Based on this defense he obtained immunity. The underworld official was Honorable Wei of Han. In the underworld he was addressed as the Perfected. Initially, I did not believe this story. Later I obtained a book, *Family Records of Han Qi's Life* [*Hanshi jiachuan* 韓氏家傳], which recorded this story. There is a saying, "One does not doubt about what is proclaimed in writings on fine silk." Given that a

---

32. Liu Fu, "Zifu zhenren ji" 紫府眞人記, in *Qingsuo gaoyi*, 1.16–17.

33. Zhang Shizheng, *Kuoyi zhi* 括異志, Sibu congkan xubian 56 (Shanghai: Shanghai shudian, 1985), 10a–11a.

slaughtered turtle could file a suit, isn't it all the more so for human beings?[34]

Ye Mengde's dating of the refurbishing work was slightly different from that of Zhang Shizheng's, which reveals the fluidity of the story's details. Ye Mengde might have felt that it was unnecessary for him to go over the widely known story in detail, but did add the new information about Han Qi's biography. Indeed, this story is recorded verbatim in the book written by his son, Han Zhongyan 韓忠彥 (1038–1109), including an additional episode regarding Emperor Shenzong. The emperor asked court officials if they heard that Han had become an immortal, detailed the story, and heaved a deep sigh.[35] After the court audience, Sun Gu 孫固 (1016–1090) personally told the emperor, "With Honorable Han's lifetime achievements, how could he not become a Perfected Man?" By bringing up the emperor in his own version of the story, Han Qi's son might have wanted to further validate the veracity of Han Qi's posthumous status.

Was Han Qi really worthy of such a prestigious position? Later, Cai Tao 蔡絛 (11th –12th cent.) brought up this issue and laid out the specific context in which he himself had heard a related story:

Mr. Wang Laozhi 王老誌 [d. 1122] talked about people's past and future lives. He had never failed in his readings of other people's fortune. Han Cuiyan 韓粹彥 [1065–1118], or Honorable Wen of Han, is my father-in-law . . . One day Han asked me to pay a visit to Wang and introduce myself. [When I got there,] Wang was delighted and immediately spoke to Han, "The Perfected in the Purple Bureau." Han was also quick to respond to him, saying: "After Honorable Wei of Han passed away, a certain magistrate, Sun Mian, supervised some cleaning work. Because he killed a huge turtle, he was indicted. Therefore an incident related to the Perfected in the Purple Bureau or what someone wrote in the *Qingsuo xiaoshuo* 青瑣小說 [i.e., *Qingsuo gaoyi*] is not incorrect." Wang Laozhi also said: "The Perfected in the Purple Bureau is not an immortal, but in fact is a noble among the underworld officials. Honorable Wei of Han's accumulated merit was his prominent virtue; he has recently arisen to heaven. Initially, he was an attendant of the Perfected of Jade

---

34. Ye Mengde, *Bishu luhua* 避暑錄話, j. shang 上, QSBJ, 2nd series, 10:239–240.

35. Han Zhongyan, *Jiachuan* 家傳, in *Han Weigong ji* 韓魏公集 (Shanghai: Shangwu yinshuguan, 1937), 19.264–265.

Radiance." . . . I alone have known about this event for a long time, and regret that other people are still ignorant of it. The world reveres only Lord of Wei, Zhongxian (魏忠獻王) [i.e., Han Qi], as the most influential court official in this dynasty for his virtue of protecting society. However, his beginning was just as an attendant of the Perfected.[36]

Cai Tao provided the names of the real people who had discussed the matter. Wang Laozhi was a renowned Daoist practitioner who was close to Cai Tao's father, Cai Jing 蔡京 (1047–1126); their intimate relationship was recorded in the *Songshi* 宋史 (A *History of the Song*).[37] Cai Jing was an older brother of Cai Bian 蔡卞 (1058–1117), Wang Anshi's son-in-law. While serving as Grand Councilor during 1102–1120, Cai Jing was instrumental in the demotion and exile of people who advocated rescinding the New Policies.[38] Cai Tao might have had a chance to meet with Wang Laozhi, at which time this recorded conversation took place. When Cai Tao wrote this story, his whole family had already fallen into the disgrace of exile, beginning in 1126, as the political winds had blown against them.[39] Setting aside the matter of the veracity of the story, Cai Tao might have wanted to find a way to deflate the posthumous reputation of Han Qi in this widely popular narrative. Cai Tao's story had some readership. Later, Zhou Hui 周煇 (fl. 12th cent.) synthesized aforementioned narratives from diverse sources in a single account under the title of "Killing Turtle."[40] He concluded the story by citing Wang Laozhi, modifying Cai Tao's rendition: "The Perfected at the Purple Bureau is prestigious amongst infernal bureaucrats; [however,] his status is less than a celestial immortal."

The evolving stories of Han Qi after his death were based on a conventional theme that encouraged the religious and moral actions of private individuals. Nevertheless, in the highly polarized political climate, the ramification of the story was far larger than one individual's morality. The producer of the play featuring Han Qi being elevated in the celestial world calculated the political

36. Cai Tao, *Tiewei shan congtan* 鐵圍山叢談 (Beijing: Zhonghua shuju, 1983), 5.85.

37. SS Liezhuan 221, 462.13527.

38. Levine, *Divided*, 150–157.

39. Ari Daniel Levine, "The Reigns of Hui-tsung (1100–1126) and Ch'in-tsung (1126–1127) and the Fall of the Northern Sung," in *The Cambridge History of China*, vol. 5, part 1: *The Sung Dynasty and Its Precursors, 907–1279*, eds. Paul Jakov Smith and Denis Twitchett (New York: Cambridge University Press, 2009), 639.

40. Zhou Hui 周煇 (fl. 12th cent.), "Shagui" 殺龜, in *Qingpo zazhi jiaozhu* 清波雜誌校注, annot. *Liu Yongxiang* (Beijing: Zhonghua, 1994), 7.328–329.

gains of debunking the New Policies. Likewise, on the other side of the political spectrum, Cai Tao wished to deflate Han Qi's reputation by retelling the story as highlighting Han's initial low status in the infernal bureau before he was promoted to a high status in the celestial world. When the conventional idea of rewards in the afterlife had been instilled in people's minds, public understanding of the deceased political leaders' whereabouts in the world-beyond had the potential to either legitimize or delegitimize their legacy.

## *Deferred Justice for the Underprivileged*

Against the background of reward in heaven and punishment in hell, there was the tribunal that all deceased should go to after their physical death. As seen in some cases, lawsuits filed by a deceased person could cause a living person to be summoned to the tribunal before his or her scheduled time of death. Many eleventh-century popular narratives dealing with the underworld court tend to emphasize the idea of deferred justice. This represents a shift in emphasis from the earlier stories contained in the *Guangyi zhi* 廣異志, an eighth-century popular literature collection, in which many underworld officers were bribed or tricked into adjusting people's allotted life spans.[41] The very notion that anyone could file a suit was very appealing to commoners, who did not any have political clout or means of access to the state's legal system. This section explores how the popular narratives featuring underprivileged people employed the theme of deffered justice in a way that posed social criticism during the eleventh century.

The conception of the underworld lawsuit is attested as early as the third century BCE in China. At this time, however, the lawsuits had less to do with the moral actions of the living and more to do with inadequate mortuary practices. By the fourth century CE, the notion of a legal court administered by a celestial bureaucratic system was found within Daoist circles.[42] In a fifth-century account of a historical event, the downfall of a previous state was interpreted as a result of a grieving spirit filing a petition.[43] However, it was not until the Tang dynasty that detailed narratives about the scenes in the tribunal

---

41. For example, Mu-chou Poo also pinpoints this aspect in the ghost stories in the Six Dynasties: Mu-chou Poo, "The Culture of Ghosts in the Six Dynasties Period," in *Rethinking Ghosts in World Religions*, ed. Mu-chou Poo (Leiden and Boston: Brill, 2009), 264.

42. Paul R. Katz, *Divine Justice: Religion and the Development of Chinese Legal Culture* (London and New York: Routledge, 2009), 34.

43. Liu Jingshu, *Yiyuan* 異苑 (Beijing, Zhonghua shuju, 1996), 6.52.

were developed.[44] By the early Song, the notion of the deceased's filing suit in the underworld court was widely accepted.

Eleventh-century narratives on this topic do not just replicate conventional motifs found in the stories of earlier times, but include social and cultural elements specific to the era. A story in the *Qingsuo gaoyi* recorded in the eleventh or early twelfth century further illustrates the complex and concrete legal process in the underworld tribunal in a way which resembles that in the social world: [45]

> [Synopsis:] Cheng Shuo 程說, a prison officer, fell ill. He saw an officer with blue clothes. He presented Cheng with a subpoena to the underworld court. Before the tribunal, Cheng met another officer who happened to be his old acquaintance. He was sympathetic to Cheng. He informed Cheng that the latter was under indictment for slaughtering fifty cows, and advised him to be honest during the trial. During the tribunal, Cheng defended himself, [saying] that he was just following an order of Governor Wang Zhen 王眞 to provide military provisions during the campaign against the Manchus. The king of the underworld court asked him to present evidence. Cheng gave the location of the handwritten letter from Wang Zhen. The letter was fetched from the human world, and immediately Wang Zhen was also summoned to verify his letter. He verified the letter, but stated that he had also followed an order from a military official. In the end, Cheng Shuo was told, "We have summoned you and cleared up the case. Your predetermined lifespan has not yet been exhausted. You can return promptly." When Cheng Shuo regained consciousness, he found that the letter had indeed disappeared.

The two worlds—the social and the imaginary—are not only porous, but also operate according to the same moral and legal principles. The prison officer in this world received a subpoena from an officer of the underworld. The process of the trial was no different from the customary practice of the Song

---

44. Paul R. Katz, *Divine Justice*, 40.

45. Li Fu, "Cheng Shuo" 程說, in *Qingsuo gaoyi*, Houji, QSBJ, 3rd series, 4:3.136–139. There have been controversies about the dating and authenticity of stories included in the "Houji" (postscript) and "Bieji" (addendum) in this book because there are versions that do not include them. However, in the preface to the *Quan Song biji* edition, the editor argues that other Song texts that included those stories with references to the *Qingsuo gaoyi* make a strong case that those stories were included in the original version.

state: subpoena, defense of the accused, presentation of evidence, verification with witness, and release. His defense was that he was just following an order from the military, which exempted him from liability for his acts.[46] As in the case of the man who killed a turtle during assigned work, the state laws stipulated that individuals were bound to carry out official duties regardless of what their conscience urged.

Given that the procedural juxtaposition had been established between the two juridical systems, how did people perceive the justice delivered in the state's legal courts? An essay entitled "Lawsuit" written by Li Zhiyan 李之彥 (fl. eleventh century) poignantly conveyed people's anger and frustration caused by mishandled cases:

Heaven and spirits do not hear people's cries. Earth and the God of Grain do not listen to people's pain. How sad! Doubtless, a lawsuit is supposed to fix what went wrong and to resolve a grievance. These days the rich win lawsuits, and the poor lose. People who have clout get support; people who don't are treated unjustly. The rich and the influential get what they want [from the lawsuit], the poor and the weak bear the injustice. How could this be a blessing of the state? I foolishly wish that there were scholar-officials in the courtroom who could intervene.[47]

If a member of the literati like Li Zhiyan was moved to lament in this way, it is not hard to imagine how people of low social strata might have felt.

The perceived injustice of the legal system drove people's fascination with the underworld justice system as the last resort for resolving their grievances. Kong Pingzhong 孔平仲 (fl. 1065) in the *Tanyuan* 談苑 (*Garden of Conversations*) reported a case in which a convict spelled out his last words on an execution ground, "Unjust killing [*yuanwang sharen* 冤枉殺人]!" [48] His reproach was a warning of what he would do after his death. Soon after, those involved in the rendering of the verdict died. Kong, the storyteller, apparently believed that the deceased had filed suit in the underworld. He commented that the death sentence might have been too harsh for the ignorant followers

---

46. In another story, a governor pronounced a death sentence for someone for the crimes of robbery and rape. He successfully defended himself by saying that he had simply followed state laws in reaching his verdict. Wen Ying, *Xu Xiangshan yelu* 續湘山野錄 (Beijing: Zhonghua shuju, 1997), 69.

47. Li Zhiyan, "Yusong" 獄訟, in *Donggu suibi* 東谷隨筆, in *Biji xiaoshuo daguan*, 6th series (Taipei: Xinxing shuju, 1975), 3:2.15.

48. Kong Pingzhong, *Tanyuan* 談苑, QSBJ, 2nd series, 5:314.

of the crime ringleader. On the other hand, an official was said to have been able to defend himself successfully in a similar case. Huang Jingguo 黃靖國 (fl. 11th cent.) was allegedly summoned to the underworld court, having been indicted for torturing a soldier to death. The dead soldier claimed that it was an "unjust killing," yet King Yama saw it otherwise. The soldier's "insult to and disobedience of authority" in the military mandated the death sentence, according to state laws. Huang Jingguo was reported to have come back to life twenty-two days after his near-death in 1072.[49]

Some people who filed petitions in the underworld were women, especially those of low social status. A story about a servant woman provides a case in point:

[Synopsis:] During the reign of Zhiping 治平 [1064–1067], a man named Gong Qiu 龔球 encountered a runaway servant woman carrying a sack with her. After her contract period was over, her master did not release her, but inflicted even more suffering on her. She begged Gong Qiu to let her stay in his house. After Gong Qiu found out that the sack was filled with gold and pearls, he sneaked away from her, taking her sack with him. One day while he was enjoying his wealth, her ghost appeared. She told Gong Qiu that a policeman had caught her while waiting for him. She was imprisoned and tortured during the interrogation about the lost jewels until her four limbs fell off and she died. She had no way to appeal her case except via the underworld court. Soon Gong Qiu was summoned to King Yama and was told that he would undergo the very kind of pain that she had suffered. Tumors grew all over his body until the four limbs fell off and he died.[50]

She was abused by her master, and then used by a man who she trusted. The legal system imposed extremely cruel punishment on her for the crime of stealing. The story captures the harsh life of servant women of the time who were outside legal protection. When they were of no use for housework due to illness, some of them were driven to commit suicide or thrown out in a wilderness.[51] Survivors of such abuse often continued to live in the house because they did not have a place to go. Their abusers did not bear any legal accountability, because those women did not have any means to bring forth their case

---

49. Liu Fu, "Congzheng yanshou" 從政延壽, in *Qingsuo gaoyi*, Buyi, QSBJ, 3rd series, 4: 265.

50. Liu Fu, "Gongqiu ji" 龔球記, in *Qingsuo gaoyi*, Houji, QSBJ, 3rd series, 4:4.144–146.

51. Peng Cheng, "Beipu huanchi" 婢僕患疾, in *Xu Moke huixi*, 24.449.

in the state's legal system. Another story of a woman that allegedly took place exposed such social inequity. An educated female was married off to a high official and lived far away from her natal family. Three days after giving birth, her father-in-law evicted her from the house. On the verge of death, she wrote her story of abuse on the wall of a transportation station because "there was no place to appeal." Her written story was read only after her death and drew public criticism of her father-in-law, which tellingly revealed the familial and social environs of women.[52]

Under these social circumstances, grieving female ghosts frequently appeared in popular narratives. Moo-chou Poo lays out three different types of ghosts who appeared in the early medieval literature: vengeful ghosts, benevolent ghosts, and ghosts in need of help.[53] By the eighth century, however, the *Guangyi zhi* rarely presents female ghosts as vengeful but mostly as exotic others available for unfettered love.[54] Some of the eleventh-century ghost stories continued to feature those earlier images, yet with a marked emphasis on retribution. A summary of the story "Mr. Chen Shuyu" in the *Qingsuo gaoyi* is illustrative:

[Synopsis:] Mr. Chen dated a singer Yinglan. He promised to marry her, lying about his current marital status. Later he threw her into a well in order to get out of the complicated situation. Pretending it was an accident, he asked Yinglan's maid to rescue her. She died as well. In the winter of the same year, Mr. Chen and his wife were walking around the Xiangguo Temple in Kaifeng. Yinglan appeared in the temple and asked him to visit her house. She told him, "If you don't come, *I will sue you in the court.* There must be a big prison." Out of fear of her threat, he went to her house without realizing that she was a ghost. That same maid welcomed him. As Chen did not come out of the house until early in the evening, other people went into the house. He was dead with his hands tied together on his back as if he had been taken to the state's execution ground, according to current law. [italics added][55]

---

52. The public response to her writing was overwhelmingly sympathetic to her, and condemning of her husband, partly because of the aesthetic elements of the writing. Shen Gua, *Mengxi bitan* 夢溪筆談, QSBJ, 2nd series, 3:24.182.

53. Mu-chou Poo, "The Completion of an Ideal World: The Human Ghost in Early Medieval China," *Asia Major*, 3rd series, 10 (1997): 69–94.

54. Glen Dudbridge, *Religious Experience and Lay Society in Tang China: A Reading of Tai Fu's* Kuang-i chi (Cambridge, UK, and New York: Cambridge University Press, 1995), 154–173.

55. Liu Fu, "Chen Shuwen" 陳叔文, in *Qingsuo gaoyi*, Houji, QSBJ, 3rd series, 4:4.141.

In this story, a marginalized singer-prostitute who hoped to be a wife uses the current legal system as the backdrop of her threat as well as for her punishment of him. The story conveys the message that those who escape the scrutiny of the state's legal system might eventually face their due punishment by a supernatural agent or ghost by the very method that the state should have imposed.[56]

Such narratives reveal that many commoners saw the world-beyond or the spirit world as the place where ultimate justice would be meted out. The legal systems in the two worlds—the social and the world-beyond—mirrored each other by sharing their logistics for resolving cases. Yet the legal system of the social world either often failed to carry out justice, or was not accessible for underprivileged people. Therefore, the notion of deferred justice in the world-beyond was a corrective for the state legal system's failure. Certain ghosts were also able to carry out retribution by themselves without recourse to the tribunal system of the world-beyond. The very fact that those stories were written by some literati indicates that they shared this notion of the underworld tribunal as the last resort for deferred justice.

## Confucian Discourses on the Supernatural

The plethora of discourses on the world-beyond and the supernatural in society was at odds with the traditional Confucian maxim of remaining silent on the issue. Some stories even feature prominent scholar-officials and highlight how they faced the supernatural beings—ghosts and spirits—about whom they were not supposed to talk. Given the rampant circulation of the stories in society, some scholar-officials felt compelled to express their opinions on the topic in their own words. As seen in the foregoing discussion, some scholars not only actively recorded, circulated, and embellished received stories, but also inserted their political and moral agenda into them. This section will illustrate the varied responses of scholar-officials on the topic of the social imaginary of the world-beyond and ghosts, and inquire into how their perspectives on this issue jibed with their ideas on Confucianism.

The traditional Confucian discourse on the world-beyond can be summed up as agnosticism on the issue of life after death, although its ritual practices

---

56. Another story whose internal date is the year 1041 features a singer-prostitute who was also lied to and killed by her lover. The murderer died in the very place and in the exactly the same way. Liu Fu, "Li Yunniang" 李雲娘, in *Qingsuo gaoyi*, Houji, 4.140. For a story of a ghost who identifies his murderer in public, see "Yangtong ji" 羊童記, in *Qingsuo gaoyi*, Houji, 4.141.

assumed the existence of the spirit world. Sima Guang and others in the eleventh century frequently quoted the famous passage of Li Dan, a Tang-dynasty figure, on this issue, which piquantly sums up their point of view: "If heaven does not exist, that is all. If it does, then virtuous people will ascend there. If hell does not exist, that is all. If it does, then morally inferior people will enter it."[57] The statement dismisses the significance of the discourse on the world-beyond rather than denying its existence. The underlined notion is that reward and punishment in heaven and hell should not serve as a strong ground for fostering moral cultivation. This position was directly challenged in the following comment of Ye Mengde 葉夢得 (1077–1148), one of the most vocal figures who recorded those stories in his collections. He wrote, "I do not just take pleasure in talking about ghosts, the world-beyond, and anomalies. I especially write about this affair [of punishment in the underworld] to teach my children that an officer should not do anything that goes against his conscience."[58] Here, to justify his interest in these narratives, he makes a point of underscoring their value as moral lessons.

Su Shi, among the prominent scholars of the time, was the best-known for his penchant for discussing this topic. The *Houqing lu* 侯鯖錄 (*Records of the Marquis's Delicacies*) records that "Su Shi used to talk about the beauty of poetry portraying ghosts."[59] Ye Mengde also noted that Su Shi "took delight in talking about immortals."[60] Ample stories on those topics in Su Shi's collected works attest to his reputation in this matter. The following anecdote written by him clearly demonstrates that he did not just record what he heard, but actively participated in the paranormal event:

> [Synopsis:] In 1080 I arrived at Huangzhou. An official in the area told me that a spirit had descended into the house of Mr. Guo. The spirit had already informed him of my coming there. In the following year, when the spirit again descended into the same house, I went there to see the spirit. Two boys were holding a plant covered in clothes with their hands using their full strength. They wrote the words of the spirit as follows: "I am He Mei from Shouyang. From my childhood I learned

---

57. Sima Guang, *Sima shi Shuyi*, 5.54–55; Chen Shan 陳善, "Tiantang diyu" 天堂地獄, in *Menshi Xinhua*, Xiaji 捫蝨新話,下集,Congshu jicheng chubian, vols. 310–311, 2.68.

58. Ye Mengde, *Yanxia fangyan*, QSBJ, 2nd series, 9:343–344.

59. Zhao Lingzhi, "Dongpo yan guishi" 東坡言鬼詩, in *Houqing lu,* QSBJ, 2nd series, 6:2.201–202.

60. Ye Mengde, *Bishu luhua* 避暑錄話, QSBJ, 2nd series, 10:232.

to read. I got married. But the prefect killed my husband and took me as a librarian of his office. The prefect's wife killed me, driven by extreme jealousy. Even after death, I did not venture to file a suit. Yet messengers of heaven saw this. In order to resolve my grievance, they allowed me to have knowledge of human affairs. There are many spirits called *Zigu shen* 子姑神 or Spirit of a Young Lady, but none can approximate my excellence. If you stay here for a while and compose odes, I would respond to them to entertain you." Ten odes were swiftly composed, all of which had wonderful meanings. I asked her about the "principles of changes" applied to immortals, ghosts, and Buddhas. All her answers were beyond the expectations of the living. One of the guests applauded and also composed a poem. The spirit got up and danced in the middle of [reading] the poem. At the end she bowed and requested of me, saying, "Your literary reputation is all over the world. Wouldn't it be regrettable if you do not have a piece of writing that allows people to know about my existence?" I heard Lady He's life and the cruel prefect. Her grievance was profound. Nonetheless, she did not give out the prefect's name. She seemed to follow etiquette. She was also knowledgeable about great writing; but she was ashamed that she was not known to the world. Coarse is this writing, yet reflecting her intention.[61]

A poetry exchange with a spirit might be bizarre to modern readers, but it was not a novelty at the time. Tai Fu, the eighth-century author/compiler of the *Guangyi zhi*, mentioned that he was once present at a party featuring such a poetry exchange.[62] From the tenth century, this practice began to be associated with the cult of *Zigu shen* 子姑神 (aka 紫姑神 or Spirit of Purple Lady).[63] Su Shi did not question the credibility of spirit talk through possession but was quick to participate in it. His unusual empathy with the female spirit might have been related to his unusual political career. Su Shi was imprisoned on political charges due to his poem criticizing the New Policies.[64] This time, around the year 1080, he was attacked for his criticism of the sweeping

---

61. Su Shi, "Zigushen ji" 子姑神記, in *Su Shi wenji* (Beijing: Zhongghua shuju, 1986), 12.406–407.

62. Dudbridge, *Religious Experience*, 1–2.

63. Judith T. Zeitlin, "Spirit Writing and Performance in the Work of You Tong 尤侗 (1618–1704)," *T'oung Pao* 84, no. 1 (1998): 103.

64. Ronald Egan, *Word, Image, and Deed in the Life of Su Shi* (Cambridge, MA: Council on East Asian Studies, Harvard University, 1994), 86–107.

cancellation of the New Policies when the opposition faction held power in the imperial court. As he entered a life of exile in Huangzhou, perhaps he might have felt sympathy with the spirit who did not file suit against her victimizers when he praised the spirit's keeping her grievance to herself.

Popular narratives written about Su Shi portray him as having firm control over ghosts, restless spirits with the potential to harm the living. In one instance, his daughter-in-law was possessed after giving birth, a vulnerable time for a woman both physically and psychologically. The ghost identified herself as a deceased maid who had stayed around Su's house for a long time as a ghost. Su replied, "I am a person who is not afraid of ghosts. There are many experts in talismans in the capital city who are certainly able to exorcize you. You'd better go. Tomorrow at dusk, I will sponsor on your behalf a Buddhist ritual of Accumulation of Merit." He kept his promise. In this incident, Su did not dismiss his daughter-in-law's possession, but confronted the ghost with a threat of exorcism.[65] Yet he also showed mercy by sponsoring a ritual so that she would be released from her current status of restless ghost.

Su Shi was also bold enough to engage with a publicly venerated spirit. He did not make an offering to the spirit of a shrine when he and his staff passed by the area where it was located.[66] As that spirit possessed one of his staff members, others suggested that Su yield to the spirit by making an offering to the spirit. When Su adamantly refused, a sudden storm swept the area as if it was the wrath of the spirit. Su Shi said, "Has the spirit become more wrathful? I am not scared." He went on to say, "Blessings and misfortune are brought by Heaven. If the spirit is angry, so be it. I will continue to walk on my journey without stopping. Can the spirit's persistence keep up with mine?" The wind calmed down and there was no harm to the group. In this anecdote, Su Shi did not doubt the existence of the publicly venerated spirit, yet identified his or her actions as being malicious. The story illustrates that Su Shi held the traditional Confucian position that the ultimate agent determining human fate was Heaven, not a spirit, though he acknowledged the latter's influence on human affairs. His integrity as a Confucian scholar was not compromised by his awareness of the power of the supernatural. His grandfather, Su Xu 蘇序 (973–1047), had expressed a similar attitude when he demolished the sculptural image of a powerful spirit along with the room where he was enshrined.[67] Later the spirit said, "I am very afraid of him [i.e., Su Xu]." He

---

65. Li Zhi, *Shiyou tanji* 師友談記, QSBJ, 2nd series, 7:35.

66. Li Zhi, *Shiyou tanji* 師友談記, QSBJ, 2nd series, 7:35–36.

67. Li Zhi, *Shiyou tanji* 師友談記, QSBJ, 2nd series, 7:54.

humbly requested that Su Xu not tear down the entire shrine so that he could survive in that region.

In the popular narratives, Su Shi is seen as a folk hero who had an affinity with the supernatural. This might have been derived from his adopting the ideas and practices of Buddhism and Daoism in his personal life while keeping one foot in the Confucian tradition. In addition to his own penchant for discoursing on the supernatural, his own unfortunate life might have contributed to his earning legendary status even during his lifetime. Su Shi himself wrote that many absurd rumors were running around, including one that he had become an immortal.[68] Soon after his death in 1101, Su Shi was thought to have become a spirit residing in a constellation.[69] Despite the government's ban on reciting and circulating his poetry during the reign of Xuanhe (1119–1125), a period of the reinstatement of the New Policies led by Cai Jing, father of Cai Tao, its popularity persisted. His spirit was celebrated by all three traditions—Confucianism, Daoism, and Buddhism. In particular, the ritual of the ghost festival was performed on his behalf at the Fantian Temple in Hangzhou.[70]

In popular narratives, Ouyang Xiu was often contrasted with Su Shi as a stereotypical scholar-official who was skeptical about the supernatural.[71] This is not surprising, because he was the leading figure in taking the decisive step of establishing the Confucian rituals as the backbone of the social and political life in the state. He declared that Buddhism had become a negative influence on Chinese culture, because it denigrated Confucian teachings.[72] He was aware that because Buddhism and Daoism were so thoroughly integrated into the lives of ordinary people, institutional measures to crack down on those religions would "scare off" commoners.[73] He therefore focused on reviving Confucianism, believing that insufficient practice of Confucianism resulted in the flourishing of Buddhism. His criticism of Buddhism was perhaps more

---

68. Su Shi, "Dongpo shengxian" 東坡昇仙, in *Dongpo zhilin*, QSBJ, 1st series, 9:2.52–53.

69. Ding Chuanjing, *Songren yishi huibian* 宋人軼事彙編 (Beijing: Zhonghua shuju, 1981), 12.636–637.

70. Ding Chuanjing, *Songren yishi huibian* 宋人軼事彙編, 12.637–638.

71. For studies of the life, thought, and literary works of Ouyang Xiu, see James T. C. Liu, *Ouyang Xiu: An Eleventh-Century Neo-Confucianist* (Stanford, CA: Stanford University Press, 1967); Ronald Egan, *The Literary Works of Ou-yang Hsiu (1007–72)* (Cambridge, UK: Cambridge University Press, 1984).

72. Ouyang Xiu, "Benlun, *zhong*" 本論,中, in *Ouyang Xiu quanji*, 2:17.288–290.

73. Ouyang Xiu, "Benlun, *xia*" 本論,下, in *Ouyang Xiu quanji*, 2:17.291.

strongly received than he meant. An account about him is quite revealing as to how people thought of him:

> A nun at the Huipu Temple in Caizhou Prefect was able to predict people's fortune, borrowing the words of the Buddha. Court officials frequented her to inquire about their fortunes, and acknowledged that her fortunetelling had efficacy. For this reason, they came to refer to her as "divine nun." Honorable Ouyang alone called her "sinister nun." He had already repudiated Buddhism from his early life with all his efforts.[74]

Ouyang Xiu in his own words took an agnostic position about the affairs of the supernatural, in accordance with the traditional Confucian doctrine. He wrote as follows:

> The sage is a human and knows human affairs only. Heaven, earth, ghosts, and spirits are not knowable. Therefore we speculate about their signs [in order to gain knowledge about them]. Human beings are knowable; therefore we talk straightforwardly about our feelings. If we speculate about the signs of Heaven, earth, and ghosts and spirits based on human feelings, there won't be anything marvelous in them. Given that, we cultivate human affairs; that will be sufficient. When human affairs are cultivated, then they are [naturally] in harmony with Heaven, earth, ghosts, and spirits.[75]

A popular narrative questions whether Ouyang Xiu would not speculate about a sign of sprit as he claimed above:

> The Honorable Ouyang was in charge of the Temple of Responding to the Celestial Tally. On the third day [of his work], a shrine manager reported that the Wulang Shrine was very efficacious and requested that Ouyang come to make an offering; if not, the spirit would possess Ouyang. Ouyang nodded [by way of accepting this challenge]. One day, while Ouyang was having a meal, the chopsticks vanished in the blink of an eye. Next day the chopsticks were in the hands of the sculptural image of the spirit. Subsequently, Ouyang ordered that the door of the

---

74. Ouyang Xiu, *Ouyang Xiu quanji*, Fulu, 6: 2.2648.

75. Ouyang Xiu, "Yi tongzi wen, *juan yi*" 易童子問, 券一, in *Ouyang Xiu quanji*, 3:76.1109.

shrine be locked and left an official seal on it. The warning posted read, "Until I remove this seal, this door will be closed." Nothing bizarre happened to Ouyang.[76]

Despite his lack of verbal acknowledgment, Ouyang's prompt reactions revealed that his agnosticism was challenged by the apparent sign, the vanished chopsticks. Although Ouyang managed not to speak about the incident, his reactions bespoke his embarrassment. Nevertheless, he confronted the malicious act of the spirit by exercising his official authority, thinking that after all it was the government that had endorsed the legitimacy of the spirit with its enshrinement. Ouyang therefore had administrative authority to close the gate of the shrine, which would suspend the making of offerings to the spirit. The storyteller pronounced Ouyang the victor by commenting that the spirit was not able to get revenge on him.[77]

In other stories, however, Ouyang Xiu demonstrated his respect for the spirits. In one, he makes a long journey to bury his deceased mother, but is unable to do so due to rain. He prays to a local mountain god, a deified former local county official. Thanking him for the fine weather that ensues, allowing the former to carry out his important family business, Ouyang later makes the deity's consideration known at the imperial court when he obtains a position in the central government.[78] This story is not inconsistent with Ouyang's overall attitudes toward the supernatural, because he acknowledges the efficacy of spirit veneration. However, another story attributed to Ouyang directly contradicts his lifelong beliefs and actions. A spirit prophesies that he will become Assistant Chief Councilor and requests that he make an offering at night while he is crossing a river in a boat. He makes Daoist offerings to the spirit, but the spirit tells him in his dream that the offering was impure. Later Ouyang learns that the spirit came to the site of the Buddhist ritual of Water-Land Purgation at night, and supposedly obtained what he needed.[79] This explicitly Buddhist apologetic account is more likely to exploit Ouyang's reputation as one of the harshest critiques of the religion.

---

76. Fang Shao, *Bozhai bian* 泊宅編, QSBJ, 2nd series, 8:6.195.

77. Judith Boltz introduces this episode by highlighting a perceived conflict between the administrative and spiritual powers. Judith Boltz, "Not by the Seal of Official Alone: New Weapons in Battles with the Supernatural," in *Religion and Society in T'ang and Sung China*, ed. Patricia Buckley Ebrey and Peter N. Gregory (Honolulu: University of Hawaii Press, 1993), 241–242.

78. Zeng Minxing 曾敏行, *Duxing zazhi* 獨醒雜志, QSBJ, 4th series, 5:5.155.

79. Huihong 惠洪, *Lengzhai yehua* 冷齋夜話, QSBJ, 2nd series, 9:1.35.

An even more explicit case in point is found in the following story:

Ouyang squarely did not believe in Buddhist doctrine. Having risen to a high position both in the administrative and military offices, one day he fell sick. In his dream, he arrived at a palace and saw ten men with imperial caps seating in a circle. One man asked, "Assistant Chief Councilor, how come you have arrived here? You should return home swiftly." Having taken several steps out of the door, Ouyang went back and asked, "You gentlemen are the so-called Ten Kings of Buddhism, aren't you?" They said, "Indeed." Therefore he asked, "People commission the copying of sutras and make food offerings to monks in order to seek blessings for the deceased. Do they actually bring any benefits?" They replied, "How could they bring anything else but benefits?" After sleeping soundly, his health recovered. Since then Ouyang believed in Buddhist teachings.[80]

It is far less likely that Ouyang would admit that he had had such an experience, not to mention his conversion to Buddhism. Rather, pro-Buddhist narratives saw his persona as an effective literary device for turning a critic into a believer. Ouyang appears in a similar account that features him in the palace in the Water Bureau of the world-beyond. In defense of Ouyang, a scholar commented on this story that it was "extraordinarily absurd, with obscure authorship."[81]Apparently many stories written about Ouyang Xiu aim to mock his famous agnosticism, as he was seen as the preeminent representative of this position at this time.

With abundant discourse on the supernatural infusing society, some scholar-officials did not restrict themselves to talking about it, but actively declared that the discourses and practices based on belief in it were a danger to society. Liu Chang 劉敞 (1019–1068) voiced this concern by basically reiterating Confucius's position on this matter:

The sage receives his commandment from Heaven. A wise man receives his commandment from the sage. Therefore, the sage's commandment is also Heaven's Commandment. . . . When one is not able to serve people, how can he serve ghosts [*gui*]? When one does not know

---

80. Ruan Yue, *Shihua zonggui*, Houji 詩話總龜, 後集 (Beijing: Renmin wenxue chubanshe, 1987), 5.285.

81. Ding Chuanjing, *Songren yishi huibian*, 8.381–382.

life, how can he know [the affairs after] death? Therefore, the sage has something that he does not talk about. A wise man has something that he does not ask about.[82]

Building upon this position, Liu Chang considered the issue in relation to society: "When a society has the *dao* 道, people are genuine; elites are noble, and ghosts become spirits [*shen* 神]. If there is no *dao*, people are deceitful; elites are lowly, and ghosts do not become spirits."[83] According to this argument, when people turn their attention to the presence of the *dao* in society, matters in the realm of the supernatural will be set right. Zhang Zai 張載 (1020–1077) concurred, approvingly quoting a famous passage in the ancient text *Zuo Zhuan* 左傳 (*Zuo's Commentary on the* Spring and Autumn Annals)[84]: "When the state is about to flourish, it listens to people; when it is about to perish, it listens to spirits."[85]

Kong Daofu 孔道輔 (985–1039) issued a warning to the prevailing culture in the era of Xiangfu (1008–1016), during which Emperor Zhenzong instituted a statewide project of performing Daoist rituals. When was Kong stationed as a military officer, people in that county believed that a snake appeared in the Zhenwu hall at the Temple of Heavenly Felicity was mysterious. Many officers and commoners visited the snake to pay their respects, thinking it was a dragon. Kong Daofu, on the other hand, declared, "When it [i.e., society] is bright, there are ritual and music. When it is dark, there are ghosts and spirits. A snake befuddles our people and disturbs our custom. Slaughter it with no mercy."[86] When he hit the snake's head with a scepter, it was destroyed. There was nothing mysterious about it. Shi Jie 石介 (1005–1045) commented on this anecdote: "In the imperial court, there are people who have flattering faces; they take side of the evil and stand against justice. Honorable Kong attacked them using the scepter."[87] Both Kong Daofu and Shi Jie saw a danger when

---

82. Liu Chang, *Gongshi xiansheng dizi ji* 公是先生弟子記, Zhibuzu zhai congshu, 2 han, Baibu congshu jicheng, vol. 243 (Taipei: Yiwen yinshuguan, 1965–1970), 26a (page number in the original edition).

83. Liu, *Gongshi xiansheng dizi ji*, 26a.

84. Zhang Zai, "Zhouli" 周禮, in *Zhang Zai ji* (Beijing: Zhonghua shuju 1978), 282.

85. Zuo Qiuming, "Zhuanggong sanshi er nian" (the thirty-second year of the Duke of Zhuang) 莊公三十二年, in *Zuo Zhuan* (Changsha: Hunan renmin chubanshe,1996), 146.

86. Tian Kuang, *Rulin gongyi* 儒林公議, QSBJ, 1st series, 5:113.

87. Tian, *Rulin gongyi*, 114.

society and state put too much weight on supernatural entities in determining human affairs and, in particular, state policies.

Amid rampant circulation of the discourse on the supernatural, some scholar-officials attempted to reinstate the Confucian doctrine of Heaven's Commandment as that which directs the lives of individuals. An anecdote related to Fan Zhongyan 范仲淹 (989–1052), a main proponent of the Minor Reforms (1043–1045), illustrates this line of thought. Fan's confrontation with a spirit exemplifies how he engaged with the spirit world:

[Synopsis:] Someone asked Honorable Wenzheng 文正 [i.e., Fan Zhongyan] to write a tomb inscription for a deceased nobleman. Fan wrote about a secret affair related to his remote acquaintance and the deceased. The deceased appeared to Fan in his dream and said, "That affair was indeed true, but was not known to people. Because of Your Honor's writing, now it was exposed to the public. I wish you could change its content." Fan said, "Because of your secret affair, someone else's reputation suffered." Then the deceased threatened Fan, saying, "If you don't change it, I will take your first son's life." Fan replied, "Life and death are predetermined by [Heaven's] Commandment." Soon after, his first son died. The deceased reappeared, and said, "Are you not going to change it after all? If you don't, I will take your second son's life." His second son, Fan Chunren 范纯仁 [1027–1101], also got sick. The man reappeared and said, "Your first son's allotted lifespan has been exhausted. How could I be able to take his life? Today, I inform Your Honor if you change the content, then your second son will be okay." Fan after all did not change it. His son recovered his health after several days. When he later became Vice Councilor, his integrity was revealed as being more than sufficient."[88]

The storyteller praised Fan Zhongyan's upholding of his integrity as a writer as well as of his faith in Heaven's Commandment, even when facing the threat of losing his two sons. Fan took seriously the request of the spirit, but discredited his power over human life. The recorder of this anecdote looked favorably upon Fan's confrontation with the spirit, in which he saw consistency with Fan's honest handling of state affairs.

Many folk narratives tended to feature high-profile scholar-officials by crystallizing their well-known positions on the supernatural: embracing,

---

88. Liu Fu, "Zhibi" 直筆, in *Qingsuo gaoyi,* Houji, QSBJ, 3rd series, 4:2.122.

disengaging, or refuting belief in the supernatural in public discourse. However, scholar-officials' responses to those discourses demonstrate that they still stood on common ground in believing in Heaven as the ultimate source of moral principles for human beings and also as the governing agent of human fate. They acknowledged that spirits had the power to intervene in human life to a certain extent; nevertheless, they stood on firm ground and maintained their moral integrity when confronted by the supernatural.

## Conclusion

The abundance of narratives about the social imaginaries of the world-beyond and the supernatural in eleventh-century China reveals that those imaginaries were so compelling that the Confucian maxim of keeping silent on that topic was widely defied. Particularly strong political messages were generated by the stories related to Wang Anshi's miserable fate in hell and Han Qi's glory in heaven. Considering the immense political tensions that arose because of Wang Anshi's New Policies, it was very likely that the producers of the stories would be his political opponents and the disgruntled populace. As those stories were incorporating forms of rumor, some literati were eager to record them, often inserting details to fill in the gaps in received narratives. During a period when individual authors and speakers in official and public discourses were frequently subject to political purges, the recording of rumors delinked authorship from accountability. Furthermore, affairs in the world-beyond were in essence unverifiable, yet generated strong psychological impacts on listeners, thus being a convenient and effective channel for the delivering of political messages.

Socially marginalized or underprivileged people also took full advantage of the social imaginaries on the world-beyond and the supernatural to express their own perceptions of the injustice prevailing in society. In particular, the tribunal system in the other world was seen as the corrective of the malfunctioning of the current legal system of the state. Popular narratives of this kind drew freely on motifs and backgrounds from various traditions such as Buddhism, Daoism, and folklore.

The responses of scholar-officials of the time diverged. While some less-rigid or less-known scholars were eager to record popular narratives conveying their political and social views, some more-rigid and more-prominent scholar-officials expressed scruples about the widespread discourse that had penetrated deeply into the social psyche. They saw an even greater danger in the belief that affairs in the world-beyond were a decisive factor in individuals' moral choice, not to mention in determining social and political affairs. They confirmed the very Confucian premise that Heaven—not any sort of deity or ghost—is the agent that determines human fate. Based upon this premise, they were convinced that they would solve social and political issues by appropriately implementing Confucian ideas in society. Nevertheless, the very existence of the narratives that mock those Confucian discourses attest to fluidity in the creation of and efficient dissemination of the social imaginaries, which lent themselves to being sites of contestation for conveying diverse social, religious, and political agendas.

## 5

# *Burial*



A CONTESTED SITE FOR SOCIAL IMAGINARIES

BURIAL IS AN integral part of Chinese funerary practices; its absolute necessity had long been understood among people across social strata regardless of religious belief. This notion was poignantly manifested in some tombs of Buddhist practitioners, with their cremated remains in urns along with exquisite burial items.[1] The burial of ancestors was a quintessential moral responsibility, and often created a heavy financial burden for poor people. Some literati and low-ranking officers also suffered that burden to cover the expenses of the burial plot, coffin, labor, and sometimes long-distance travel to bring the body to the ancestral hometown. On the other hand, rich people spent exorbitant resources for tomb construction and exquisite burial items, which was seen as wasteful at the societal level. The Song government responded to these two contrasting problems by providing poor people with public graveyards and by reining in rich people's overconsumption.

Given the indisputable individual responsibility of ancestral burial, what would be proper and good burial was a galvanizing issue of the time. One of the main triggers of this issue was that rich commoners and merchants began to perform the so-called lavish burial (*houzang* 厚葬), which had long been reserved for royal and aristocratic families. This type of burial was sharply contrasted with "simple burial," the standard Confucian practice as defined in the classical ritual codes. In this chapter, I will inquire into why burial became a focal point of some scholar-officials' efforts to build a socio-moral order

---

1. An example is found in a very small tomb filled with various figurines; see Liu Zhiyuan and Jian Shi, "Chuanxi de xiaoxing Songmu" 川西的小型宋墓, *Wenwu cankao ziliao*, no. 9 (1955): 92–98.

based on Confucian norms. In order to engage this inquiry, I will first lay out the sociocultural contexts of the time, during which some scholar-officials took issue with the previously tolerated negligence of burial by emphasizing the moral accountability of individuals for their failure and by implementing institutional measures to address the problem. Then I will investigate how polarizing tendencies in burial practices associated with two social groups—rich merchants and scholar-officials—implied contesting social imaginaries of the world-beyond and conflicting notions on the functions of burial in establishing the deceased's place either in the world-beyond or in the social world. I will also examine some exceptional cases that did not fit into the general pattern of the correlations between social groups and burial practices in order to illustrate how an individual's beliefs and self-identity factored into choices of burial practices.

## *The Duty of Burial*

At the heart of the heavy emphasis on burial as an individual's moral responsibility lay the fear of the consequences of its failure. Such fear was derived from the traditional belief that souls whose physical bodies were not buried properly would fail to become spirits, and thus could cause misfortunes to the living, especially to direct descendants. They might hover over the world of the living and make unwelcome appearances. Therefore the presence of abandoned corpses was seen not only as a sign of moral failure of individuals but also as a psychological and health threat to the general public. During the eleventh century, some individual scholar-officials began to be more publicly critical of the problems associated with inadequately performed burials, as recorded in various types of literature.

Public anxiety over unrestful souls is typically projected in many Chinese ghost stories, in which these souls approach the living to ask for a proper burial so they may be at peace. Eleventh-century ghost narratives continued to feature the conventional motifs and plots of the stories of previous times. Ghosts usually appear to a close family member or sometimes to an unrelated other who has the resources to perform a burial.[2] A ghost can also request a proper burial of his or her murderer as a way of making amends for the crime.[3] They often hover around the area where their remains have been abandoned and

---

2. Liu Fu, "Zanggu ji" 葬骨記, in *Qingsuo gaoyi*, QSBJ, 3rd series, 4:1.15.

3. Zhang Qixian, "Luoyang rangong jian yuangui" 洛陽染工見冤鬼, in *Luoyang jinshen jiu wenji* 洛陽搢紳舊聞記, QSBJ, 1st series, 2: 4.189–190.

approach travelers who happen to pass by.[4] Typically, the accuracy of directions given by the ghost for locating his or her abandoned remains is confirmed. Upon the completion of the burial, the ghost usually reappears to the person to express gratitude and report on his or her peaceful status.[5] These stories tend to reflect the collective fear of dying without proper care of the dead body, but they do not address what kinds of punishment one would receive for the failure to carry out an ancestral burial.

One story widely circulated during the eleventh century tellingly addresses the issue of accountability. The spirit of Chen Ji 陳洎 (fl. 1041), former Vice-commissioner of State Finance, possessed a twelve-year-old servant boy in order to communicate with Xue Xiang 薛向 (fl. 1060), the current Commissioner of State Finance.[6] Xue asked Chen: "Your Honor had hardly ever offended the Heavenly Thearch (*shangdi*) or done anything unfilial. How could you receive such a punishment [of becoming a ghost]?" Chen Ji answered, "I had not offended the Heavenly Thearch, but hadn't buried my ancestors of three generations." In a slightly different rendition of the story in the *Jiang Linji zazhi* 江隣幾雜志 (*Miscellaneous Records of Jiang Linji*), the author, Jiang Xiufu 江休复 (1005–1060), says that he heard it from Shen Wentong 沈文通 (1025–1067). Chen Ji said: "I committed a sin of neglecting to bury my parents. [Otherwise,] I could have obtained the status of venerable spirit. I have now become a lowly ghost with legs covered by long hair."[7] This narrative makes it clear that Chen's failure was significant enough to cost him his high status in the spirit world. In another collection, *Houqing lu* 侯鯖錄 (*Records of the Marquis's Delicacies*), the author highlights that he recorded this story to admonish many of his fellow scholar-officials and relatives who had failed to bury their parents.[8] He meant to chide people in his circle for their customary procrastination, which often led to abandoning the remains in repository without ever providing burial. The thesis of the story resonated with many people's ideas to establish burial as the foremost duty of individuals, without which other virtues and career accomplishments could not merit a blessed afterlife. Diverse

---

4. Su Shi, "Yu Zhu Kangshu ershi shou, *shiba*" 與朱康叔二十首, 十八, in *Su Shi wenji* (Beijing: Zhonghua shuju, 1986), 59.1791–1712.

5. Su Shi, "De you houbo" 德有厚薄, in *Su Shi wenji* (Beijing: Zhonghua shuju, 1986), 73.2378–2379.

6. Fan Zhen, *Dongzhai jishi* 東齊記事 (Beijing: Zhonghua shuju, 1980), 5.41.

7. Jiang Xiufu, *Jiang Linji zazhi* 江鄰幾雜志, QSBJ, 1st series, 5:148.

8. Zhao Lingzhi, *Houqing lu*, QSBJ, 2nd series, 6:4.222.

renditions of the same story attest that it stimulated responses from readers and listeners who shared these concerns.

Some scholar-officials were alarmed by the cultural tolerance of the postponement and negligence of ancestral burial, which prevailed even among esteemed officials like Chen Ji. Later, government officers came in for not just moral blame, but also legal consequences for delaying the burial of ancestors. For example, Li Ji 李稷 (d. 1082) was impeached in 1076 for leaving his father's remains for over twenty years in a Buddhist repository, and was subsequently demoted from a civil position to a less prestigious military position.[9] The impeachment statement specified that the state had already established ten years as the maximum length of time government officers could postpone such burials.

In the public sphere, the disregard of the cultural norm of respectfully treating human remains was also observed. In particular, the exhumation of tombs was abhorred, based on the passage in the *Records of Rituals* (*Liji*): "Burial is to hide the dead body so that it cannot be seen by people."[10] Ouyang Xiu, a pioneer advocate in the reviving of Confucian rituals, best illustrates this by his pursuit of a legal case against some government workers who were involved in a state project of new canal construction in 1059. It turned out they had destroyed many tombs and demolished private houses, which resulted in laying bare skeletons along the levee.[11] Ouyang reported the "sad and frightening" situation to the emperor, and accused certain officers of misleading the imperial court by failing to report the presence of tombs and private houses in the path of the construction project. Ouyang therefore persuaded the emperor to cancel the entire plan and instead to rebuild the old canal. Although Ouyang argued that the new canal would not solve the water shortage problem anyway, his core justification for the cancellation was that the sanctity of human remains outweighed any possible benefit to the living. An even more astonishing story was reported by Fan Zhiming 范致明 (d. 1119) about two people who secretly used human bones from a public graveyard in order to supplement the insufficient amount of animal bones during a public project of renovating a building.[12] Subsequently, one person died, but shortly thereafter came back

---

9. CB 278.6795 and 280.6859; SS Li 27, 124.2912.

10. Sun Xidan, ed., *Liji jijie* 禮記集解, "Tangong, *shang*" 檀弓,上 (Beijing: Zhonghua shuju, 1989), 9.227.

11. Ouyang Xiu, "Lun Mengyanghe kaiju fenmu zhazi" 論孟陽河開掘墳墓劄子, in *Ouyang Xiu quanji*, 4:111.1689–1690.

12. Fan Zhiming, *Yueyang fengtuji* 岳陽風土記, QSBJ, 2nd series, 7: 88.

to life, allegedly on the basis of the defense in the underworld tribunal that he had just gone along with the other person, who had plotted the plan. Soon after, the allegedly responsible individual and his family members also died. These two stories indicated the tension between two groups of people who had different attitudes toward the treatment of human remains: those who were negligent of the cultural norm and those who were strongly committed to it.

One particular legal case demonstrates that the state's judicial system acknowledged the socially and culturally shared notion of a tomb as an inviolable site. The *Dongxuan bilu* 東軒筆錄 (*Essays from an Eastern Balcony*) reports that a high-profile official, Shi Jie 石介 (1005–1045), died at the age of forty in his hometown, where he was exiled after having been embroiled in political strife.[13] His opponents made the allegation that Shi Jie had surrendered to the Khitans, leaving behind a decoy tomb. During the arguments of this case, it was proposed that his tomb be opened so that his death could be verified. This measure, however, was perceived to be fraught with complications. If his corpse were to be found, the government would have ended up breaking the cultural taboo of tomb invasion in vain. Therefore, the court selected the more onerous method of summoning several hundred witnesses who were involved in the burial, and finally verified his death.

The above accounts reveal that during the eleventh century, many people tended to be quite tolerant of burial failure both at individual and institutional levels, despite the strong cultural norm for the absolute necessity of burial. However, some scholar-officials felt the situation was no longer tolerable and took it as a sign of moral failure prevalent in society. They delivered the strong message that those individuals who failed to fulfill their ancestral burial duties or desacralized human remains would be held accountable. From this perspective, burial practice was no longer just a private matter, but was the very foundation of the socio-moral order.

## *Caring for the Anonymous Dead*

Despite such a heavy moral weight on the treatment of human remains, the presence of unclaimed and abandoned corpses was prevalent. Many corpses were piled up in Buddhist temples where the repositories of coffins were located.[14] Worse, some were simply thrown into a river, or laid bare on roads. Some people died on the street without having any survivors to take care of

---

13. Wei Tai, *Dongxuan bilu* 東軒筆錄, QSBJ, 2nd series, 8: 4.69–70.

14. SDZLJ, 222.859.

their remains. During the eleventh century, those who took issue with this situation did not just advocate moral obligation of individuals, but also recognized that poor people simply were not able to afford burials due to a lack of land. Therefore, they took on the social responsibility for granting minimal decency to those who died without burial while they held positions in local governments.

In the very beginning of the dynasty, the inadequate treatment of human remains was addressed by the state law, the *Song Penal Traditions* (*Song xingtong* 宋刑統), promulgated in 963:

> For damaging a corpse by cremation or throwing into water, punishment for "killing during affray," reduced by one degree, shall be applied. As for abandoning a corpse that has not yet been lost, and for damaging it by shaving its head, punishment for "killing during affray," reduced by one additional degree, shall be applied for each case.[15]

Cremation and water burial were interpreted as acts of damaging and abandoning a corpse rather than forms of burial, based upon the Confucian notion of the sacred nature of human remains. However, the heavy punishment for this crime as being comparable to a "killing" was unfair while many people were not able to afford burial plots.[16] Because the Song legal system allowed for flexibility in its application, local officials exercised their discretion in taking into consideration regional situations.[17] In 999, about thirty years after the promulgation of the above-mentioned laws, it was not unusual to encounter dead bodies laid on the roads within the two major cities, Kaifeng and Luoyang.[18] This indicated that in the early Song people did not take the laws seriously.

Frequent warfare in the borderlands and natural disasters in other areas created especially dire situations. From the beginning of the Song dynasty, the imperial court dealt with the problems in certain areas by issuing ad hoc edicts that demanded the government offices collect abandoned corpses.[19] Emperor

---

15. Dou Yi, *Song xingtong* 宋刑統 (Beijing: Zhonghua shuju, 1984), 18.286–287.

16. Patricia Buckley Ebrey, "Cremation in Song China," *American Historical Review* 95, no. 2 (1990): 406–428.

17. Brian McKnight, *Law and Order in Sung China* (Cambridge, UK: Cambridge University Press, 1992).

18. SDZLJ 222.859.

19. SDZLJ 222.859.

Zhenzong (r. 997–1022) institutionalized a more systematic program for collecting corpses:

> In Xiangfu 5 [1012], Li Zonge 李宗諤 [964–1012] along with Ding Wei served as the Vice Commissioner of Provisioner for [the event of installing] the sculptured image of Zhenzong [at the Jade Hall]. Li returned home [after having assumed the role]. His Majesty came over to the Jade Hall and asked how Li's trip was. Li therefore presented a memorial, saying, "In the Bian Canal, corpses flow. They come all the way down, hidden in the stream, and lay bare on the levee. Eventually fishes and birds eat them without any restraints." When His Majesty heard this, he felt compassion and sighed. He therefore proceeded to make the "Bian River Liturgical Petition" with the imperial seal, and ordered the prefect to engrave the writings on a stone and to establish it at the pavilion of the ferry. Each year the government gave one hundred strings of coins and offered both Buddhist and Daoist death rituals, each for seven days, for the deceased's repentance and absolution. For each corpse, the local government granted three bamboo mats and a copper coin, and also granted wine, paper, dried meat, and a meal. Immediately, the emperor ordered the collection of unclaimed corpses for burial, and established this order as the definitive model of this kind.[20]

Li Zonge's memorial highlighted the public health threat of the massive number of floating corpses, and then addressed how human dignity was damaged when fishes and birds ate them. Several more edicts addressing the issue were announced during Zhenzong's reign.[21] From that era, there are numerous records of officials, both in the central and local governments, performing the duties of offering both burial and memorial services for unclaimed corpses.[22] In 1040 the central government announced that the local governments would collect and bury unclaimed corpses that had been stored within the temples for a long time.[23] Buddhist temples played crucial roles in those services, and were compensated by incentives toward the state-administered ordination

---

20. Wen Ying, *Yuhu qinghua* 玉壺清話 (Beijing: Zhonghua shuju, 1997), 4.37.

21. SDZLJ 222.859.

22. CB 83.1884, 126.2975, 170.4084 and 174.4198; SS Benji 9, 9.179.

23. CB 126.2975.

of monks.[24] To this end, both Daoist and Buddhist rituals, Buddhist Water-Land Purgation in particular, were chosen to ensure the salvation of massive number of souls in anonymity.[25] This measure was taken to render minimal decency to the deceased without invoking specifically Confucian norms for burial.

At the local level, the cultural innovation of the public graveyard appeared during the eleventh century.[26] It was the result of a gradual process initiated by local officials who created graveyards in their areas of administration out of their awareness of the needs of poor people who simply could not afford burial plots. The family record of Han Qi 韓琦 (1008–1075) credited him for establishing a public graveyard in his governing area in order to change the local custom of cremation and to solve the problem of unclaimed corpses left in repositories run by Buddhist shrines.[27] He ordered that a stone stele be erected to announce this new program and banning of cremation in the region. He indeed might be the first person who initiated this program, because there is another record complimenting his exemplary achievement in this regard.[28] Fu Bi 富弼 (1004–1083) made his own contribution to this program, when he governed an area in present-day Shandong around 1050. Seeing so many skeletons around due to severe flooding, he ordered that they be buried in a collective graveyard (*congzhong* 叢塚) and personally wrote a liturgical text for their memorial service. In one story, a travelling scholar stayed overnight in a stranger's house. The host explained that the town was called a "collective hometown" (*congxiang* 叢鄉) for the homeless constructed by Honorable Fu and his officers.[29] The host, who later turned out to be a ghost, complimented the virtue of Honorable Fu. Su Shi in 1095 also contributed to a mass burial for several hundreds of unclaimed skeletons administered by the prefect of

---

24. Mark Robert Halperin, "Buddhist Temples, War Dead, and the Song Imperial Court," *Asia Major* 12, 3rd series, no. 2 (1999): 71–99; Ebrey, "Cremation."

25. CB 273.6690, 291.7136.

26. For different terms referring to public graveyards, see Silvia Freiin Ebner von Eschenbach, "Public Graveyards of the Song Dynasty," in *Burial in Song China*, ed. Dieter Kuhn (Heidelberg: Forum, 1994), 215–216.

27. Han Zhongyan, *Jiachuan* 家傳, in *Han Weigong ji* 韓魏公集 (Shanghai: Shangwu yinshuguan, 1937), 13.202. Regarding Han Qi's posthumous celebrity status in popular narratives, see Chapter 4, 132–138.

28. Zhang Shizheng, "Han Zhigui jin fenshi" 韓稚圭禁焚屍, in *Juanyou zalu* (Shanghai: Shanghai guji chubanshe, 1993), 26; SS Li 28, 125.2918–2919.

29. Liu Fu, "Congzhong ji" 叢冢記; "Congzhong ji xubu" 叢冢記續補, in *Qingsuo gaoyi*, 1.12.

Huizhou by writing a tomb inscription tablet for them.[30] In another context, he composed a "Petition for a Burial of Parched Skeletons" to be used in the Water-Land Purgation.[31]

It was not until 1079 that the central government officially undertook the construction of charitable graveyards, Mercy Gardens (*louzeyuan* 漏澤圓), in the suburban areas of the capital city, coupled with announcing standardized logistics for their uses.[32] The government program also included supporting poor commoners who were unable to afford burials by granting land and lending money without interest. They could personally conduct relevant rituals by using the facility within the public graveyard.[33] The policy specified that Buddhist temples would be involved in collecting the unclaimed dead bodies and conducting burials for them.[34] A more concrete program was launched in 1104 to reestablish the Mercy Gardens and expand the program to the levels of prefecture and county as a part of the nationwide welfare system to support the Public Hospitals for the Poor (*anjifang* 安濟坊) and Public Nursing Homes (*juyangyuan* 居養院).[35]

An archeological discovery of a Mercy Garden at Shanzhou Prefect in Henan Province provides detailed information about the facility, which operated from 1104 to 1116.[36] As of 1994, 849 grave pits, numbered and lined up in rows and columns, had been excavated from half of the graveyard, occupying 12,650 square meters. A single body was buried in a pit with or without two conjoined earthenware jars particularly designed for burial;[37] 238 tombs contain brick tomb inscription tablets with generic phrases simply filling out basic information about the deceased's identity,

---

30. Su Shi, "Zang kugu shu" 葬枯骨疏, in *Su Shi wenji* (Beijing: Zhonghua shuju, 1986), 62.1911.

31. Su Shi, "Huizhou guanzang pogu ming" 惠州官葬暴骨銘, in *Su Shi shiwen huibian*, in *Su Shi wenji*, 1.2420–2421.

32. Patricia Ebrey, "The Response of the Sung State to Popular Funeral Practice," in *Religion and Society in T'ang and Sung China*, eds. Patricia Buckley Ebrey and Peter N. Gregory (Honolulu: University of Hawaii Press, 1993), 223–224; CB 297.7217, 289.7069 and 296.7210; SS Benji 12, 12.248; SHY Shihuo 60.4a.

33. SHY Shihuo 60.4b.

34. CB 297.7217.

35. The Public Nursing Home during the Song was institutionalized in 1098. SHY Shihuo 60.4a–b; SS Benji 30, 30.562.

36. Sanmenxiashi wenwu gongzuodui, ed., *BeiSong Shanzhou louzeyuan* 北宋陝州漏澤圓 (Beijing: Wenwu chubanshe, 1999).

37. Sanmenxiashi wenwu gongzuodui, ed., *BeiSong Shanzhou Louzeyuan*, 11–36 and 340–384.

including his or her name, age, date and place of death, and occupation, if known. Information on the administration agency that handled the funeral was often provided, such as name of administration unit and date of inspection, occasionally with the name and title of each officer who took charge of transporting, dressing, and inspecting the dead body. Soldiers deployed for construction constituted the largest number of the identified tomb occupants.[38] Their records show that fatal incidents took their lives in their twenties while they worked together with criminals. The Public Hospitals for the Poor were the largest suppliers of the burials, including the identified tomb occupants, which testified to a historical record about specifying the purpose of institutionalizing this type of graveyard.[39] In addition, many elderly people in their seventies or above buried in the graveyard were from public nursing housing such as Public Nursing Homes (*juyangyuan* 居养院), House for the Poor (*pinziyuan* 貧子院), and House of Benevolence First (*renxianyuan* 仁先院). Travelers and possibly homeless people found dead in inns and postal stations were buried there as well. Given this information, this graveyard functioned as an auxiliary facility of public institutions where people died without families to take care of their body.

Local gazetteers of many regions during the twelfth century demonstrate that this trend of building public graveyards spread to many regions.[40] Nevertheless, dire situations were still observed in the twelfth century. Ye Mengde 葉夢得 (1077–1148), commander of Jiankang, wrote: "On the streets, dead bodies of the homeless and labor workers are laid out. Some starved to death or got sick because of hot weather."[41] Ye's comment emphasizes that the failed burial was also an outcome of the social problem of poverty and that it represented a public health issue. He added more public graveyards in his governing area, appropriating unused land in rather remote places.[42]

With some scholar-officials' attempt to make burial the basis of the socio-moral order, it was necessary to make it affordable. The establishment of public graveyards, initiated by scholar-officials in local governments, was to cope with the prevailing reality that poor people had no choice but to tolerate the

---

38. Sanmenxiashi wenwu gongzuodui, ed., *BeiSong Shanzhou Louzeyuan*, 403–404.

39. SS Benji 30, 30.562; SHY Shihuo 60.4b–6b.

40. Silvia Freiin Ebner von Eschenbach, "Public Graveyards of the Song Dynasty," in *Burial in Song China*, ed. Dieter Kuhn (Heidelberg: Forum, 1994), 215–252.

41. Ye Mengde, *Bishu luhu* 避暑錄話, QSBJ, 2nd series, 10: 239–240.

42. Ebner von Eschenbach, "Public graveyards," 238.

presence of unburied dead bodies in their environs. It was an attempt to narrow the huge gaps between cultural norms and social reality. The result was to shift burial away from being solely a matter of an individual's moral responsibility to being handled via state policy. Conceptually speaking, it was to turn ghosts into spirits by institutional intervention, which would in turn reduce public anxiety about ghosts. Although mass burials were for those unfortunates who had died anonymously, the latter did obtain the minimal decency of resting in peace.

## *To Engrave Legacy in Social Memory*

Ancestral burial loomed large in the lives of scholar-officials and literati, but what constituted proper burial was an open question to them. During the early Song, people were rather flexible about when and where to bury, and under whose care a grave would be left. However, there were growing concerns expressed by individual scholar-officials, who wished to define proper burial against the background of cultural conventions. This section explains the primary concerns of scholar-officials in their definition of proper burial, when they adopted or rejected certain mortuary practices. In particular, the focus will be on the use of the tomb inscription tablet, because it was the centerpiece of their burial practice as an identity marker of individuals in death.

Against the background of scholar-officials' efforts to define the ideal burial lay the state's program of granting a Buddhist cloister for the care of tombs and graveyards for distinguished officials. For example, to the rear of the White Horse Temple (*baima si* 白馬寺) in Luoyang, tombs of the ten early Song Grand Councilors were ensconced, including that of Li Hang 李沆, who vehemently criticized Zhenzong's Daoist ritual practices, as discussed in Chapters 1 and 2 of this book.[43] Even Sima Guang, an adamant proponent of Confucian ritual, ended up having his grave under a Buddhist cloister's care, which was highly unlikely to have been his wish.[44] Ouyang Xiu also resisted having his father's tomb under a Buddhist cloister's care, as he detested the religion; alas, the tombs of his both parents ended up being under a Daoist shrine's care through Han Qi's arrangement.[45] A more dreadful case was reported—the alleged cremation of Wang Anshi's remain by his son-in-law,

---

43. Jiang Xiufu, *Jiang Linji zazhi*, QSBJ, 1st series, 5: 5.161.

44. Kida Tomo, *Shiba Kō to sono jidai* 司馬光とその時代 (Tokyo: Hakutei sha, 1994), 285–289.

45. Zeng Minxing, *Duxing zazhi* 獨醒雜志, QSBJ, 4th series, 4: 5.141.

Cai Bian 蔡卞 (1048–1117), which was a huge scandal at the time. Allegedly it happened during Cai's commissioning of the construction of the Emperor Shenzong's mausoleum, within proximity of which Wang's original tomb was located.[46] Wang's cremation itself is not verifiable with available textual evidence, yet at the very least it could have been relocated, because *The Ordinances of Funerals and Burials* (喪葬令 *Sangzang ling*) did not allow any other tomb to be built within the perimeter of one *li* of the emperor's mausoleum.[47]

Another prevailing practice was to postpone burial, even for years, based on belief in geomancy. Su Shi criticized the custom as one which would neither prevent disaster nor bring about blessings.[48] He also lamented that some scholar-officials did not perform burials because they had not yet received text for the tomb inscription tablet (*muzhi* 墓誌) from celebrity scholar-officials because of their "bottomless vanity" in seeking reputation.[49] Taking issue with this practice, Su Shi approvingly quoted Zi Si's 子思 (circ. 483–402 BCE) dictum: "Without burial, one cannot take off mourning garments." On the other hand, some poverty-stricken people had no choice but to leave a dead body in a temporary repository, because they were not able to afford the expense.[50] The heaviness of the financial burden was well expressed in Su Shi's desperate letter to his relative to solicit a donation to support his niece, who had just exhausted all her resources for her husband's burial, including the expensive long-distance travel to his ancestral hometown for final rest in accordance with the Confucian norm.[51] Su Shi also found himself in financial trouble when his father passed away; Han Qi and Ouyang Xiu sent 300 and 200 silver tales, respectively, which Su declined to accept.[52]

These social and cultural realities naturally caused some people to be concerned about their own future burials. A will left by Song Qi 宋祁 (998–1061), Grand Councilor, clearly illustrates this. His text "Rules and Admonitions"

---

46. Zhao Lingzhi, *Houqing lu*, QSBJ, 2nd series, 6: 3.217–218.

47. Zhongguo shehui kexueyuan, Lishi yanjiusuo, annot., *Tianyige cang mingchaoben Tianshengling jiaozheng: Fu Tangling fuyuan yanjiu* 天一閣藏明鈔本天聖令校證: 附唐令復原研究 (Beijing: Zhonghua shuju, 2006), 29.351.

48. Su Shi, "Da Bi Zhongju, *ershou*" 答畢仲舉, 二首, in *Su Shi wenji*, 56.1671.

49. Su Shi, "Da Li Fangshu shu" 答李方叔書, in *Su Shi wenji*, 49.1430–1431.

50. Su Shi, "Shang Han Weigong, *yi shou*" 上韓魏公, 一首, in *Su Shi wenji* (Beijing: Zhonghua shuju, 1986), 50.1443.

51. Su Shi, "Yu Tangxiong, *yi shou*" 與堂兄, 一首, in *Su Shi diewen huibian* 蘇軾佚文彙編, in *Su Shi wenji*, 4.2523.

52. CB 216.5263.

(*zhijie* 治戒) demonstrates his notion of a proper burial that would convey Confucian ideals against prevailing cultural conventions:

> After I die, properly handle the funeral relevant to a mourning family. Gather a clean used crane-feather coat, silk cap, and stringed footwear. Three days after my death, put the body into a coffin; after three months, have the burial. Never impose any taboo restrictions [on the burial] based on geomancy. Use low-quality wood for the coffin, varnish it four times, and paint it three times only. In this way, several decades later the skeleton will be dried up and the clothes will be rotten. That is all. . . . Dig the tomb pit about ten meters in depth. That small pit will be my tomb chamber. Detest the use of an embellished coffin and spirit articles [*mingqi* 明器]. On the left side, place clean water: two bowls of water and two jugs of wine. On the right side, place two bundles of rice noodles, a suit of court garments, a suit of personal garments, and a pair of my shoes. Inscribe my personal information on the left side [of the tomb inscription tablet] and a motto of my life on the right side. Then hide the inscription tablet inside the tomb. Just be simple and frugal. No gold, copper, or miscellaneous stuff to be placed inside the tomb. . . .. It is inappropriate to ask famous people to compose writings for the tomb inscription tablet and inscription stele on the pathway to the tomb. In the ground, plant five cypress trees. The mound is three feet or about one meter in height. Do not install stone sculptured images of guardian deities and apotropaic beasts [*shiweng zhongshou* 石翁仲獸]. Doubtless those things placed to demarcate the tomb are not meant to last forever. Do not perform Buddhist and Daoist death rituals. This is what I have wished for throughout my life. *If you cannot but go against my command, [know that] your violations amount to killing my [moral] self.* It amounts to making me pursue ignorance. . . . Do not make a figurine of the exorcist [*fangxiang* 方相]. [Just] lay out clothes and utensils. This arrangement will reveal my frugality. Throughout my life I have been the kind of person who does not speak carelessly. Do not dare make any collections of my writings.[53] [italics added]

This lengthy text clearly reveals a scholar's fear that he would be buried improperly against his wishes. He spells out explicitly what his descendants might attempt to do for his sake, which would unfortunately damage his

---

53. Song Qi, *Song Jingwengong biji* 宋景文公筆記, QSBJ, 1st series, 5: 70–71.

reputation by making him pursue "ignorance." His concerns resonated with his publicly articulated ideals, as he was an ardent critic of Zhenzong's performing Buddhist and Daoist rituals at the court, arguing that they were not only excessive but also uncanonical.[54]

His checklist of the characteristics of an improper burial includes its postponement, an oversized tomb, a coffin of high-quality wood with embellishment, "spirit articles," and seeking the composition of a tomb inscription from a high-profile figure. Among the burial items of which he disapproves are "spirit articles" (明器), as opposed to "commemorative articles" (*shengqi* 生器).[55] The latter were what the deceased used during life, such as the used clothes and shoes listed in Song Qi's will. Typical items contained in the tombs of literati were brushes and inkstones. Toys found in a child's tomb of the early Northern Song bespeak the nature of "commemorative articles."[56] In contrast, "spirit articles" were expected be used exclusively in the spirit world and therefore were not made to be usable in the world of the living. Song Qi declared that *mingqi* would not be allowed. He also specified the particular sculptural images that should not be installed: the statue of the Dispeller of Evil Spirits inside the tomb and the stone statues of guardian deities and apotropaic creatures (*shiweng zhongshou* 石翁仲獸) outside the tomb.

The ideal burial for Song Qi can be summed up as a "simple burial" (*bozang* 薄葬); as he declared, "Just be simple and frugal." He wanted only to take some basic provisions to fulfill the soul's needs for its journey: clothes, shoes, noodles, water, and wine. This preparation of perishable items reveals that Song Qi was aware that burial goods could function to accommodate the soul's needs. Nevertheless, he refused the notion that the images of the spiritual beings would offer the soul special protection. He presented a conventional Confucian justification for a frugal burial: the physicality of the burial, including human remains and accompanying items, was meant to be dispersed rather than last forever. Song Qi clearly placed emphasis on what would be left behind him among the living, not on the presumed well-being of the soul brought about by the material equipment within the tomb. His main concern, therefore, was what should be written on his tomb inscription tablet (*muzhi* or *muzhiming* 墓誌銘). This item is a square-shaped stone tablet with

---

54. CB 125.2942–2943.

55. For a definition of these two items, see Wu Hung, *The Art of the Yellow Springs: Understanding Chinese Tombs* (Honolulu: University of Hawai'i Press, 2010), 87–91.

56. Liu Jianzhou, "Zhengzhou Nanguan wai faxian yizuo Songmu" 鄭州南關外發現一座宋墓, *Wenwu*, no. 8 (1965): 52–53.

an engraved inscription of the deceased's biography (*zhi* 誌) and a matching cover slab. Song Qi highlights that his spirit of humility should be extended to the inscription by making it not too flattering. He himself wrote a short, modest biography and rhymed epitaph (*ming* 銘), to be engraved on the left and right sides, respectively, of the tomb inscription tablet:

> Biography: Qi is his name, and Song is his family name. He studied Confucianism, which displayed in his public service. At the age of sixty-four, he managed to walk around perfectly by himself. In the southern area of Sanfeng, he is buried, following after his father.

> Epitaph: In life I do not live; in death I do not die. I also fool myself; [therefore] I seek clarity in my reasoning.[57]

These phrases are contained in the collections of his work, following right after the above-cited instructions. Nevertheless, the very existence of his collected works illustrates that people did not take his request not to make his literary collection at face value but rather as humbling remarks.

Song Qi's great concerns about his own inscription tablet echoed with a cultural trend that Song scholar-officials included such a tablet as the crucial burial item. Its prominent significance, albeit absence in canonical reference, represents a vantage point to illumine what primary concerns were implied in the burial practice of scholar-officials. Some modern scholars suggest that the tradition of burying the stone inscription tablet may have been triggered by the government's ban on erecting commemorative steles in 278 CE under the Western Jin Dynasty (265–371), although the use of its prototypical form could be traced back to the Eastern Han (20–220 CE).[58] Timothy M. Davis argues that its primary purpose was to protect the dead with its radiating "numinous potency" and to enhance the dead's status in the spirit world by providing information of their lineage and virtue.[59] He, however, notes that after tomb inscription texts became a prominent literary genre during the Liang Dynasty (502–587), their function shifted to commemorating the dead among the living, as opposed to protecting the dead, by having them as its primary audience.[60]

---

57. Songqi, *Song Jingwengong biji*, 71.

58. Timothy M. Davis, "Potent Stone: Entombed Epigraphy and Memorial Culture in Early Medieval China" (PhD diss., Columbia University, 2008), 236–240 and 256.

59. Davis, "Potent Stone," 170–178.

60. Davis, "Potent Stone," 232–281 and 284.

The tomb inscription tablet served as the definitive identity marker, with its recording of the name and official title(s) of the occupant, which also served a very practical function by identifying the dead in case the tomb was damaged. In the case of a woman, the title of her husband or father was given. Because only officeholders were permitted to use tablets, their absence indicated that the tomb occupant did not hold any official positions. Sima Guang, in his *Shuyi* 書儀 (written in the 1070s), specified that only people of the fifth rank and above were eligible.[61] However, about four decades later in year 1111, the government's regulations presented in the *Zhenghe wuli* 政和五禮 (*The Five Rituals of the Zhenghe Reign*), specified that the ninth rank and below were not eligible.[62] Sima Guang might have applied a higher standard for eligibility. It also might be the case that the government regulations reflected the social reality that the use of the tomb inscription tablet had been extended to officers in lower ranks over time. About a century later, Zhu Xi took a further liberal position by allowing low-ranking officers and commoners to use the tomb inscription tablet so long as it is abbreviated.[63]

A tomb inscription in a form of a funerary biography opens with identifying the deceased, usually in the context of family genealogy, and then narrates his achievements, including the records of state exams, public service, and moral character. In case of a woman, its focus rests mainly with her family caregiving as the primary virtue. It ends with a list of survivors, which is often coupled with information about their career accomplishments. Angela Schottenhammer argues that many Song tomb inscriptions add a more personal tune to the genre's formulaic style developed during the Tang and also deemphasize genealogy, especially when the deceased came from a humble background.[64] As she rightly argues, the biographical part of the inscription was greatly expanded during the Song. In some cases, genealogy was omitted altogether, as seen in many of Su Shi's writings, presumably for people who did not have anything glorious to talk about in their family history.[65] Some

---

61. Sima Guang, *Sima shi shuyi*, 7.80.

62. Zheng Juzhong (1059–1123) et al., "Zang" 葬, in *Zhenghe wuli xinyi*, Siku Quanshu edition, 216.4b.

63. Patricia Ebrey, *Chu Hsi's Family Rituals: A Twelfth-century Chinese Manual for the Performance of Cappings, Weddings, Funerals, and Ancestral Rites* (Princeton, NJ: Princeton University Press, 1991), 108–109.

64. Angela Schottenhammer, "Characteristics of Song Epitaphs," in *Burial in Song China*, ed. Dieter Kuhn (Heidelberg: Forum, 1994), 263.

65. For collections of *muzhiming* authored by Su Shi, see *Su Shi wenji*, 15.459–473.

notable events displaying the deceased's integrity were often recounted in great detail, accompanied by the comments of the author. For example, the recently discovered tomb inscription tablet for Fu Bi 富弼 (1004–1083), Grand Councilor, detailed his involvements in court politics in pivotal historical moments in chronological order, using nearly 7,000 characters.[66] It includes long citations of Fu Bi's memorials to the emperors, debates on policies, and concrete information about their political circumstances.

Making a tomb inscription tablet required social networking, often involving many people. Usually, someone who thought highly of the deceased composed the text. A calligrapher then wrote the composition in ink on paper, after which it would be copied and engraved in stone by a professional stone engraver. Another calligrapher could be added for the tablet cover. The names and official titles of those who were involved in the process were recorded on the tomb inscription tablet. A text and calligraphy done by prominent figures validated the deceased's good social standing and thus enhanced the prestige of his or her survivors. For example, Fan Chunren 范純仁 (1027–1101), Fan Zhongyan's son and Sima Guang's protégée, wrote the abovementioned Fu Bi's tomb inscription, and Sima Guang's calligraphy was used for the inscription tablet cover. Su Shi also was one of the high-profile figures associated with Fu Bi's tomb inscription, writing a text with 6,700 words to be engraved on the "inscription stele on the pathway to the tomb" (*shendaobei* 神道碑), placed outside of the tomb.[67] Fan Chunren also wrote the tomb inscription for Wang Shanggong 王尚恭 (d. 1084), for which Sima Guang offered calligraphy.

This information of the people involved in the production of the tomb inscription tablet for Fu Bi reveals a close-knit social and political circle surrounding him. It is relevant to recall here what Song Qi wrote: "It is inappropriate to ask famous people to compose writings for a tomb inscription tablet and a stele." In the spirit of a truly frugal burial, Song Qi cast a critical eye on the practice of writing funerary biography as a way of displaying social and political capital. Sima Guang directed even more severe criticism at embellished and flattering tomb inscriptions: "Some people use artful and splendid words for exaggeration and embellishment. The deceased's accomplishments equal those of Lü Wang 呂望 [ca. 1128–1015 BCE]; and their virtue is comparable with Confucius. It merely begs for mockery."[68] This may explain why

---

66. Shi Jiazhen et al., "Fu Bi jiazu mudi fajue jianbao" 富弼家族墓地發掘簡報, *Zhongyuan wenwu*, no. 6 (2008): 4–18.

67. Su Shi, "Fu Zhenggong shendaobei" 弼鄭公神道碑, in *Su Shi wenji*, 18.525–539.

68. *Shuyi*, 7.80.

Sima Guang offered only his calligraphy for the inscription tablets of both Wang Shanggong and Fu Bi. Su Shi, having been a celebrated writer, composed many tomb inscriptions, yet did not spare harsh criticism of the current custom of vying to receive one from a famous person at the cost of delaying the burial, as mentioned earlier.

A tomb inscription located the deceased's life precisely in the social context by highlighting what was worthy of remembering. In this sense, some inscriptions placed a heavy emphasis on information about the surviving family. For example, roughly one-third of the inscription of Yang Chengxin 楊承信 (917–961) was information about his seven brothers (out of eleven altogether), eleven sisters, a daughter, and, most importantly, one son.[69] As the inscription or funerary biography had already become an established genre of writing, it occupied a topical heading within the collected works of an individual. The social nature of tomb inscription was most acutely demonstrated when they were circulated in public in a collection of an author's works, not in that of the deceased. Thus, receiving composition from a high-profile figure increased the chance of its circulation. For example, the biographical inscription for Fu Bi contained in the collected works of its author, Fan Chunren, is virtually identical with that in the discovered tomb inscription tablet. The high expectations for scholarly integrity in the writing of tomb inscriptions were poignantly addressed in a ghost story related to Fan Zhongyan in Chapter 4 of this book. In that story, Fan refused to yield to the demand of a spirit, even at the threat of the death of his two sons, including Fan Chunren, to delete a dishonorable secret about the deceased.

Song Qi's will best illustrates the ideal Confucian burial of the time, that is, a "simple burial" in a simple pit with a tomb inscription tablet.[70] The simplicity of the tomb, without decorative items, reveals that the inner space of the tomb would be expected to eventually rot away. This tendency to downplay images, especially those of humans and imaginary creatures, derived from the Confucian tradition's rejecting the social imaginaries of the world-beyond. Just as the Confucian social imaginary of the unknown world was blank, so was the tomb space. On the other hand, the biography engraved in stone was meant to last forever; it did not mention the deceased's status as a spirit but his or her lifetime achievements, especially in an official capacity. Official rank in

---

69. Zhao Shigang, "BeiSong Yang Chengxin muzhi ba" 北宋楊承信墓志跋, *Kaogu yu wenwu*, no. 1 (1985): 55–58.

70. For various cases of scholar-officials' tombs, see Dieter Kuhn, *A Place for the Dead: An Archaeological Documentary on Graves and Tombs of the Song Dynasty (960–1279)* (Heidelberg: Forum, 1996), 101–119.

the inscription clearly serves the goal of distinguishing scholar-officials, with their prestigious positions, from the rest of the population. However, the spirit of material frugality in the Confucian burial was not paralleled in simplicity of literary expressions, as some people who sought literary embellishments and expanded the length of the text. They simply shifted the areas of vanity from the material furnishings of the tomb to reputation in social memory.

## *Eternal Happiness Bought with Money: A Merchant's Tomb at Baisha*

On the other side of the spectrum in Song mortuary practices, there were people who chose the "lavish burial." In death, the deceased entered a subterranean house with a vaulted ceiling, often filled with luxurious "spirit articles." The sturdy construction of those tombs has enabled them to survive far better than simple pit tombs. The lavish burial was an enduring mortuary tradition primarily associated with royal and aristocratic families prior to the Song. However, a major shift occurred during the eleventh century in that rich commoners and merchants began to practice it as well. What were the main motives of investing their resources in the material aspects of the tomb? To answer this question, I shall take a well-known Song tomb at Baisha as a representative case illustrating the social imaginary of the world-beyond shared by rich merchants of the time, and their notions of the tomb space in order to position themselves in that imaginary world.[71]

Three Song tombs in close proximity were discovered in 1951 and 1952 at Baisha in Henan, a town located forty-seven miles away from a major trade route that connected Luoyang and Kaifeng. They had not been plundered, and retained much of their original pictorial images at the time of discovery. The tombs are surmised to be a family tomb compound, as they share common pictorial motifs and an architectural style. The brick tombs have a hexagonal corbeled dome style covered with earth, which was widely adopted in Henan province and its northern environs.[72] Stone was not only illegal for tomb construction but also hard to come by in this area. The architectural details of the three tombs, such as their intricate vaulted ceilings with multilayered brickwork, manifest the level of luxury. Among the three, the

---

71. For discussion of the tomb occupants as rich merchants, see Su Bai, *Baisha Songmu* 白沙宋墓 (Beijing: Wenwu chubanshe, 1957), 103–104.

72. A study of this type of tomb architecture is Wei-Cheng Lin, "Underground Wooden Architecture in Brick: A Changed Perspective from Life to Death in 11th-through 13th-century Northern China," *Archives of Asian Art* 61 (2011): 3–36.

double-chamber tomb labeled tomb no. 1 dated in 1099 is the largest;[73] the two others (no. 2 and no. 3) have a single chamber. A comprehensive archeological report on these tombs, *Baisha Songmu* 白沙宋墓 (*The Song Tombs at Baisha*), was published by Su Bai in 1957 by presenting the material details of the tombs. While special attention was given to identifying material objects that appeared in the mural paintings in tomb no. 1, Su Bai failed to consider that those paintings were intended to convey meanings in the spirit world rather than depicting the occupants' lifestyle. Instead of looking at many several paintings as isolated pieces, I suggest looking at them as a whole pictorial program, one that conveys a coherent theme. Such contextualization sheds a new light on certain images which have been previously neglected. Based on materials presented in *Baisha Songmu*, I will attempt to decode the pictorial program of tomb no. 1.

The tomb occupants are a married couple buried in the same chamber, a typical practice in the Sichuan area but often criticized by some scholar-officials as noncanonical.[74] The tomb's architectural structure recalls an underworld wooden house with a gate. The tomb gate demarcates the tomb space from the entryway with its stairs connected to the ground above. Passing the gate, a one-meter-long passageway leads to a gate of the house (i.e., tomb), whose front and rear chambers are connected by the corridor. The imitated gate and windows with drapes enhance the sense of a real house. Carved into the back door of the rear chamber, a woman in bas-relief statue is entering the house, which is a popular motif employed in Song tombs. Coupled with the two imitation windows on the north side of the front chamber, it creates the image of open space within the house leading toward the outside of the building. This design enhances the tomb architecture, rendering a realistic aura of a house of the living. There are not many burial objects besides one silver ingot, some porcelain pots, and a few pieces of iron. One important object is a stone land deed laid next to the bodies of the deceased in the rear chamber. Although about half the content is no longer legible, it identifies the tomb occupants as a certain Zhao family without an official title.

---

73. The entire length of the tomb is 670 cm; entrance, 100 cm in length, 110 cm in height; front chamber, 190 cm in length, 340 cm in height; passage, 140 cm in length, rear chamber, 240 cm in length, 320 cm in height. The dates of burial for the second and third tombs are not known. A coin in the second tomb indicates that the tomb cannot be dated earlier than 1068. Given material evidence including architectural styles and elements in paintings, Su Bai surmises that these two tombs could be dated to the early 12th century. Kuhn, *A Place for the Dead*, 303; Su Bai, *Baisha Songmu*, 99–102.

74. Halga Stahl, "Su Shi's Orthodox Burial: Interconnected Double Chamber Tombs in Sichuan," in *Burial in Song China*, ed. Dieter Kuhn (Heidelberg: Forum, 1994), 161–214.

Because of the scant burial items, the rich pictorial images on the walls are the primary conduits for the expression of the ideas of the tomb occupants or its designer. The tomb employs several popular motifs in tomb mural paintings in the region during the time: a banquet, a dining table, food preparation, and a woman entering a house. The pictorial program starts from the painting on the west wall of the passageway. In a scene of setting off on a journey, three men are standing along with a saddled horse without a rider whose feet are set on the ground. They have facial expressions of being engaged in serious discussion. One man carries a wine jar, and another is holding a folded umbrella. The image of the umbrella is more clearly shown in tomb no. 2.[75] On the opposite side of the passageway appear three men. Two are moving with fast steps toward their destination, one with two strings of coins on his shoulder and another holding a grain sack. The third man, on the other hand, poses with his hand on the gate and with a rather frightened or worried face looking inside the gate. They are moving toward the gated house. On both sides of the south wall (southeast and southwest) of the front chamber, three guards are shown standing with the entrance to the house in the background. A vague image of the strings of coins is shown on the shoulder of one of them, which may indicate that he accepts money from visitors.[76]

The journey scenes with three horsemen and travelers carrying some items and money seem quite mundane. By highlighting this mundane aspect, both Su Bai and Valerie Hansen argue that the grain sack and wine are repayment for what people owed to the Zhaos, which serves as evidence for their social status as landowners or merchants.[77] However, this journey, I argue, echoes with the traditional theme of the soul's transition to the world-beyond in some tomb paintings dating from the Han dynasty forward.[78] The horse without a rider in this painting resonates with the traditional theme of the entourage of the soul's journey featuring a saddled horse without a rider, presumably ridden by the deceased's soul.[79] For example, in the famous mural relief in a tomb at Cangshan, the soul's journey is represented as a grandiose procession with chariots.[80] The soul is greeted by celestial beings at a station leading to

---

75. Su, *Baisha Songmu*, figure 41a.

76. Su, *Baisha Songmu*, 35.

77. Su, *Baisha Songmu*, 34–35, 41; Valerie Hansen, *The Open Empire: A History of China to 1600* (New York: W. W. Norton, 2000), 272–275.

78. Wu, *The Art of the Yellow Springs*, 192–217.

79. Wu, *The Art of the Yellow Springs*, 204–208.

80. Wu, *The Art of the Yellow Springs*, 197.

Two paintings of the journey theme (images in the western and eastern wall in the passageway)
Su, *Baisha Songmu*, figure 27.

the celestial world. The guards in this tomb mark the boundary of the space, where the soul ends his or her journey and enters another realm.

The items carried by the travelers reappear in the corridor that connects the two chambers, which indicate that they have been successfully transferred to the house. On the east wall of the corridor, there is a grain sack with a label that reads "Great Master Zhao in the second year of Yuanfu [1099]," indicating the year of burial and the identity of the tomb occupant.[81] On the west wall of the corridor, there are images of two wine jars, a pair of scissors, iron, a piece of a silver or gold ingot, and a pendant ornament for women. Scissors, items women use for tailoring clothes, had been one of the commemorative articles for deceased females since the Han dynasty.[82] The two wine jars might indicate that they are being used for the ritual of the contract

---

81. Su, *Baisha Songmu*, figure 31a.

82. Wu, *The Art of the Yellow Springs*, 166.

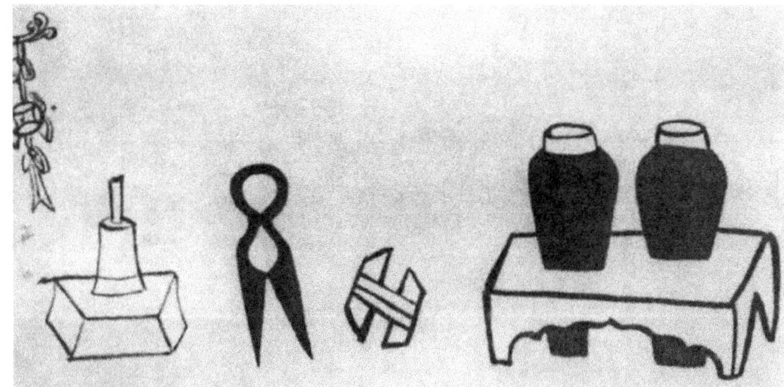

Pendant ornament, iron, scissors, silver ingot, wine jars (image at the bottom of the western wall of the corridor)
Su, *Baisha Songmu*, figure 31b.

between the buyer and seller of the tomb site in accordance with burial customs.[83] In a tomb of the late twelfth century, a wine jar placed on top of a land deed explicitly indicates the connection between the two items.[84]

Whereas real coins were widely used in burials, a pictorial image of them being carried in bulk is highly uncommon. This motif has not yet been found in other Song tombs, to my knowledge, except for two other Zhao tombs in the same compound at Baisha. In tomb no. 3, one traveler carries a basket full of strings of coins; another traveler carries them in his hand, along with a grain sack on his shoulder.[85] In tomb no. 2, strings of real coins are laid on top of the stomach of the deceased—perhaps initially on the top of the coffin.[86]

As one enters the front chamber, one sees an image of the husband and wife sitting on chairs in a luxurious living room and gazing at the performance scene on the western wall. A piece of a silver ingot is in front of the man's legs under the table, and another piece is under the woman's chair.[87] These images of ingots are a visual expression that they are literally

---

83. Terry Kleeman, "Land Contracts and Related Documents," in *Chūgoku no shūkyō, shisō to kagaku: Makio Ryōkai hakase Shōju kinen ronshū* 中国の宗教,思想と科学: 牧尾良海博士頌寿記念論集, ed. Makio Ryōkai (hakushi shōju kinen ronshū kankōkai) (Tokyo: Kokusho kankōkai, 1984), 16–17; Valerie Hansen, *Negotiating Daily Life in Traditional China* (New Haven: Yale University Press, 1996), 153.

84. Sichuansheng bowuguan, "Sichuan Guangyuan shike Songmu qingli jianbao," 四川廣元石刻宋墓清理簡報, *Wenwu*, no. 6 (1982): 57.

85. Sichuansheng bowuguan, "Sichuan Guangyuan shike Songmu qingli jianbao," figure 48.

86. Sichuansheng bowuguan, "Sichuan Guangyuan shike Songmu qingli jianbao," figure 44.

87. Sichuansheng bowuguan, "Sichuan Guangyuan shike Songmu qingli jianbao," 38–39.

The Zhaos watching the performance (image on the southern wall of the front chamber)

Su, *Baisha Songmu*, figure 5.

sitting on money, because silver ingots were used as monetary transactions during this time. Under the table, a blaze keeps the couple warm. Four people standing behind them serve the couple with tea and fruit. On the screens behind the table, there are scripts of pseudo-characters, with the exception of three real characters, *bu* (不, not) and *mache* (馬車, horse sedan). Traditionally, pseudo-characters were an indication that the writings belonged to the spirit world, in which the imitation of the real tended to hold true.[88] Their different gazes and facial expressions make it clear that only the couple is enjoying the performance, being served by all the rest. The musical band in the image on the western wall is of considerable size, consisting of eleven men and women playing different types of instruments. Hosting a banquet with a performing band was the epitome

---

88. For a discussion of the religious uses of illegible writings in China, see James Robson, "Signs of Power: Talismanic Writing in Chinese Buddhism," *History of Religions* 48, no. 2 (2008): 130–169. For reversed writings in mortuary practice, see Wu Hung, *Monumentality*, 259–262.

of wealth display during the Song, to the extent that government sumptuary laws stipulated the number of musicians and musical instruments, in accordance with the host's official rank.[89] Nevertheless, the level of luxury ostentatiously manifest in the banquets hosted by grand merchants or big landowners often exceeded that of high officials,[90] which conspicuously exhibited the gap between the two social groups. The mural painting poignantly reflects this social phenomenon.

The southwestern wall presents a painting in which Mrs. Zhao is doing her makeup in front of a mirror stand while in a sitting position. The facial expressions of the four serving women and their holding of the makeup paraphernalia illustrate their close attentiveness to Mrs. Zhao's needs. Mrs. Zhao is in another scene in the painting on the southeastern wall. She is sitting in a room with drapes surrounded by two women and two men, all of whom are here also standing. A silver ingot is laid on a small table next to Mrs. Zhao.[91] She is talking with a man who offers her a plate stuffed with some valuable objects. A standing woman next to Mrs. Zhao also holds a piece of a silver ingot.[92] Two silver ingots in this painting have an image similar to the one in the corridor. Another man is holding strings of coins about to be presented to her. Clearly, this scene portrays Mrs. Zhao receiving money and silver ingots from these two men. Her posture of sitting in front of the others who are standing shows her superior status. The motif in this painting is unconventional, though it can fit into the broad category of the illustration of daily life, a popular motif of the time. Within this rather elastic category, the tomb designer has inserted what the couple values most: money, especially that received as payment from others.

The pictorial images in the mural paintings in the tomb are hardly exotic or otherworldly. They appear to portray an ideal life of comfort and pleasure in this world, one marked by the enjoyment of conveniences, services, and entertainment. For the Zhao family, it is money that brings happiness—this is the main theme that the paintings highlight explicitly, with the strings of coins and silver ingots that appear in differing paintings. Note here that a real silver ingot was one of the scant burial items within this tomb. The two other tombs of the Zhao family are also extensively decorated with pictorial expressions of this theme, which reveals monetary gains to be the extended families' shared

---

89. CB 299.7268–7269.

90. Shen Gua, "Renshi, *yi*"人事, 一, in *Mengxi bitan* 夢溪筆談, QSBJ, 2nd series, 3: 74–75.

91. Su Bai states that she is holding an ingot: Su, *Baisha Songmu*, 40.

92. Su, *Baisha Songmu*, 40.

Mrs. Zhao receiving money (image on the southeastern wall of the rear chamber)
Su, *Baisha Songmu*, figure 32b.

concerns, culminating in the scene of Mrs. Zhao receiving money from male visitors. It is likely that the Zhao family actually had enjoyed such a life, considering their capacity to build this expensive tomb. For this reason, Both Su Bai and Valerie Hansen see the paintings as portraying the tomb occupants' day-to-day existence, such as traveling for trade and monetary transactions. On the other hand, Dieter Kuhn in *A Place for the Dead* argues that they are generic images presenting life on the *fenglai* island, the idealized place where the immortals live.[93] Although Kuhn is right to see that the scene is related to life after death, he does not see the thematic particularity of this tomb in his generalization about Song tombs; he also downplays motifs taken from everyday life.

Rather, the journey theme of the passageway indicates that the travelers are bringing provisions and necessities to be used in the house where the souls will reside. The tomb chambers could be a resting place for the *po*-souls (魄) that are conventionally understood to reside in the burial space. Taken together with the journey motif in the passageway, the pictorial program may also express the *hun*-souls' (魂) journey to the world-beyond, where they will continue to enjoy a life of comfort.[94] With the possession of money as the

---

93. Kuhn, *A Place for the Dead*, 346–347.

94. For the *hun*-soul's journey, see Ying-shih Yü, " 'O Soul, Come Back!' A Study in the Changing Conceptions of the Soul and Afterlife in Pre-Buddhist China," *Harvard Journal of Asiatic Studies* 47, no. 2 (1987): 363–395.

central theme, I argue that the pictorial program illustrates a merchant's wish that the money earned in this world would be transferred to the other world, where he and his wife could continue to enjoy a life of comfort, being served by other people. That is how they understood heaven.

## *Materializing the Sprits and Their World*

The "lavish burial," as exemplified by the tomb at Baisha, was the type of practice that Song Qi detested. The tomb of lavish burial tended to have the structure of a subterranean house with an entryway leading to one or more burial chambers, usually equipped with interior designs, mural decorations, and burial objects. It had been an enduring practice of people of the upper echelon of society—royals, aristocrats, and high-ranking officials—because they were the ones who had the necessary resources. The problem arose during the eleventh century, when a new social group, rich merchants, was also able to afford lavish burials. The state's sumptuary laws, as well as some scholar-officials' strong objection to this practice, failed to solve the problem. Why did some people invest so many resources, in terms of material furnishings in the tomb, despite the social and legal constraints? In order to answer this question, I turn now to the decipherment of the significance of specific material components of lavish tombs by examining selected individual tombs.

From the state's perspective, a lavish burial was a pure waste of resources. Out of this concern, the government under the reign of Renzong promulgated the *Ordinances of Funerals and Burials* in 1029.[95] It regulated the number of items used in the various stages of the funeral and burial rites in accordance with official rank and specified the sizes of the tomb and grave plot.[96] The ordinances decreed that wealthy people of lower rank should not practice rituals of higher ranks; the other way around was acceptable.[97] Some items were banned for all ranks. For example, stone could not be used for making a coffin, casket, or tomb chamber. The coffin and casket could not have any decorative carvings, color paintings, or window frames; luxurious goods, such as jade, pearl,

---

95. For studies of various aspects of these ordinances, see Gouli Taiwan shifan daxue, lishi xuexi, ed., *"Tianshengling" lunji: Xin shiliao, xin guandian, xin shijiao* 天聖令論集 新史料新觀點新視角 (Taibei: Yuanzhao chuban youxian gongsi, 2011); for studies of both the Tang and Song ordinances, see Huang Zhengjian, ed., *Tiansheng ling yu Tang Song zhidu yanjiu* 《天聖令》與唐宋制度研究 (Beijing: Zhongguo shehui kexue chubanshe, 2011).

96. *Tianyige cang Mingchaoben Tianshengling jiaozheng* (cited fn. 47, above), 29.351; 29.356.

97. *Tianyige cang Mingchaoben Tianshengling jiaozheng*, 29.358.

and gold, could not be placed inside the coffin.[98] The ordinances were loosely based on Confucian ritual norms, especially in the sense that official rank was the defining factor for limiting consumption. There were some discrepancies between the government ordinances and individuals' understanding of the Confucian ritual laws, especially because the former were not clearly defined among scholar-officials. For example, the government ordinances of 1029 did not address the tomb's architectural style. Sima Guang, on the other hand, stated that the subterranean house structure tomb with entryway was reserved for the emperor only, according to the ancient ritual custom.[99]

Archaeological discoveries, however, indicate that the government ordinances were not strictly enforced. Although the ordinances themselves did not specify the punishment for violations, the applicable punishment was listed in an article in the *Song Penal Traditions* (*Song xingtong*), promulgated in 963, because no further revised laws on this subject were issued:

> Those who violate all the ordinances on the construction or manufacturing of temple hostels, carriages, clothes, utensils, tombs, and stone sculptural creatures and their ilk will be punished with 100 strokes of cane. Although an official is able to pardon a violator, he should still order him to fix or remove illegal items. [(Note:) *Tombs shall not be altered.*] Sellable items are to be auctioned. If a violator has not fixed, removed, or sold the prohibited items within 100 days after the pardon, he shall be punished with 100 strokes of a cane.[100]

It was less likely that 100 strokes of cane were immediately imposed in the case of burial violations, considering that there was understood to be flexibility in the application of laws in the Song era.[101] The law itself facilitated the suspension of punishment under the condition that the problems were fixed. Furthermore, a caveat written in a form of a note stated that an already-built tomb would not be altered, based on the norm of inviolability of tomb space. Given that, it was more likely that neither a sealed tomb nor burial items underwent institutional scrutiny, which meant a commissioner of burials had considerable liberty in designing tomb spaces, despite the stated regulations.

---

98. *Tianyige cang Mingchaoben Tianshengling jiaozheng*, 29.355.

99. *Shuyi*, 7.79

100. Dou, *Song xingtong*, 26.417.

101. John D. Langlois, Jr., "'Living Law' in Sung and Yuan Jurisprudence," *Harvard Journal of Asiatic Studies* 41, no. 1 (1981): 170 and 181–192.

Spirit articles or *mingqi* were particularly abundant in Song tombs with the subterranean house structure, which lent itself to the impulse to fill in its void. Spirit articles offer significant insights into the way of life and beliefs of the deceased. We recall here that Song Qi did not want to have any *mingqi* in his tomb, without clarifying what they were. The Song state simply specified the number of *mingqi* allowed for each official rank and for commoners in the beginning of the dynasty.[102] What could be legitimately included in the category of spirit articles was not clearly defined within the Confucian tradition. The *mingqi* could include both nonrepresentational items like utensils and representational items like *yong* 俑 or figurines of deities, apotropaic beasts, animals, and human beings. The *Records of Rituals* endorses both nonrepresentational and representational *mingqi* of smaller than life size. Such figurines usually were expected to play certain roles in the spirit world, mostly to protect or serve tomb occupants. In particular, human figurines endowed the tomb space with a particular aura of a dwelling place, as though they could be animated. Nevertheless, Confucius took issue especially with human figurines, based on his distaste for their likeness to human beings, because they might invoke the ancient custom of human sacrifice: "It is alright to use straw figurines. To use human figurines is not kind; isn't it similar to using human beings?[103] Therefore Confucius decried the use of wooden or clay human figurines, because they were overly representational, and suggested using less-representational figurines made of straw.

Aware of the difficulty in defining *mingqi*, Sima Guang, in the following discussion of them in the *Shuyi*, chose not to quote the famous passage of Confucius, and did not mention human figurines as being illegitimate:

*Mingqi*: It refers to carved wooden images of a carriage, horse, servant, and maid. Each is in charge of services for the deceased. Its appearance is like that of the living but smaller. Its quantity depends on the deceased's rank.

Comments: Bamboo cannot be used. Clay cannot be glazed. Wood cannot be ornamented . . . The clay carriage and grass figurines have been used since ancient times. In accordance with the *Ordinances of Funerals and Burials* [of the Song state], for the deceased of the fifth and sixth ranks thirty items are permitted for use; for those who have not reached the [ranks of] court officials, fifteen items. But utensils used [for the

---

102. SS Li 7, 124.2910; Li 28,125.2919.

103. Sun, *Liji jijie*, "Tangong, *xia*" 檀弓,下, 1:10.265.

burial] such as a bowl, plates, jars, and basins are all counted toward the number of the items.[104]

His silence regarding human figurines could indicate that they were not much in use by contemporary scholar-officials and literati, his assumed readers, or that he did not feel strong objections about their use. He rather quickly concludes his discussion of *mingqi* by arguing that utensils counted toward the maximum number of items set by the government ordinances. He could imply that those utensils would be sufficient to fill the limited number without necessarily denouncing the representational items that were endorsed in the classical text. Sima's position was quite different from that of Song Qi, who flatly rejected the use of any *mingqi* for his burial, not to mention tomb figurines. On the other hand, Zhu Xi later, in the *Family Rituals*, also followed Sima Guang's position on this issue. However, in another text Zhu mentions that his family did not use any *mingqi*,[105] which echoed the Song scholar-official's general tendency of avoiding discussion of human figurines, and sometimes *mingqi* altogether.

Although the *Book of Rituals* endorses only wood and clay, easily perishable materials, for the making of tomb figurines and other *mingqi*, a variety of materials had been used since antiquity. During the northern Song, durable materials such as ceramic, stone, and glass were commonly used for making realistic representations of various images, albeit smaller than life-size. The tomb at Jiangsu of a rich merchant, Li Bin 李彬 (d. 1091), and his wife provides an excellent example of maximizing the use of *mingqi* for delivering a statement of the deceased.[106] The two brick chambers, one meter apart, share the same pit. Being a commoner, he was eligible to have up to twelve items of *mingqi*, according to the government regulation,[107] yet the two chambers combined contain as many as ninety-one items. Among them is a miniature shoulder carrier held up by two human figurines, evidencing their role of transporting the soul. Another thirty-four items are various figurines representing the four directional apotropaic beasts, deities of different stars, eight

---

104. *Shuyi*, 7.81.

105. Patricia B. Ebrey, *Chu Hsi's* Family Rituals: *A Twelfth-Century Chinese Manual for the Performance of Cappings, Weddings, Funerals, and Ancestral Rites* (Princeton, NJ: Princeton University Press, 1991), 109.

106. Zhenjiangshi bowuguan and Liyangxian wenhuaguan, "Jiangsu Liyang Zhuze BeiSong Li Bin fufu mu" 江蘇溧阳竹簣北宋李彬夫妇墓, *Wenwu*, no. 5 (1980): 34–39.

107. SS Li 28, 125.2918.

out of the twenty-eight deities of the constellations, the Perfected Warrior (*Zhenwu* 眞武), military officers, Buddha, Bodhisattva Vajrapāṇi, and an officer in the Personnel Evaluation Section (*gongcao* 功曹). The assemblage, as is the case in many other Song tombs, reflects a pick-and-choose approach of taking various deities from different religious traditions. In particular, Li Bin's commitment to Buddhism is testified to in the tomb inscription: "At ordinary times, he recites Buddhist scriptures and counts their volumes [of recitation] every day."

Li Bin's tomb contains some unique burial items, miniatures of various buildings and facilities within his house. In addition to a ceramic piece representing a granary, there are seven glass pieces: a two-story building, three pavilions on the water, a gate, a pavilion, and a performance stage. Their significance in his life is clearly stated in the tomb inscription tablet.

> He loves to take care of the residential house surrounded by a two-story building, pavilion, balcony, and water pavilion, and filled with wonderful trees and variegated plants. Seen from afar, its soaring appearance in magnificence is above and beyond that of houses in wealthy urban neighborhoods, villages, and hamlets.

The architecture and landscape of his house manifest his wealth publicly in a way that dwarfs the holdings of people with prestigious official titles. The granary filled with grain might have functioned as a depository for his business of cornering and lending grain. The performing stage in the beautiful garden with a water pavilion was more likely to be used for hosting musical bands. The inscription also clarifies that the source of his wealth is from his family business, which is now in its fourth generation. Note here that Li Bin was not qualified to have a tomb inscription tablet, yet he might have felt that he deserved one. The material furnishings in his tomb celebrate his life in wealth and also express his wish for it to be continued in his life after death.

Some scholar-officials also used tomb figurines. The tomb of Fan Zhongwen 范仲溫 (985–1050), a half-brother of Fan Zhongyan (989–1052), contains the stone figurines of fourteen humans, a bird, and a horse.[108] Each figurine has a nametag engraved in its foundation panel that specifies its assumed function in the spirit world: one, for example, is "Horse rider of Fan Fujun (Commandery Governor) of the Song." The nametags clearly testify

---

108. Liu Yusheng, "Henansheng Fangchengxian chutu Songdai shiyong" 河南省方城縣出土宋代石俑, *Wenwu*, no. 8 (1983): 40–43.

to Fan's belief in the world-beyond, en route to which those figurines would assist the soul in various ways. This belief was the main reason that some scholar-officials did not want to include the *mingqi* among their grave goods, although they were not banned by the government.

The image of the deceased was often materialized through mural portrait paintings in subterranean house tombs, as seen in the tomb at Baisha. Because a simple pit grave did not have enough room for wall structures, Confucian texts of the period did not even mention pictorial images as something to avoid. Sima Guang, however, criticized the popular custom of placing a portrait image of the deceased behind the "soul cloth" that was placed to the south of the dead body immediately after washing and dressing of it. Nevertheless, Sima reluctantly approved of putting the portrait image of a male that was drawn during his life, albeit labeling it a "current vulgar custom"; he absolutely forbade it, however, for a female.[109] He was also against decorating the soul cloth with a cap, clothes, and shoes, because it was "treating the dead like the living." Considering Sima's aniconicism, on the basis of which he objects to images of the deceased in a ritual context, he would certainly not endorse the tomb mural portrait.

A more serious example of materializing the image of the deceased is manifested by the full-body stone sculpture of a civil officer, supposedly that of the tomb occupant, in an undated Song tomb in Sichuan.[110] It is a rare and extreme case of a realistic three-dimensional representation of the image of the deceased in the tomb space. In another tomb at Chongqing in Sichuan, a group of people's images in bas relief were carved in tomb walls as if looking over the deceased's chamber from a balcony.[111] These images of human beings, either tomb occupants or their attendants, keenly reveal an impulse to materialize the soul's continuing life after death.

The lavish burial also includes the use of expensive materials like gold and pearl and the use of a large amount of stone for making the coffin and chamber, which is banned by the government. Although a majority of scholar-officials had simple pit tombs with a small number of burial items, certain wealthy scholar-officials or their family members used those materials, which were banned. One such example is the tomb of Madame Shi (d. 1109), wife of Xiong Ben 熊本 (d. 1090), who served as Grand Master of the Palace, Edict

---

109. *Shuyi*, 5.54

110. A stone statue is found in the tomb of Wang Jian 王建 (847–918), emperor of the Former Shu 蜀 Kingdom, which is located in the same region. Wu, *The Art of the Yellow Springs*, 126.

111. Chongqing Dazu shike yishu bowuguan, "Chongqing Dazu Longshuizhen mingguang-cun Mo'erpo Songmu qingli jianbao" 重慶大足龍水镇明光村磨兒坡宋墓清理簡報, *Sichuan wenwu*, no. 5 (2002): 3–7.

Attendant at Longtu Pavilion (rank 4b2).[112] Her single-chamber tomb is a very sturdy structure, using granite for both walls and ceiling. Despite having been plundered, this tomb still contained some nonrepresentational items made of gold, silver, bronze, iron, and crystal upon its discovery by archaeologists. In particular, the five gold items had a total weight of 115. 2 grams. Prior to being looted, the tomb might have contained even more valuables. The tomb inscription tablet indicates that Madame Shi's wealth was from her natal family, as both her father and grandfather held high-ranking positions.

Another example is a single-chamber tomb in Nanjing with arched brick vaults filled with exquisite items made of silver. The partially legible tomb inscription indicates that the tomb occupant was someone who lived during Emperor Yingzong's reign (1063–1067), having the official positions of Supervisor in the Transit Authorization Bureau of the Department of State Affairs (rank 6a), and later of Gentleman for Court Services (rank 6a–7a).[113] Despite these mid-ranking positions, he was able to afford a lavish burial thanks to his prestigious family background, as his tomb-inscription tablet clearly states the official positions of his grandfather and father. The items of silver consist of a kettle, bowls, a tray, a basin, plates, chopsticks, and a spoon that seem to have been used during his life. As silver was used as currency of high value, burying such a large amount is considered a lavish burial, broadly defined. In the beginning of the Song dynasty, following the example of the Tang, the government banned the use of silver along with gold for death rituals of both scholar-officials and commoners.[114] Zhenzong in fact prohibited the manufacture of silver products by the general populace in 1001.[115]

The stone chamber and coffin were also proscribed items for people of all official ranks, in accordance with government regulations. A case of the violation of these regulations is the tomb of Mr. Zhang, who had no official title, located near Luoyang.[116] He either died or was buried in 1106. The impressive stone coffin is large: 2.2 meters long, 1.3 meters high in the front (1.04 meters high in the back), and 1.1 meters wide in the front (0.85 meters wide in the back). A particularity of this burial is the tomb inscription engraved on the

---

112. Xu Jiadong, "Jiangxi Boyang Songmu" 江西波阳宋墓, *Kaogu*, no. 4 (1977): 286.

113. Li Wenming and Li Huren, "Nanjing Luying Songmu qingli jianbao," *Dongnan wenhua*, no. 2 (1995): 15–21.

114. SS Li 28, 125.2917–2918.

115. CB 48.1051.

116. Huang Minglan and Gong Dazhong, "Luoyang BeiSong Zhang Jun mu huaxiang shiguan" 洛陽北宋張君墓畫像石棺, *Wenwu*, no. 7 (1984): 79–81.

coffin cover. This exquisite coffin is also decorated with the engraving of an image of a well-known story of filial piety and the ascension of the immortals. The ascension motif illustrates the Daoist ideal of a soul's eternal life in the celestial world, which the durability of stone could represent better than a conventional wooden coffin.

Interestingly, the above-mentioned tomb of Fu Bi also includes a stone coffin room, entryway, and mural paintings. Although he had attained the highest position possible in the bureaucratic system of the state—Grand Councilor—he was not permitted to have a stone coffin room, because it was banned for all ranks. In addition, the architectural structure with entryway was not acceptable for nonroyal family members, according to the Confucian ritual codes. The single-chamber brick tomb is quite large, its entire length being 24.6 meters.[117] This already plundered tomb might have originally contained exquisite burial items. Its mural paintings have also been damaged, so that there is no information to be gleaned from its pictorial motifs. Nevertheless, its architectural design and the materials used present clues about the level of luxury of this tomb. Apparently, the material conditions of the tomb alone were not sufficient to fulfill the wishes of Fu Bi or the supervisor of burial, as the impressive tomb inscription tablet has remarkably lengthy texts written by influential figures. Suffice it to say that Fu Bi was one of those people who provoked the laments of Sima Guang and Song Qi about the current vulgar custom practiced even by people in the upper echelon of society. Fu Bi's tomb is proof that the government's ordinances on burials were not strictly implemented, even at the highest level. Those people who employed lavish burials subscribed to the wishful thinking that in death they would enjoy the happiness of eternal life and that the magnified materiality of the tomb space would be translated into magnified happiness.

In sum, the "lavish burial" of wealthy people, namely certain officeholders and many rich commoners and merchants, was an expression of their hope that the burial itself influenced the soul's transition to or its status in the spirit world. According to this line of thinking, the tomb occupied a special space wherein figurative items were animated in order to play certain roles in the service of the deceased. Nonrepresentational luxury items were also included, because of their durability or simply their value, to accompany the soul in eternity.

---

117. According to the state regulation, an official of the first rank could have a tomb of a radius of about 90 *bu*, or 32.8 meters. The size of his tomb would be roughly within this limit; see SS Li 27, 124.2910.

## *Asserting Beliefs in the Tomb Space*

As we have seen, the unique voice of an individual tomb, either that of the occupant or the designer, was often expressed through particular choices from multiple conventional options available for architectural styles, burial objects, and motifs in mural paintings. Dieter Kuhn classifies the architectural types of the excavated tombs, including information on the social status of tomb occupants, in his analysis of available archaeological data as of 1990. He argues that there was a general tendency for most Song people with official titles to choose simple pit tombs with tomb inscription tablets, whereas rich people with no official title disproportionately chose lavish burials with land deeds.[118] Kuhn's observation has not been challenged by archaeological reports issued since his study. Given that the social group of the deceased was the primary dividing factor in choosing the two different mortuary items—the tomb inscription tablet or the land deed—this section inquires into what the main motives were that drove such group behaviors. I will first discuss how land deeds used mostly by nonofficeholders served as one of the most significant indicators of belief in the spirit world in a way that contrasted markedly with the use of tomb inscription tablets. I will then discuss some tombs that do not fit the general pattern, in order to illustrate how personal beliefs and self-proclaimed identity factored into people's choices of burial practices.

Among many burial items, the land deed was quintessentially associated with the tomb occupant's belief in the spirit world. Its wide use was definitely a cultural phenomenon of the Song period, although its earliest extant example dates to 82 CE.[119] Despite its wide use, it was not problematized either by the government or by individual scholar-officials. Nevertheless, it deserves close attention as part of our efforts to detect the tomb occupant's understanding of the presumed impacts of mortuary practices on the spirit's well-being. A key characteristic of the land deed is that it was used mostly by people without official titles and was mutually exclusive with a tomb inscription tablet, as both listed the name of the deceased along with official titles, if any. Therefore, many lavish luxurious tombs of rich commoners tended to include land deeds, as seen in the tomb at Baisha.

---

118. Kuhn, *A Place for the Dead*, 86–100; "Decoding Tombs of the Song Elite," in *Burial in Song China*, 50–79.

119. Kleeman, "Land Contracts and Related Documents," 1.

The use of the land deed was based on the notion that the deceased needed to buy a burial plot either from the underworld bureaucracy or from whoever had previously been buried in the spot, so as to avoid the "culpability" of intruding on and polluting the land.[120] Therefore, the buyer and the deities made a contract by specifying the amount of money paid, often strings of 99,999 copper coin cash. After the contract document was signed, payment was made by burning a facsimile of paper money. The contract was written on a land deed, a tablet resembling a tomb inscription tablet. Although diverse materials were used to make it, such as paper, brick, wood, clay, and iron, the predominant material used during the Song was stone, based on the archaeological data. In certain cases, real coins were laid on top of the land deed or right next to the body of the deceased.[121] A wine jar, an item for the contract, was often also placed near the land deed.[122]

The text of the land deed followed conventional formulae, albeit with some variations.[123] It typically opens with precise information about the time of burial, including the hour, date, month, and year, based on the notion that they were the decisive factors in terms of the auspiciousness of the burial. Then it states the identity of the deceased, including elements such as their name and the time of death. With the statement of the purchase of the land, the demarcation of the location is specified in two different ways. One type of conventional formula states the location of the deceased in the spirit world and declares that its boundaries should not be breached. An alternative is to describe the physical location of the burial plot with references to landmarks such as a mountain and a river. This is followed by a declaration protecting the deceased in the burial plot, thereby locating him or her securely in the realm of the spirits. The names of the seller, writer, witness, and guarantor of the contract are designated from the pool of deities, with some variations in the assignment of their roles. The most common name of the deities are Zhang Jiangu 張堅固, Li Dingdu

120. Kleeman, "Land Contracts and Related Documents," 12; Ina Asim, "Status Symbol and Insurance Policy: Song Land Deeds for the Afterlife," in *Burial in Song China*, ed. Dieter Kuhn (Heidelberg: Forum, 1994), 311; Hansen, *Negotiating Daily Life*, 155–159.

121. Sichuansheng bowuguan, "Sichuan Guangyuan shike Songmu qingli jianbao" 四川廣元石刻宋墓清理簡報, *Wenwu*, no. 6 (1982): 57.

122. Chengdushi wenwu kaogu gongzuodui, "Chengdu Beijiao Ganyoucun faxian BeiSong xuanhe liunian mu" 成都北郊甘油村發現北宋宣和六年墓, *Sichuan wenwu*, no. 3 (1999): 114–117.

123. For translations of some land deeds, see Asim, "Status Symbol and Insurance Policy," 334–361.

李定度, Shi Gongcao 石功曹 (Mr. Shi from the Personnel Evaluation Section), Xi Wangmu 西王母 (Queen Mother of the West), Dong Wangfu 東王父 (King Father of the East), and Jin Zhubu 金主簿 (Register Mr. Jin). A land deed written in 1124 specifies their roles: "Having written the document, they flew to heaven. Having read the contract, they enter the Yellow Spring. No [other] deities can snatch away the contract. Hastily, hastily like ordinances."[124] It declares that the contract cannot be altered; thus the burial place is made secure.

As to the gain in the popularity of the use of land deeds during the Song, Valerie Hansen argues that the burgeoning of contracts, both in legal affairs and in business transactions, engendered a parallel conception in dealings with gods.[125] On the other hand, Ina Asim suggests that those who were not eligible to have tomb inscription tablets increasingly used land deeds, because both functioned to present the deceased's identity in the spirit world.[126] However, I argue that the intended functions of the two items during the Northern Song were vastly different. A common phrase in the ending part of land deeds of the Northern Song sums up their purpose: "The writer of this contract eternally guarantees peace and luck to the lost soul in the netherworld; and great luck, longevity, and prosperity to the male and female descendants."[127] This formulaic phrase declares its purpose to be the soul's smooth transition to and well-being in the world-beyond; its end results to the living are luck and prosperity.

More importantly, the land deed does not bear any societal function, because it is a contract between the buyer (the deceased) and seller (a designated deity) of the burial plot. A document written in the thirteenth century identifies the name of the living landowner who would ask the deities, on behalf of a buyer, to sell the land.[128] Likewise, the name of the (human) author of the document is not given, because it is alleged to be a designated deity. However, some land deeds do include the name of the engraver of the tablet.[129] The tomb occupant's biography and genealogy and information about

---

124. Zeng Qinghua, "Jingyangxian BeiSong Huang Nian silang mu qingli jianxun" 井研縣北宋黃念四郎墓清理簡, *Sichuan wenwu*, no. 1 (2002): 95; Yao Meiling, "Tang Song maidiquan xiyu kaoxi" 唐宋買地券習語考釋, *Yuncheng xueyuan xuebao* 22, no. 1 (2004): 60.

125. Hansen, *Negotiating*, 3 and 222–223.

126. Asim, "Status Symbol and Insurance Policy," 363.

127. Long Teng, "Pujiang BeiSong Song Sui mu chutu wenwu" 蒲江北宋宋燧墓出土文物, *Sichuan wenwu*, no. 5 (1996): 61; Ruichangxian bowuguan, "Jiangxi Ruichang faxian liangzuo BeiSong jinian mu" 江西瑞昌發現兩座北宋紀年墓, *Wenwu*, no. 1 (1986): 71.

128. Asim, "Status Symbol and Insurance Policy," 362; Ikeda On, "Chūgoku rekidai boken ryakukō" 中国歷代墓券略考, *Tōyō bunka kenkyūjo kiyō* 86 (1981): 253.

129. Long, "Pujiang BeiSong," 61.

survivors are by and large absent, because they are not germane to a contract document. The land deed functions purely as a mortuary item, one that is not to be circulated among the living. In this regard, it is markedly different from the tomb inscription tablet, the content of which is personalized and which was often circulated for the purpose of keeping the deceased in social memory.

Sima Guang (and later Zhu Xi also) was silent about land deeds in his array of criticism of contemporary practices, which is an indication that scholar-officials and literati, his readership, tended not to adopt it in their burial practice. Archaeological reports corroborate the generalization that that most officeholders preferred tomb inscription tablets to land deeds. However, there were some exceptional individuals who did not follow the expected practice of their social group, and thus the deciphering of their motives deserves our attention. In the tomb of Yang Cunzhong 楊存忠 (d. 1131), Palace Eunuch of the Left Duty Group (左班殿直, fourth highest of the twelve ranks of titles for eunuchs), both a land deed and a tomb inscription tablet are found, in two different chambers.[130] His chamber contains a tomb inscription tablet; in the chamber of his first wife, who passed away before him, there is a land deed. In the second wife's chamber, there is neither. Having been an eunuch, he might not have felt a strong commitment to Confucian orthodox burial, as he was most likely to have been in charge of the tomb's construction when his first wife passed away. Moreover, the paintings of the musical band's performances in his burial chamber illustrate his belief in the quality of life after death, as seen in the above-mentioned tomb at Baisha.

A unique case in which both the tomb inscription tablet and land deed were written by the same calligrapher is found in the tomb of Jiang Jun 江君 (d. 1073), Assistant Director of Palace Library (秘書丞) (rank 7b), at Anji in Jiangxi.[131] This looted tomb does not contain many burial items but does have a bronze mirror. Because the archaeological report fails to provide the content of the inscription, Mr. Jiang's life and personal beliefs are unknown. Nevertheless, the simultaneous presentation of the two items written by the same calligrapher indicates that the conductor of the burial subscribed to the

---

130. Luo Zongzhen, "Jiangsu Huai'an Songdai bihua mu" 江蘇淮安宋代壁畫墓, *Wenwu*, Z1 (1960): 45–46 and 51.

131. Peng Shifan and Tang Changpo, "Jiangxi faxian jizuo BeiSong jinian mu" 江西發現幾座 北宋紀年墓, *Wenwu*, no. 5 (1980): 31.

belief implied by the land deed, and yet did not want to give up the use of the tomb inscription tablet, the exclusive privilege of officeholders.

A century later, the tomb of Zhu Jinan 朱濟南 (d. 1197), Grand Master for Court Audience (rank 6), includes a land deed. It does not include a tomb inscription tablet but rather a tombstone (*mubei* 墓碑), on which only Zhu's name—there is no funerary biography—is written.[132] His tomb includes seventy pieces of spirit articles, consisting of various ceramic figurines of the Deities of Twelve Double Hours and human beings in various functions. Such a high volume of figurines far exceeded the allowed limit for Zhu's official rank, which illustrates his great concern about his soul's well-being in the spirit world. In particular, the figurines of the deities mentioned in the land deed contract are also entombed to perform their roles as stated in the document. His preference for a land deed over an inscription tablet indicates that he placed a heavier weight on his personal belief in the spirit world than in the cultural conventions and norms associated with social status.

On the other hand, there were some people who included tomb inscription tablets, although they were not qualified to do so. As mentioned earlier, this practice was reserved for people with official titles—those up to the eighth rank, according to the state regulations issued in year 1111, and previously those up to the fifth rank, according to Sima Guang in the 1070s. The tomb of Madame Yi Baniang (d. 1090) of Pengze in Jiangxi is an example. Her tomb inscription does not include the official title of either her husband or her father, but does mention that she is from an "illustrious clan" (*haozu* 毫族), an umbrella term referring to an aristocratic family.[133] Gold and silver jewelry buried in the tomb attest to the accuracy of the claim of "illustrious clan." The wooden inner coffin is large—318 centimeters in length and 160 in height—and it is put inside the stone casket, an item banned by the state. On a cypress-man figurine is written a text intended to prevent the filing of an underworld lawsuit related to her burial, which reveals her belief in the social imaginary underlined in that practice.[134] Another tomb in the same province, Jiangxi, contains the tomb inscription tablet of Mr. Wu Zhu 吳助, who had no official title and who died in 1117. Despite his having the status of commoner, he or his surviving family were able to afford a sturdy tomb constructed of brick and stone. Inside his

---

132. Chen Dingrong and Xu Jinchang, "Jiangxi Linchuanxian Songmu" 江西川臨縣宋墓, *Kaogu*, no. 4 (1988): 329–334.

133. Peng and Tang, "Jiangxi faxian," 29.

134. For a discussion of the functions of the cypress-man figurine in mortuary ritual, see Hansen, *Negotiating Daily Life*, 290–292.

tomb are many human figurines, such as those of military and civil officers and servants of both genders. The figurines of spiritual beings include the Deities of Twelve Hours (*shiershi shen* 十二時神), dragon-head-and-human-body imaginary creatures, and a deity of "listening to the earth by kneeling down" (*guifu yong* 跪伏俑).[135] These two tombs are clearly examples of lavish burial practice on the part of rich people who held no official title. The accompanying burial items suggest that the deceased subscribed to the idea that burial would affect the spirit's well-being in the world-beyond, yet they chose tomb inscription tablets rather than land deeds. Here tomb inscription tablets are mainly perceived as status symbols, as is well illustrated by the self-proclamation of belonging to an "illustrious clan," a status not necessarily tied to official rank.

Some literati who had not held offices also used inscription tablets, as illustrated by the tomb of Zhao Huojie 趙火桀 (d. 1120). According to the inscription, he "loved studying" and sat for the national exams several times.[136] Although he did not pass the extremely competitive exam leading to a governmental career path, making it to the national examination was itself an accomplishment for a scholar. Though he did not have any official post, he was still able to afford a luxurious tomb, the structure of which was similar to that of the tomb at Baisha. On all eight walls of the tomb, there are paintings of a banquet, its preparation, and making a bed assisted by female servants. His lack of commitment to Confucian ritual requirements was explicitly spelled out in the tomb inscription tablet: "He believed in Daoism and loved wine." Mr. Zhao is representative of many literati who failed to obtain scarce governmental posts and did not see why tomb inscription tablets should be limited to those who had them.

Because the land deed was perceived to be crucial for the securing of a place for the deceased in the spirit world, many people who subscribed to this social imaginary entombed it along with other items such as figurines and mural paintings. Because it was a contract document, the personal voice of and information on the life of the deceased were absent from it. By contrast, the tomb inscription tablet laid out a life in social and genealogical contexts, while refusing to place the deceased in the social imaginaries of the world-beyond. Although the tomb inscription tablet itself was a privilege of officeholders, some wealthy commoners and literati without ranking

---

135. Peng and Tang, "Jiangxi faxian," 29–30.

136. Wei Jun and Zhang Daosen, "Anyang Songdai bihuamu kao" 安陽宋代壁畫墓考, *Huaxia kaogu*, no. 2 (1997): 103–104 and 55.

government positions also included one in their tombs of lavish burial. On the other hand, some wealthy officeholders who subscribed to the social imaginary of the world-beyond also tended not to give up their privilege of having a tomb inscription tablet in their tombs with banned items. The few exceptional cases of officeholders who prioritized the land deed over the tomb inscription tablet demonstrated compelling reasons for doing so, derived from their concerns for the deceased's well-being in the spirit world. These exceptional cases conversely confirm that the majority of scholar-officials of the eleventh century who received a "simple burial" defied the social imaginaries of the world-beyond, and, in particular, refused to express those imaginaries through burial practices.

## *Conclusion*

During the eleventh century of the Song dynasty, some scholar-officials brought burial practices to the forefront of their efforts to establish a socio-moral order based on Confucianism with recourse to the tradition's ritual norms and the government's regulations. For the poor, they established public mass graveyards in order to put an end to the prevailing custom of abandoning or cremating dead bodies. In addition, they set in opposition two types of burial, "simple burial" and "lavish burial," and decreed the latter to be immoral. Based upon the Confucian tradition's dictum of not speaking about the spirit world, the simple burial abstained from material representation of the life after death, the imagination of the world-beyond, and supernatural beings. Perishable materials used in the simple burial resonate with the tradition's notion of the ultimate dissipation of the soul. Its focus on funerary biographical writing, a nonmaterial item, reveals that the foremost concern of the scholar-officials of the time was the long-term survival of their reputations in social memory. Their prestige in death was measured by their official titles and virtue, not wealth. In contrast, the practice of the lavish burial was based on the belief that various forms of material furnishings of the tomb would actually assist the soul's transitional process to the world-beyond and its existential conditions in that place. When rich merchants and commoners chose this type of burial during this time, they highlighted their wealth as the foundation of their happiness in this world and the one beyond.

Burial was a site of contestation for the posing or defying of social imaginaries of the world-beyond and for asserting one's primary values in life and after death. Broadly speaking, two social groups—scholar-officials and wealthy merchants—were at odds, with the former attempting to enforce Confucian norms regarding burial practice and the latter often disregarding those norms. Nevertheless, there were some exceptional cases that did not fit into the general pattern of correlations between social groups and burial practices. Those exceptional cases illustrate the fact that tombs in eleventh-century China in essence remained private spaces where individuals would rest in peace in accordance with their beliefs and self-identity. Conversely, it was for this very reason that some Confucian ritualists took steps to pressure people to follow the tradition's ritual norms.

# Conclusion

IT IS COMMONLY understood that the revival of Confucianism in China in the eleventh century paved the way for the rise of neo-Confucianism, narrowly defined as Zhu Xi's school of Confucianism, which emerged in the twelfth century. This study locates the impetus for the revival of Confucianism in the reactions of scholar-officials to Emperor Zhenzong's massive project of creating new state rituals with heavy Daoist undertones throughout the state. During Renzong's reign, some officials maneuvered in the imperial court to return Confucian canonical rituals to their place of primacy with regard to noncanonical (Daoist and Buddhist) rituals and finally succeeded in invalidating the cult of the Sacred Ancestor as official state ritual. A crucial moment in the revival of Confucianism was marked by Ouyang Xiu's declaration that the legitimacy of imperial authority resided in the orthopraxis of ritual as prescribed in the Confucian classical texts. The ongoing debates and legal cases related to death ritual practices stimulated the study of the canonical ritual texts as scholar-officials used them as a source of references for justifying their positions. Later, a faction of scholar-officials took further steps in this direction by taking a lead in reviving Confucian family rituals among scholar-officials and also condemning non-Confucian rituals prevailing in society at large as well in state-sponsored programs.

The debates centering on ritual at the imperial court gave voice to a crucial task in Song state formation: the negotiation of how power was to be distributed between the emperor and court officials. At the social level, scholar-officials faced competition in displaying prestige with wealthy merchants. The distribution of power, social status, and prestige in traditional China was symbolically presented both in imperial rituals and in family rituals. Given these cultural preconditions, three different social groups preferred to employ different types of death rituals, ones that which implied conflicting social imaginaries reflecting the groups' varied interests and visions of society.

Each group chose to deploy different types of authority—royal, canonical, and supernatural—in defining the cause, aim, and content of death ritual performance. These spheres of authority often came into conflict.

Emperor Zhenzong created a rupture in the tradition of grounding imperial authority in the Confucian doctrine of the Mandate of Heaven when he sought stronger ideological support for royal authority. He wished to increase monarchical power in order to compensate for the loss of prestige he as emperor had suffered due to military setbacks and the subsequent treaty made with a "barbarian" state. To this end, he and his close staff invented the myth of the Sacred Ancestor, which identified the imperial lineage with the bloodline of a Daoist high deity. Whereas the doctrine of the Mandate of Heaven allowed for public criticism concerning the emperor's virtue and governance as Heaven's agent, this new myth did not, in making the emperor the direct descendent of a divine being. Zhenzong did in fact largely ignore the criticism of him leveled by prominent scholar-officials. Because there was no textual basis for the myth, unchallenged royal authority was central to the process of mythmaking as well as to its goal. This imaginary was very much of the social world, relegating the celestial world to being merely the background of the origin of the divinity. Hoping that people at large shared the social imaginary of the divine origin of the imperial family, the central government implemented various official cultural programs in which state officers and the general populace were required to participate. The civil ritual of veneration of the Sacred Ancestor along with other deceased emperors by ordinary people broke away from the Confucian liturgical tradition, in which only the reigning emperor could offer rituals to royal ancestors. Institutionalizing this new cult as a permanent civil ritual was routinizing citizens' expression of their subordination to royal authority in a tangible way. The emperor and his close staff made a heavy investment in ritual affairs in terms of time and resources, based on their belief in ritual's capacity to ensure national security and prosperity.

Scholar-officials, led by Ouyang Xiu and some others, were relentless in their calls for orthopraxis of imperial rituals and finally invalidated the cult of royal ancestor veneration as a legitimate state ritual, reducing it to a private ritual of the royal families. Their critiques of royal authority relied upon and emphasized textual authority, because the canonical status of some Confucian texts had long been upheld within the legal-political tradition of the imperial states. Working from this assumption, they cited particular textual references in criticizing the emperors so as to depersonalize their opinions and to invoke the doctrine of the Mandate of Heaven. As public criticism became a significant function within the imperial court during the reign of Emperor Renzong, the authority of the canonical and classical texts was further strengthened as the basis for judging both an individual's morality and governmental conduct. Nevertheless, those texts of more than a millennium earlier often failed to provide clear-cut answers in some ambiguous cases. As a result, the matter of interpretation sparked debates and disputes among scholar–officials in the imperial court, which in turn triggered further study of the various texts.

Confucian ritualists, with Sima Guang as their most prominent representative, took ritual discourse further in conceptualizing the state formation. They envisioned a virtuous government run by bureaucrats, with the emperor being at the summit of the structure—not beyond it. Sima Guang derived the model for his ideal society from the prescriptions of the Confucian rituals, which aimed to order society through a structure of official ranks. The social imaginary that Sima and his sympathizers put forth entailed the reforming of society through ritual practice and the reestablishing of Confucian ethics as social norms. They naturally saw themselves as the role models for this society to come, due to their moral perfection, textual knowledge, and expertise in ritual performance. For them, rituals not only represented the social order in symbolic form but also reinforced that order as it ought to be. In other words, the order presented in rituals became the paradigm for social reality on earth. To address practices across all strata of society, they took the lead in reforming death rituals such as creating public graveyards, writing a new Confucian family ritual manual, condemning non-Confucian death rituals, and taking legal action against violators of the state laws.

Also coming in for criticism by scholar-officials were the newly emergent social group of rich merchants, who displayed their monetary power through their consumption of luxurious housing, private hosting of entertainment, and ostentatious rituals to compensate for their lack of political and cultural capital. On the one hand, they were not obliged to observe exclusively Confucian rituals; on the other, their death rituals could not be on a par with those performed by officials in terms of grandeur, according to state regulations. Despite the state's sumptuary laws, the wealthy merchants were often able to avoid charges and continued their burial practices unimpeded to a great extent. In performing non-Confucian death rituals and lavish burials, they appealed to supernatural authority as the agent to bestow blessings on supplicants and their ancestors. They subscribed fervently to the elaborate social imaginaries of the world-beyond and the concept of salvation through ritual performance. Through ritual performance, the invisible authorities became manifest and thereby became social reality to those who believed in them. In so doing, wealthy merchants proposed that there was another order of reality in which they might occupy a superior position, thanks to their material investment in ritual performance. Their primary desires included assuring their ancestors' material well-being in the world-beyond and their descendants' prosperity in this world. In particular, the idea that the salvation of the deceased could be achieved through ritual performance by the living flew in the face of the Confucian conception of the purpose of ritual. Although their social imaginary was oriented toward the other world, in the end their specific wishes demonstrated their desires to transgress the norms of the society they inhabited, which prioritized official rank over material wealth.

Social imaginaries were located at the core of state formation in the royal myth, the Confucian vision of ideal society, and rich merchants' belief in the world-beyond. The varied social imaginaries were at once a result of the process of state formation in the mid-Northern Song dynasty and a driving force to further shape its political and social culture. Each social imaginary contained implications for how society ought to be constructed, and for where a particular individual desired to be situated within that imagined world. In this sense, social imaginaries were not merely a reflection of social reality but in fact constituted the very heart of that reality, as Cornelius Castoriadis proposed in *The Imaginary Institution of Society*. When one group's interests were in conflict with those of another, the social imaginaries portrayed by each group would naturally be at odds with one another. Through the manipulation of the very channel where invisible social and political powers were made manifest, some ritual agents were able to enhance their own power and status through effective staging of the medium.

Scholar-officials of the eleventh century launched a series of attacks against competing social imaginaries. During Renzong's reign, they succeeded in limiting the royal family's performance of non-Confucian death rituals to a large extent, and successfully generated a consensus among the members of the imperial court on the issue of supremacy of the Confucian imperial rituals. Later, when intellectual and political disagreements brought divisions among scholar-officials, especially during the era of New Policies, a faction expanded their criticism to the state policies of religious pluralism that retained Buddhist and Daoist rituals as part of the official rituals. Based on the notion of orthopraxis of Confucian rituals, they also criticized fellow scholar-officials for adopting non-Confucian rituals in their family rituals as well as flexible applications of the canonical ritual codes. Their censorship of ritual performance was in essence their way of exerting control over other people's social imaginaries. Conversely, the practices of death rituals that violated Confucian prohibitions evidenced the resistance to the norms reinforced by institutional censorship.

In conclusion, I turn to Jonathan Z. Smith's contention in his *Imagining Religion* that ritual functions to reconcile the disparities between perceived reality and imagined ideals. This study of death rituals during the Northern

Song dynasty provides answers for questions which Smith chooses not to pursue: how and where does this reconciliation of disparities takes place?[1] Narrowing the gap did occur at the level of cognition of the ritual participants, who perceived that ritual actions and statements held true or were efficacious in reality. Ritual discourse provided a conceptual mechanism for evaluating the claims put forth in ritual practice as truthful, or for advancing the contention that social reality ought to be modeled upon ritual practice. Through the discourse on Confucian rituals, practitioners came to see the performance of ritual as that which prescribed ideal social relations. They believed that the disparities or ambiguities in those social relations would be corrected by the performance of ritual. In contrast, death rituals oriented to the other world undermined the rituals' functions of modeling and adjusting social relations. Violators of Confucian rituals believed in the rituals' capacity to engender magical efficacy in the world-beyond, where ritual participants and their ancestors could secure a better position. In this way, ritual agents attempted to narrow the gap between social reality and social ideals not only at the level of their own perception but also at the level of social reality. Yet social ideals were, as is often the case in human societies, multiple, and thus those ideals could be in conflict with one another, since they intertwined with politics and group interests.

In eleventh-century China, where ritual was one of the core elements constituting the social and political fabric, death rituals served not only as a means of effectively displaying existing power relations, but also as a tool by means of which practitioners could construct power and status. Through debates concerning and practices of imperial rituals, scholar-officials were able to limit the monarchical power to a certain extent during Renzong's era. Amid ebbs and flows of shift in political power within factions among scholar-officials, continuing legal and intellectual disputes over the performance of proper death rituals in turn contributed to a revival of Confucianism as the dominant value system of Chinese society in the period that followed.

---

1. Jonathan Z. Smith, *Imagining Religion* (Chicago: University of Chicago Press, 1982), 90–101.

# Bibliography

## Abbreviations

CB      *Xu zizhi tongjian changbian* 續資治通鑑長編
QSBJ      *Quan Song biji* 全宋筆記
QSW      *Quan Song wen* 全宋文
SDZLJ      *Song da zhaolingji* 宋大詔令集
SHY      *Song huiyao jigao* 宋會要輯稿
SS      *Songshi* 宋史
*Shuyi*      *Sima shi shuyi* 司馬氏書儀
SSJBM      *Songshi jishi benmo* 宋史紀事本末
TCJBM      *Tongjian changbian jishi benmo* 通鑑長編紀事本末

### PREMODERN CHINESE SOURCES

Ban Gu 班固 (32–92). *Hanshu* 漢書. Beijing: Zhonghua shuju, 1962.

Cai Tao 蔡絛 (11th–12th cent.). *Tiewei shan congtan* 鐵圍山叢談. Beijing: Zhonghua shuju, 1983.

Chen Bangzhan 陳邦瞻 (d. 1623). *Songshi jishi benmo* 宋史紀事本末. Beijing: Zhonghua shuju, 1977.

Chen Menglei 陳夢雷 (1650–1741) and Jiang Tingxi 蔣廷錫 (1669–1732), eds, *Gujin tushu jicheng* 古今圖書集成. Shanghai: Tushu jicheng yinshuju, 1884.

Cheng Ju 程俱 (1078–1144), ed. *Minggong shupan qingming ji* 明公書判清明集. Beijing: Zhonghua shuju, 2002.

Ding Chuanjing 丁傳靖 (1870–1930), ed. *Songren yishi huibian* 宋人軼事彙編, 3 vols. Beijing: Zhonghua shuju, 1981.

Dou Yi 竇儀 (914–966) et al. *Song xingtong* 宋刑統. Beijing: Zhonghua shuju, 1984.

Fan Zhen 范鎮 (1007–1088). *Dongzhai jishi* 東齋記事. Beijing: Zhonghua shuju, 1980.

Fan Zhiming 范致明 (fl. 1100). *Yueyang fengtuji* 岳陽風土記. In QSBJ, 2nd series, vol. 7.

Fan Zhongyan 范仲淹 (989–1052). *Fan Zhongyan quanshu* 范仲淹全書. Nanjing: Fenghuang chuban she, 2004.

Fang Shao 方勺 (b. 1066). *Bozhai bian* 泊宅編. In QSBJ, 2nd series, vol. 8.

Han Qi 韓琦 (1008–1075). *Han Weigong ji* 韓魏公集. Shanghai: Shangwu yinshuguan, 1937.

He Wei 何薳 (1077–1145). *Chunzhu jiwen* 春渚紀聞. Beijing: Zhonghua shuju, 1983.

Hong Mai 洪邁 (1123–1202). *Yijian zhi* 夷堅志. Beijing: Zhonghua shuju, 1981.

Huihong 惠洪 (1070–1128). *Lengzhai yehua* 冷齋夜話. In QSBJ, 2nd series, vol.9.

Jiang Xiaoyu 江少虞 (d. ca. 1131). *Songchao shishi leiyuan* 宋朝事實類苑. Shanghai: Shanghai guji chubanshe, 1981.

Jiang Xiufu 江休復 (1005–1065). *Jiang Linji zazhi* 江鄰幾雜志. QSBJ, 1 series, vol. 5.

Kong Pingzhong 孔平仲 (fl. 1065). *Tanyuan* 談苑. In QSBJ, 2nd series, vol. 5.

Li Gou 李覯 (1009–1059). *Li Gou ji* 李覯集. Beijing: Zhonghua shuju, 1981.

Li Tao 李燾 (1115–1184). *Xu zizhi tongjian changbian* 續資治通鑑長編, 34 vols. Beijing: Zhonghua shuju, 1979–1993.

Li Xinchuan 李心傳 (1167–1224). *Jianyan yilai chaoye zaji* 建炎以來朝夜雜記. Beijing: Zhonghua shuju, 2000.

Li You 李攸 (fl. 1134). *Songchao shishi* 宋朝事實. Taipei: Guangwen shuju, 1980.

Li Yuangang 李元剛 (fl. 11–12th cent.). Houde lu 厚德錄. In Shuofu 說郛, edited by Tao Zongyi, j. 94. Shanghai: Shanghai shangwu, 1927.

Li Zhi 李廌 (1059–1109). *Shiyou tanji* 師友談記. In QSBJ, 2nd series, vol. 7.

Li Zhiyan 李之彥 (fl. 11th cent.). *Donggu suibi* 東谷隨筆. In *Biji xiaoshuo daguan*, 6th series, vol. 3. Taipei: Xinxing shuju, 1975.

Liu Fu 劉斧 (fl. 11th cent.), *Qingsuo gaoyi* 青瑣高議. In QSBJ, 3rd series, vol. 4.

Liu Jingshu 劉敬叔 (fl. 404). *Yiyuan* 異苑. Beijing, Zhonghua shuju, 1996.

Nie Chongyi 聶崇義 (fl. 10th cent.). *Sanlitu jizhu* 三禮圖集注. In *Yingyin Wenyuangge Siku quanshu*, vol. 129. Taipei: Taiwan shangwu yinshuguan, 1983–1986.

Ouyang Xiu 歐陽修 (1007–1072). *Ouyang xiu quanji* 歐陽修全集, 6 vols. Beijing: Zhonghua shuju, 2001.

Peng Cheng 彭乘 (985–1049). *Xu Moke huixi* 續墨客揮犀. Rpr. with Zhao Lingzhi, *Houqing lu* 侯鯖錄, and Peng Cheng, *Moke huixi* 墨客揮犀. Beijing: Zhonghua shuju, 2002.

Ruan Yuan 阮元 (1764–1849), ed. *Yili zhushu* 儀禮註疏. In *Shisan jing zhushu: Fu jiaokanji* 十三經註疏, 附校勘記. Beijing: Zhonghua shuju, 1980.

Ruan Yue 阮閱 (fl. 1127). *Shihua zonggui houji* 詩話總龜後集. Beijing: Renmin wenxue chubanshe, 1987.

Shao Bo 邵博 (d. 1158). *Shaoshi wenjian houlu* 邵氏聞見後錄. In QSBJ, 4th series, vol. 6.

Shao Bowen 邵伯温 (1057–1134), *Shaoshi wenjian lu* 邵氏聞見錄. Beijing: Zhonghua shuju, 1997.

Shen Kuo 沈括 (1030–1095). *Mengxi bitan* 夢溪筆談. In QSBJ, 2nd series, vol. 3.

Shi Su 施宿 (1164–1222). *Kuaiji zhi* 會稽志. Yingyin Wenyuange Siku quanshu, vol. 486. Taipei: Taiwan Shangwu yinshuguan, 1983.

Sima Guang 司馬光 (1019–1086). *Sima shi shuyi* 司馬氏書儀. Congshu jicheng, vol. 35, Changsha: Shangwu yinshuguan, 1935–1937.

————. *Sima Wengong wenji* 司馬溫公文集. Shanghai: Shangwu yinshu guan, 1937.

————. *Sushui jiwen* 涑水記聞. In QSBJ, 1st series, vol. 7.

————. *Zizhi tongjian* 資治通鑑. Beijing: Zhonghua shuju, 1981.

Song Minqiu 宋敏求 (1019–1079). *Cunming tuicaolu* 春明退朝錄. Beijing: Zhonghua shuju, 1980.

Song Minqiu 宋敏求 (1019–1079) and Song Shou 宋綬 (991–1040), eds. *Song da zhaoling ji* 宋大詔令集. Beijing: Zhonghua shuju, 1962.

Song Qi 宋祁 (998–1061). *Song Jingwengong biji* 宋景文公筆記. In QSBJ, 1st series, vol. 5.

Su Shi 蘇軾 (1037–1101). *Su Shi wenji* 蘇軾文集. Beijing: Zhonghua shuju, 1986.

————. *Dongpo zhilin* 東坡志林. In QSBJ, 1st series, vol. 9.

Su Zhe 蘇轍 (1039–1112). *Su huangmen Longchuan lüezhi* 蘇黃門龍川略志. In *Congshu jicheng chubian*, vol. 3887. Shanghai: Shangwu yinshuguan, 1935–1940.

Sun Sheng 孫升 (1038–1099). *Sungong tanpu* 孫公談圃. In QSBJ, 2nd series, vol. 1.

Sun Xidan 孫希旦 (1736–1784), ed. *Liji jijie* 禮記集解, 3 vols. Beijing: Zhonghua shuju, 1989.

Sun Zongjian 孫宗鑒 (fl. 1119). *Xishi suolu* 西畬瑣錄. In QSBJ, 3rd series, vol. 4.

Tao Zongyi 陶宗儀 (1360–1368), ed. *Shuofu* 說郛. Ming chaoben jiaozheng paiyin ben 明鈔本校正排印本. Shanghai: Shanghai shangwu, 1927.

Tian Kuang 田況 (1003–1061). *Rulin gongyi* 儒林公議. In QSBJ, 1st series, vol. 5.

Tuotuo 脫脫 (1313–1355). *Songshi* 宋史. Beijing: Zhonghua shuju, 1977.

Wang Anshi 王安石 (1021–1086). *Wang Linchuan ji* 王臨川集. Shanghai: Shangwu yinshuguan, 1933.

Wang Cun 王存 (11th cent.). *Yuanfeng jiuyu zhi* 元豐九域志. Taipei: Wenhai chubanshe, 1963.

Wang Su 王素 (1007–1073). *Wenzheng Wanggong yishi* 文正王公遺事. In QSBJ, 1st series, vol. 4.

Wang Yong 王栐 (fl. 1227). *Yanyi yimou lu* 燕翼藝謀錄. Rpr. with Wang Zhi 王銍, *Moji* 默記. Beijing: Zhonghua shuju, 1997.

Wang Yucheng 王禹偁 (954–1001). *Xiaoxu ji* 小畜集. Taipei: Taiwan shangwu yinshuguan, 1963.

Wei Tai 魏泰 (fl. 11th–12th cent.). *Dongxuan bilu* 東軒筆錄. In QSBJ, 2nd series, vol. 8.

Wei Xinzi 委心子 (fl. 1169), ed. *Xinbian fenmen gujin leishi* 新編分門古今類事. 3 vols. Shanghai: Shangwu yinshuguan, 1937.

Wen Ying 文瑩 (11th cent.). *Xu Xiangshan yelu* 續湘山野錄. Beijing: Zhonghua shuju, 1997.

————. *Yuhu qinghua* 玉壺清話. Beijing: Zhonghua shuju, 1997.

Wu Jian 吳幵 (fl. 11–12th cent.). *Mantang suibi* 漫堂随筆. In *Shuofu* 說郛, edited by Tao Zongyi, j. 64. Shanghai: Shanghai shangwu, 1927.

Xiao Song 蕭嵩 (8th cent.) et al. *Da Tang Kaiyuan li* 大唐開元禮. In *Yingyin Wenyuangge Siku quanshu*, vol. 646. Taipei: Taiwan shangwu yinshuguan, 1983–1986.

Xu Song 徐松 (1781–1848) et al. *Song huiyao jigao* 宋會要輯稿. Beijing: Zhonghua shuju, 1957.

————. *Song huiyao jigao bubian* 宋會要緝稿補編. Beijing: Xinhua shuju, 1988.

Xunzi 荀子 (c. 310–c. 220 BCE). *Xunzi* 荀子. Taipei: Taiwan shangwu yinshuguan, 1969.

Yang Bojun 楊伯峻, ed. *Chunqiu Zuozhuan zhu* 春秋左傳注, 4 vols. Beijing: Zhonghua shuju, 1981.

Yang Zhonglang 陽仲良 (13th cent.). *Tongjian changbian jishi benmo* 通鑑長編紀事本末. Taipei: Wenhai chubanshe, 1967.

Ye Mengde 葉夢得 (1077–1148). *Bishu luhua* 避暑錄話. In QSBJ, 2nd series, vol. 10.

————. *Shilin yanyu* 石林燕語. Beijing: Zhonghua shuju, 1984.

Zeng Minxing 曾敏行 (1118–1175). *Duxing zazhi* 獨醒雜志. In QSBJ, 4th series, vol. 4.

Zeng Zaozhuang 曾棗莊 et al. *Quan Song wen* 全宋文, 360 vols. Shanghai: Shanghai Cishu chubanshe; Hefei: Anhui Jiaoyu chubanshe, 2006.

Zhang Qixian 張齊賢 (943–1014). *Luoyang jinshen jiu wenji* 洛陽搢紳舊聞記. QSBJ, 1st series.

Zhang Shizheng 張師正 (b. 1016). *Kuoyi zhi* 括異志. Sibu congkan xubian, vol. 56. Shanghai: Shanghai shudian, 1985.

————. *Juanyou zalu* 倦遊雜錄. Rpr. with Yang Yi 楊億, *Yang Wengong Tanyuan* 楊文公談苑. Shanghai: Shanghai guji chubanshe, 1993.

Zhang Zai 張載 (1020–1077). *Zhang Zai ji* 張載集. Beijing: Zhonghua shuju 1978.

Zhao Lingzhi 趙令畤 (1051–1107). *Houqing lu* 侯鯖錄. In QSBJ, 2nd series, vol. 6.

Zhao Ruyu 趙汝愚 (1140–1196), ed. *Songchao zhuchen zouyi* 宋朝諸臣奏議. Shanghai: Shanghai guji chubanshe, 1999.

Zheng Juzhong 鄭居中 (1059–1123) et al. *Zhenghe wuli xinyi* 政和五禮新儀. In *Yingyin Wenyuangge Siku quanshu*, vol. 647. Taipei: Taiwan shangwu yinshuguan, 1983–1986.

Zhongguo shehui kexueyuan, Lishi yanjiusuo 中國社會科學院歷史研究所, annot. *Tianyige cang mingchaoben Tianshengling jiaozheng: Fu Tangling fuyuan yanjiu* 天一閣藏明鈔本天聖令校證:附唐令復原研究, Beijing: Zhonghua shuju, 2006.

Zhou Hui 周煇 (b. 1126). *Qingpo zazhi jiaozhu* 清波雜誌校注, annotated by Liu Yongxiang 劉永翔. Beijing: Zhonghua, 1994.

Zhu Yi'an 朱易安 et al., ed. *Quan Song biji* 全宋筆記. Ser. 1–4, 40 vols. Zhengzhou: Daxiang chubanshe, 2003–2008.

Zhu Yu 朱彧 (d. ca. 1148). *Pingzhou ketan* 萍洲可談. In QSBJ, 2nd series, vol. 6.

Zuo Qiuming 左丘明 (ca. 502–422 BCE). *Zuo Zhuan* 左傳. Changsha: Hunan renmin chubanshe, 1996.

MODERN SOURCES

Ahern, Emily Martin. *Chinese Rituals and Politics.* Cambridge, UK: Cambridge University Press, 1981.

Allen, Sarah M. *Shifting Stories: History, Gossip, and Lore in Narratives from Tang Dynasty China.* Cambridge, MA: Harvard Asia Center, 2014.

Asim, Ina. "Status Symbol and Insurance Policy: Song Land Deeds for the Afterlife." In *Burial in Song China,* edited by Dieter Kuhn, 307–370. Heidelberg: Forum, 1994.

Bai Wengu 白文固. "Songdai de gongdesi he fensi" 宋代的功德寺和墳寺. *Qinghai shehui kexue* 青海社会科学, no. 5 (2000): 76–80.

Bell, Catherine M. *Ritual Theory, Ritual Practice.* New York: Oxford University Press, 1992.

______. *Ritual: Perspectives and Dimensions.* New York: Oxford University Press, 1997.

Benn, Charles. "Religious Aspects of Emperor Hsüan-tsung's Taoist Ideology." In *Buddhist and Daoist Practices in Medieval Chinese Society,* edited by David W. Chappell, 127–145. Honolulu: University of Hawaii Press, 1987.

Bloch, Maurice, and Jonathan Parry, eds. *Death and the Regeneration of Life.* Cambridge; New York: Cambridge University Press, 1982.

Bol, Peter. "The Sung Examination System and the *Shi.*" *Asia Major* 3, 3rd series, no. 2 (1990): 149–172.

______. *This Culture of Ours: Intellectual Transition in T'ang and Sung China.* Stanford, CA: Stanford University Press, 1992.

______. "Government, Society, and State: On the Political Visions of Ssu-Ma Kuang and Wang An-shih." In *Ordering the World: Approaches to State and Society in Sung China,* edited by Robert Hymes and Conrad Schirokauer, 177–181. Berkeley: University of California Press, 1993.

______. "The Examinations and Orthodoxies: 1070 and 1313 Compared." In *Culture and State in Chinese History: Conventions, Accommodations, and Critiques,* edited by Theodore Huters, R. Bin Wong, and Pauline Yu, 29–57. Stanford, CA: Stanford University Press, 1997.

Boltz, Judith. "Not by the Seal of Official Alone: New Weapons in Battles with the Supernatural." In *Religion and Society in T'ang and Sung China,* edited by Patricia Buckley Ebrey and Peter N. Gregory, 241–305. Honolulu: University of Hawaii Press, 1993.

Bossler, Beverly Jo. *Powerful Relations: Kinship, Status, and State in Sung China (960–1279).* Cambridge, MA: Harvard Asia Center, 1998.

______. "Gender and Entertainment at the Song Court." In *Servants of the Dynasty: Palace Women in World History,* edited by Anne Walthall, 261–279. Berkeley: University of California Press, 2008.

Bourdieu, Pierre. *Distinction: A Social Critique of the Judgment of Taste,* translated by Richard Nice. Cambridge, MA: Harvard University Press, 1984.

Brashier, K. E. "Text and Ritual in Early Chinese Stele." In *Text and Ritual in Early China*, edited by Martin Kern, 249–284. Seattle: University of Washington Press, 2005.

———. *Public Memory in Early China*. Cambridge, MA: Harvard University Asia Center, 2014.

Brook, Timothy. "Funerary Ritual and the Building of Lineage in Late Imperial China." *Harvard Journal of Asiatic Studies* 49, no. 2 (1989): 465–495.

Brown, Miranda. *The Politics of Mourning in Early China*. Albany: State University of New York Press, 2012.

Bruun, Ole. *An Introduction to Feng Shui*. New York: Cambridge University Press, 2008.

Cahill, Suzanne. "Taoism at the Sung Court: The Heavenly Text Affair of 1008." *Bulletin of Sung and Yüan Studies* 16 (1980): 23–44.

Cai Shangsi 蔡尚思. *Zhongguo lijiao sixiang shi* 中國禮教思想史. Hong Kong: Zhonghua shuju, 1991.

Campany, Robert. *Strange Writing: Anomaly Accounts in Early Medieval China*. Albany: State University of New York Press, 1996.

———. "Tales of Strange Events." In *Early Medieval China: A Sourcebook*, edited by Wendy Swartz, Robert Campany, Yang Lu, and Jessey J. C. Choo, 576–591. New York: Columbia University Press, 2014.

Casey, Edward S. *Imagining: A Phenomenological Study*. Bloomington and London: Indiana University Press, 1979.

Castoriadis, Cornelius. *The Imaginary Institution of Society*, translated by Kathleen Blamey. Cambridge, UK: Polity Press, 1987.

———. "Radical Imagination and the Social Instituting Imaginary." In *Rethinking Imagination: Culture and Creativity*, edited by Gillian Robinson and John Rundell, 136–154. London and New York: Routledge, 1994.

Chaffee, John W. *The Thorny Gates of Learning in Sung China: A Social History of Examinations*. Albany: State University of New York Press, 1995.

———. "The Rise and Regency of Empress Liu (969–1033)." *Journal of Sung–Yuan Studies* 31 (2002): 1–25.

Chaffee, John W., and Denis Twitchett, eds. *The Cambridge History of China*, vol. 5, part 2: *Sung China, 960–1279*. Cambridge, UK: Cambridge University Press, 2015.

Chao, Shin-yi. *Daoist Rituals, State Religion, and Popular Practices: Zhenwu Worship from Song to Ming (960—1644)*. London and New York: Routledge, 2011.

Chen Dingrong 陳定榮 and Xu Jianchang 徐建昌. "Jiangxi Linchuanxian Songmu" 江西川臨縣宋墓. *Kaogu* 考古, no. 4 (1988): 329–334.

Cheng Ju 程俱. *The Enlightened Judgments: Ch'ing-ming Chi: The Sung Dynasty Collection*, translated by Brian E. McKnight and James T. C. Liu, annotated by Brian E. McKnight. Albany: State University of New York Press, 1999.

Chengdushi wenwu kaogu gongzuodui 成都市文物考古工作隊. "Chengdu Beijiao Ganyoucun faxian BeiSong Xuanhe liunian mu" 成都北郊甘油村發現北宋宣和六年墓. *Sichuan wenwu* 四川文物, no. 3 (1999): 114–117.

Chien, Edward T. "The Neo-Confucian Confrontation with Buddhism: A Structural and Historical Analysis." *Journal of Chinese Philosophy* 9 (1982): 307–328.

Chikusa Masaaki 竺沙雅章. "Sōdai bunji kō" 宋代墳寺考. *Toyo gakuho* 東洋學報 61 (1979): 35–66.

————. "Sōsho no Seiji to shūkyo 宋初の政治と宗教." In *Collected Studies on Sung History Dedicated to Professor James T. C. Liu in Celebration of His Seventieth Birthday* (劉子健博士頌寿紀年宋史研究論集), edited by Tsuyoshi Kinagawa, 179–195. Kyoto: Tohosa, 1989.

Cheng Ya-ju 鄭雅如, *Qinggan yu zhidu: WeiJin shidai de muzi guanxi* 情感與制度: 魏晉時代的母子關係. Taipei: Guoli Taiwan daxue chuban weiyuanhui, 2001.

Choi, Mihwa. "State Suppression of Buddhism and Royal Patronage of the Ritual of Water and Land in the Early Chosŏn Dynasty." *Seoul Journal of Korean Studies* 22, no. 2 (2009): 181–214.

————. "Extreme Asceticism: Confucian Practice and Riesebrodt's Religious Virtuoso." *Journal for the Scientific Study of Religion* 51, no. 3 (2012): 456–467.

————. "Materializing Salvation: A Liturgical Program and Its Agenda." *Journal of Daoist Studies* 6 (2013): 29–57.

Chongqing Dazu shike yishu bowuguan 重慶大足石刻藝術博物館. "Chongqing Dazu Longshuizhen mingguangcun Mo'erpo Songmu qingli jianbao" 重慶大足龍水镇明光村磨兒坡宋墓清理簡報. *Sichuan wenwu* 四川文物, no. 5 (2002): 3–7.

Chou, Kai-Wing. "Between Canonicity and Heterodoxy: Hermeneutical Moments of the Great Learning (Ta-hsueh)." In *Imagining Boundaries,* edited by Kai-wing Chow, On-Cho Ng, and John Henderson, 147–163. Albany: State University of New York Press, 1999.

————. *The Rise of Confucian Ritualism in Late Imperial China: Ethics, Classics, and Lineage Discourse.* Stanford, CA: Stanford University Press, 1994.

Cole, Alan. "Upside Down/Right Side Up: A Revisionist History of Buddhist Funerals in China." *History of Religions* 35, no. 4 (1996): 310–338.

Collins, Steven. *Nirvana and Other Buddhist Felicities.* New York: Cambridge University Press, 1998.

Davis, Edward L. *Society and the Supernatural in Song China.* Honolulu: University of Hawaii Press, 2001.

Davis, Richard L. *Court and Family in Sung China, 960–1279: Bureaucratic Success and Kinship Fortunes for the Shih of Ming-chou.* Durham: Duke University Press, 1986.

Davis, Timothy M. "Potent Stone: Entombed Epigraphy and Memorial Culture in Early Medieval China." PhD diss., Columbia University, 2008.

De Pee, Christian. *The Writing of Weddings in Middle-Period China: Text and Ritual Practice in the Eighth through the Fourteenth Centuries.* Albany: State University of New York Press, 2007.

————. "Purchase on Power: Imperial Space and Commercial Space in Song-Dynasty Kaifeng, 960–1127." *Journal of the Economic and Social History of the Orient* 52, no. 4–5 (2009): 760–794.

Ding Chuanjing 丁傳靖, ed. *A Compilation of Anecdotes of Sung Personalities*, translated by Chu Djang and Jane C. Djang. Collegeville, MN: St. John's University Press, 1989.

Duby, Georges. *The Three Orders: Feudal Society Imagined*, translated by Arthur Goldhammer. Chicago: University of Chicago Press, 1980.

Dudbridge, Glen. *Religious Experience and Lay Society in T'ang China: A Reading of Tai Fu's* Kuang-i chi. Cambridge: Cambridge University Press, 1995.

Ebner von Eschenbach, Silvia Freiin. "Public Graveyards of the Song Dynasty." In *Burial in Song China*, edited by Dieter Kuhn, 215–252. Heidelberg: Forum, 1994.

Ebrey, Patricia Buckley. "Education through Ritual: Efforts to Formulate Family Rituals During the Sung Period." In *Neo-Confucian Education: The Formative Stage*, edited by Wm. Theodore de Bary and John W. Chaffee, 277–306. Berkeley: University of California Press, 1989.

———. "Cremation in Song China." *American Historical Review* 95, no. 2 (1990): 406–428.

———. *Chu Hsi's "Family Rituals": A Twelfth-century Chinese Manual for the Performance of Cappings, Weddings, Funerals, and Ancestral Rites*. Princeton, NJ: Princeton University Press, 1991.

———. *Confucianism and Family Rituals in Imperial China: A Social History of Writing about Rites*. Princeton, NJ: Princeton University Press, 1991.

———. "The Response of the Sung State to Popular Funeral Practice." In *Religion and Society in T'ang and Sung China*, edited by Patricia Buckley Ebrey and Peter N. Gregory, 209–239. Honolulu: University of Hawaii Press, 1993.

———. "The Liturgies for Sacrifices to Ancestors in Successive Versions of the Family Rituals." In *Ritual and Scripture in Chinese Popular Religion*, edited by David Johnson, 104–136. Berkeley, CA: Publications of the Chinese Popular Culture.

———. "Portrait Sculptures in Imperial Ancestral Rites in Song China." *T'oung Pao* 87, no. 1 (1997): 42–92.

———. "Taking out the Grand Carriage Imperial Spectacle and the Visual Culture of Northern Song Kaifeng." *Asia Major* 12, 3rd series, no. 1 (1999): 33–65.

Egan Ronald. *The Literary Works of Ou-yang Hsiu (1007–72)*. Cambridge, UK: Cambridge University Press, 1984.

———. *Word, Image, and Deed in the Life of Su Shi*. Cambridge, MA: Council on East Asian Studies, Harvard University, 1994.

Eliade, Mircea. *Myth and Reality*, translated by Willard R. Trask. New York: Harper & Row, 1963.

———. *The Myth of the Eternal Return: Cosmos and History*, translated by Willard R. Trask. Princeton, NJ: Princeton University Press, 1971.

Elvin, Mark. *The Pattern of the Chinese Past*. Stanford, CA: Stanford University Press, 1973.

Faitler, Demerie Paula. "Confucian Historiography and the Thought of Ssu-ma Kuang." PhD diss., University of Michigan, 1991.

Fan Lidan 范立丹. "Songru dui lixiang shehui de gouxiang" 宋儒對理想社會的構想. *Hangzhou daxue xuebao zhexue shehui kexue* 杭州大學學報 哲學社會科學 27, no. 3 (1997): 99–105.

Faure, Bernard. *Visions of Power: Imagining Medieval Japanese Buddhism*, translated by Phyllis Brooks. Princeton, NJ: Princeton University Press, 1996.

Fisher, Carney T. "The Ritual Dispute of Sung Ying-tsung." *Papers on Far Eastern History* 36 (1987): 109–137.

Fujikawa Masakazu 藤川正數, *Gishin jidai ni okeru mofuku rei no kenkyû* 魏晉時代おける喪服禮の研究. Tokyo: Keibunsha, 1961.

Gardner, Daniel K. "Ghost and Spirit in the Sung Neo-Confucian World: Chu Hsi on *Kuei-Shen*." *Journal of the American Oriental Society* 115, no. 4 (1995): 598–611.

Glahan, Richard von. *The Sinister Way: The Divine and the Demonic in Chinese Religious Culture*. Berkeley: University of California Press, 2004.

Golas, Peter J., "The Sung Fiscal Administration." In *The Cambridge History of China*, vol. 5, part 2: *Sung China, 960–1279*, edited by John W. Chaffee and Denis Twitchett, 139–213. Cambridge, UK: Cambridge University Press, 2015.

Goldin, Paul. "The Consciousness of the Dead as a Philosophical Problem in Ancient China." In *The Good Life and Conceptions of Life in Early China and Graeco-Roman Antiquity*, edited by R. A. H. King, 59–92. Berlin: De Gruyter, 2015.

Gregory, Peter N., and Daniel A. Getz, Jr., eds. *Buddhism in the Sung*. Honolulu: University of Hawaii Press, 1999.

Gregory, Peter N., and Patricia B. Ebrey. "The Religious and Historical Landscape." In *Religion and Society in T'ang and Sung China*, edited by Patricia Buckley Ebrey and Peter N. Gregory, 1–44. Honolulu: University of Hawaii Press, 1993.

Gruzinski, Serge. *The Conquest of Mexico: The Incorporation of Indian Societies into the Western World, 16th–18th Centuries*, translated by Eileen Corrigan. Cambridge, MA: Blackwell, 1993.

———. *Images at War: Mexico from Columbus to Blade Runner (1492–2019)*, translated by Heather MacLean. Durham and London: Duke University Press, 2001.

Gu Kuixiang 顧奎相, *Sima Guang* 司馬光. Harbin: Heilongjiang Renmin chubanshe, 1985.

Gu Quanfang 顧全芳. "Sima Guang yu Wang Anshi bianfa" 司馬光與王安石變法. *Jinyang xuekan* 晉陽學刊, no. 2 (1984): 67–74.

Haeger, John Winthrop, ed. *Crisis and Prosperity in Sung China*. Tucson: University of Arizona Press, 1975.

Hagen, Kurtis. "Xunzi and the Nature of Confucian Ritual." *Journal of the American Academy of Religion* 71, no. 2 (2003): 371–403.

Halperin, Mark Robert. "Buddhist Temples, War Dead, and the Song Imperial Court." *Asia Major* 12, 3rd series, no. 2 (1999): 71–99.

Hansen, Valerie. *Changing Gods in Medieval China, 1127–1276*. Princeton, NJ: Princeton University Press, 1990.

———. *Negotiating Daily Life in Traditional China; How Ordinary People Used Contracts, 600–1400*. New Haven: Yale University Press, 1995.

_______. *The Open Empire: A History of China to 1600*. New York: W. W. Norton, 2000.

Hartwell, Robert M. "The Evolution of the Early Northern Sung Monetary System, A. D. 960–1025." *Journal of the American Oriental Society* 87, no. 3 (1967): 280–289.

_______. "Financial Expertise, Examinations, and the Formulation of Economic Policy in Northern Sung China." *The Journal of Asian Studies* 30, no. 2 (1971): 281–314.

_______. "Demographic, Political, and Social Transformations of China, 750–1550." *Harvard Journal of Asiatic Studies* 42, no. 2 (1982): 365–442.

Hawkes, David, trans. *Ch'u Tz'u: The Songs of the South: An Ancient Chinese Anthology*. Boston: Beacon Press, 1962.

He Shuyi 何淑宜. "Yi li hua su: WanMing shishen de sangsu gaige sixiang ji qi shijian" 以禮化俗—晚明士紳的喪俗改革思想及其實踐. *Xin shixue* 新史學 11, no. 3 (2000): 49–100.

Henderson, John. "Strategies in Neo-Confucian Heresiography." In *Imagining Boundaries*, edited by Kai-wing Chow, On-Cho Ng, and John Henderson, 107–120. Albany: State University of New York Press, 1999.

Holzman, Donald. "The Image of the Merchant in Medieval Chinese Poetry." In *Immortals, Festivals and Poetry in Medieval China*, 92–108. Brookfield, VT: Ashgate, 1988.

Hong Jinchun 洪錦淳. *Shuilu fahui yigui* 水陸法會儀軌. Taipei: Wenjin chubanshe, 2006.

Hou Chinglang. *Monnaies d'offrande et la notion de trésorerie dans la religion chinoise*. Paris: Collège de France, Institut des Hautes Etudes Chinoises, 1975.

Huang Chi-chiang. "Imperial Rulership and Buddhism in the Early Northern Sung." In *Imperial Rulership and Cultural Change in Traditional China*, edited by Fredrick P. Brandauer and Chi-chiang Huang, 149–158. Seattle: University of Washington Press, 1994.

Huang Minglan 黃明蘭 and Gong Dazhong 宮大中. "Luoyang BeiSong Zhangjun mu huaxiang shiguan" 洛陽北宋張君墓畫像石棺. *Wenwu* 文物, no. 7 (1984): 79–81.

Huang Qijiang 黃啓江. "Wang Qinruo yu Daojiao" 王欽若與道教. *Jiangxi Shehui kexue* 江西社會科學, no. 5 (1994): 59–61.

Huang Zhengjian 黃正建, ed. *Tiansheng ling yu Tang Song zhidu yanjiu* 《天聖令》與唐宋制度研究. Beijing: Zhongguo shehui kexue chubanshe, 2011.

Hucker, Charles O. *A Dictionary of Official Titles in Imperial China*. Stanford, CA: Stanford University Press, 1985.

Hymes, Robert P. *Statesmen and Gentlemen: The Elites of Fu-Chou, Chiang-Hsi, in Northern and Southern Song*. Cambridge, UK: Cambridge University Press, 1986.

_______. "Personal Relations and Bureaucratic Hierarchy in Chinese Religions: Evidence from the Song Dynasty." In *Unruly Gods: Divinity and Society in China*, edited by Meir Shahar and Robert Weller, 37–69. Honolulu: University of Hawaii Press, 1996.

______. "Sung Society and Social Change." In *The Cambridge History of China,* vol. 5, part 2: *Sung China, 960–1279,* edited by John W. Chaffee and Denis Twitchett, 526–664. New York: Cambridge University Press, 2015.

Hymes, Robert P., and Conrad Schirokauer, eds. *Ordering the World: Approaches to State and Society in Sung China.* Berkeley: University of California Press, 1993.

Ikeda On 池田温. "Chūgoku rekidai boken ryakukō" 中国歴代墓券略考. *Tōyō bunka kenkyūjo kiyō* 東洋文化研究所紀要 86 (1981): 193–278.

Ing, Michael. *The Dysfunction of Ritual in Early Confucianism.* New York: Oxford University Press, 2012.

Inglis, Alister D. *Hong Mai's* Record of the Listener *and Its Song Dynasty Context.* Albany: State University of New York Press, 2006.

Ji, Xiao-bin. *Politics and Conservatism in Northern Song China: The Career and Thought of Sima Guang (A.D. 1019–1086).* Hong Kong: Chinese University Press, 2005.

Johnson, David G. "The Last Years of a Great Clan: The Li Family of Chao chün in Late T'ang and Early Sung." *Harvard Journal of Asiatic Studies* 37, no. 1 (1977): 5–102.

Kearney, Richard. *Poetics of Imagining: Modern to Post-modern.* New York: Fordham University Press, 1998.

Kida Tomoo 木田知生. *Shiba Kō to sono jidai* 司馬光とその時代. Tokyo: Hakutei sha, 1994.

______. "Shiba kō no bukkyo kan: Sōdai shitaifu no bukkyō juyō no ichi keitai" 司馬光の仏教觀—宋代士大夫の仏教受容の一形態. *Ryūkoku daigaku ryonshū* 龍谷大學論集 448 (1996): 207–228.

Kleeman, Terry. "Land Contracts and Related Documents." In *Chūgoku no shūkyō, shisō to kagaku: Makio Ryōkai hakase shōju kinen ronshū* 中国の宗教,思想と科学: 牧尾良海博士頌寿記念論集, edited by Makio Ryōkai hakushi shōju kinen ronshū kankōkai, 1–34. Tokyo: Kokusho Kankōkai, 1984.

Knapp, Keith N. "Borrowing Legitimacy from the Dead: The Confucianization of Ancestral Worship." In *Early Chinese Religion, Part Two: The Period of Division (220–589 AD),* edited by John Lagerwey and Lü Pengzhi, 1: 143–192. Leiden: Brill, 2010.

Kojima Tsuyoshi 小島毅. "Sōdai tenkenron no seiji shisō" 宋代天譴論の政治思想. *Tōyō bunka kenkyūjo kiyō* 東洋文化研究所紀要 107 (1988): 1–87.

______. "Koshi seido no hensen" 郊祀制度の變遷. *Tōyō bunka kenkyūjo kiyō* 東洋文化研究所紀要 108 (1989): 123–219.

Kracke, Edward A., Jr. *Civil Service in Early Sung China: 960–1067.* Cambridge, MA: Harvard University Press, 1953.

______. "Sung K'ai-feng: Pragmatic Metropolis and Formalistic Capital." In *Crisis and Property in Sung China,* edited by John Winthrop Haeger, 49–77. Tucson: University of Arizona Press, 1975.

Kroll, Paul W. "Spreading Open the Barrier of Heaven." *Asiatische Studien/Etudes Asiatiques* 40, no. 1 (1986): 22–39.

Kuhn, Dieter. "Decoding Tombs of the Song Elites." In *Burial in Song China*, edited by Dieter Kuhn, 11–159. Heidelberg: Forum, 1994.

———. *A Place for the Dead: An Archeological Documentary on Graves and Tombs of the Song Dynasty (960–1279)*. Heidelberg: Forum, 1996.

Kutcher, Norman. *Mourning in Late Imperial China: Filial Piety and the State*. New York: Cambridge University Press, 1999.

Lagerway, John. *Taoist Ritual in Chinese Society and History*. New York: Macmillan, 1987.

Lai, Guolong. "The Diagram of the Mourning System from Mawangdui." *Early China* 28 (2003): 45–99.

Langlois, John D., Jr. "'Living Law' in Sung and Yuan Jurisprudence." *Harvard Journal of Asiatic Studies* 41, no. 1 (1981): 165–217.

Le Goff, Jacques. *The Medieval Imagination*, translated by Arthur Goldhammer. Chicago and London: University of Chicago Press, 1985.

Levering, Miriam. "Ta-hui and Lay Buddhists: Ch'an Sermons on Death." In *Buddhist and Daoist Practices in Medieval Chinese Society*, edited by David W. Chappell, 181–209. Honolulu: University of Hawaii Press, 1987.

Levine, Arie Daniel. *Divided by a Common Language: Factional Conflict in Late Northern Song China*. Honolulu: University of Hawaii Press, 2008.

Lewis, Mark Edward. "The *Feng* and *Shan* Sacrifices of Emperor Wu of the Han." In *State and Court Ritual in China*, edited by Joseph P. McDermott, 50–80. Cambridge: Cambridge University Press, 1999.

Li Wenming 李文明 and Li Huren 李虎仁. "Nanjing Luying Songmu qingli jianbao" 南京陸營宋墓清理簡報. *Dongnan wenhua* 東南文化, no. 2 (1995): 15–21.

Liao, Hsien-Huei. "Visualizing the Afterlife: The Song Elite's Obsession with Death, the Underworld, and Salvation." *Hanxue yanjiu* 漢學研究 20, no. 1 (2002): 399–440.

———. "Encountering Evil: Ghosts and Demonic Forces in the Lives of the Song Elite." *Journal of Song–Yuan Studies* 37 (2007): 89–134.

Lin, Wei-Cheng. "Underground Wooden Architecture in Brick: A Changed Perspective from Life to Death in 11th- through 13th-century Northern China." *Archives of Asian Art* 61 (2011): 3–36.

Lincoln, Bruce. *Authority: Construction and Corrosion*. Chicago: University of Chicago Press, 1994.

Lippiello, Tiziana. *Auspicious Omens and Miracles in Ancient China: Han, Three Kingdoms and Six Dynasties*. Sankt Augustin, Germany: Monumenta Serica Institute, 2001.

Liu Fusheng 劉復生. "BeiSong zhongqi ruxue fuxing yundong" 北宋中期儒學復興運動. *Wenxian* 文献, no. 1 (1991): 151–159.

Liu, James T. C. *Ou-yang Hsiu: An Eleventh-century Neo-Confucianism*. Stanford, CA: Stanford University Press, 1967.

________. "How did a Neo-Confucian School Become the State Orthodoxy?" *Philosophy East and West* 23, no. 4 (1973): 483–506.

________. "The Sung Emperors and the Ming-t'ang or Hall of Enlightenment." In *Études Song: In Memoriam Étienne Balazs*, Série II, edited by Françoise Aubin, 45–57. Paris: Mouton, 1973.

Liu Jianzhou 劉建洲. "Zhengzhou Nanguan wai faxian yizuo Songmu" 鄭州南關外發現一座宋墓. *Wenwu* 文物, no. 8 (1965): 52–53.

Liu Jingzhen 劉靜貞. "Quanwei de xiangzheng: Song Zhenzong dazhongxiangfu shidai tansuo" 權威的象徵–宋真宗大中祥符時代探索. *Dongwu wenshi xuebao* 東吳文史學報 7 (1989): 55–90.

Liu Yongping. *Origins of Chinese Law: Penal and Administrative Law in Its Early Development*. Hong Kong: Oxford University Press, 1998.

Liu Yusheng 劉玉生. "Henansheng Fangchengxian chutu Songdai shiyong" 河南省方城懸出土宋代石俑. *Wenwu* 文物, no. 8 (1983): 40–43.

Liu Yusheng 劉玉生 and Wei Renhua 魏仁華. "Henansheng Fangcheng Jintangzhai BeiSong Fan Zhixiang mu" 河南省方城金湯寨北宋范致祥墓. *Wenwu* 文物, no. 11 (1988): 61–65 and 39.

Liu Xing 劉興 et al. "Jiangsu Liyang Zhuze BeiSong Li Bin fufu mu" 江蘇溧陽竹簀北宋李彬夫婦墓. *Wenwu* 文物, no. 5 (1980): 34–39.

Liu Zhiyuan 劉志遠 and Jian Shi 堅石. "Chuanxi de xiaoxing Songmu" 川西的小型宋墓. *Wenwu cankao ziliao* 文物參考資料, no. 9 (1955): 92–98.

Lo, Winston Wan. *An Introduction to the Civil Service of Sung China: With Emphasis on Its Personnel Administration*. Honolulu: University of Hawaii Press, 1987.

Loewe, Michael. "State Funerals of the Han Empire." *Bulletin of the Museum of Far Eastern Antiquities* 71 (1999): 572.

Long Teng 龍騰. "Pujiang BeiSong Song Sui mu chutu wenwu" 蒲江北宋宋燧墓出土文物. *Sichuan wenwu* 四川文物, no. 5 (1996): 59–61.

Lu Weijing. "Abstaining from Sex: Mourning Ritual and the Confucian Elite." *Journal of the History of Sexuality* 22, no. 2 (2013): 230–252.

Lü, Zongli. *Power of Words: Chen Prophecy in Chinese Politics AD 265–618*. Bern: Peter Lang, 2003.

Luo Zongzhen 羅宗真. "Jiangsu Huai'an Songdai bihua mu" 江蘇淮安宋代壁畫墓. *Wenwu* 文物 Z1 (1960): 45–6 and 51.

Makita Tairyō 牧田諦亮. "Suiroku'e shōkō 水陸會小考." *Tōhō shūkyō* 東方宗教 12 (1957): 14–33.

Mannheim, Karl. *Ideology and Utopia: An Introduction to the Sociology of Knowledge*, translated by Louis Wirth and Edward Shils. San Diego, New York, and London: Harcourt Brace Jovanovich, 1985.

Matsumoto Koichi 宋本浩一. "Sōrei sairei ni miru Sōdai shūkyōshi no ichi keikō" 葬禮·祭禮にみる宋代宗教史の一傾向." In *Sōdai no shakai to bunka*

宋代の社会と文化, edited by Sōdaishi kenkyūkai, 169–194. Tokyo: Kyūko Shoin, 1983.

McCauley, Robert N. "Philosophical Naturalism and the Cognitive Approach to Ritual." In *Thinking through Rituals: Philosophical Perspectives*, edited by Kevin Schilbrack, 148–171. New York and London: Routledge, 2004.

McDermott, Joseph P. "Emperor, Elites, and Commoners: The Community Pact Ritual of the Late Ming." In *State and Court Ritual in China*, edited by Joseph P. McDermott, 299–351. Cambridge: Cambridge University Press, 1999.

McKnight. Brian E. *Law and Order in Sung China*. New York: Cambridge University Press, 1992.

McMullen, David. "Bureaucrats and Cosmology: The Ritual Code of Tang China." In *Rituals of Royalty: Power and Ceremonial in Traditional Societies*, edited by David Cannadine and Simon Price, 181–236. Cambridge and New York: Cambridge University Press, 1987.

Meyer, Christian. "Negotiating Rites in Imperial China: The Case of Northern Song Court Ritual Debates from 1034 to 1093." In *Negotiating Rites*, edited by Ute Hüsken and Frank Neubert, 99–115. Oxford and New York: Oxford University Press, 2011.

Mote, F. W. *Imperial China: 900–1800*. Cambridge, MA, and London: Harvard University Press, 1999.

Neskar, Ellen. "The Cult of Worthies: A Study of Shrines Honoring Local Confucian Worthies in the Sung Dynasty (960–1279)." PhD diss., Columbia University, 1993.

Olsson, Karl F. "The Structure of Power under the Third Emperor of Sung China: The Shifting Balance After the Peace of Shan-Yuan." PhD diss., University of Chicago, 1974.

Peng Shifan 彭適凡 and Tang Changpo 唐昌朴. "Jiangxi faxian jizuo BeiSong jinian mu" 江西發現幾座北宋紀年墓. *Wenwu* 文物, no. 5 (1980): 28–33.

Pines, Yuri. "Disputers of the *Li*: Breakthroughs in the Concept of Ritual in Preimperial China." *Asia Major* 13, 3rd series, no. 1 (2000): 1–41.

Poo, Mu-chou. "Ideas Concerning Death and Burial in Pre-Han and Han China." *Asia Major* 3, 3rd series, no. 2 (1990): 25–62.

Puett, Michael. *To Become a God: Cosmology, Sacrifice, and Self-divinization in Early China*. Cambridge, MA: Harvard University Asia Center , 2004.

Qi Xia 漆俠. *Zhongguo jingji tongshi* 中國經濟通史, vols 10–11, *Songdai jingji juan* 宋代經濟卷, Beijing: Jingji ribao chubanshe, 1999.

Rappaport, Roy. *Ritual and Religion in the Making of Humanity*. Cambridge and New York: Cambridge University Press, 1999.

Rawski, Evelyn. "A Historian's Approach to Chinese Death Ritual." In *Death Ritual in Late Imperial and Modern China*, edited by James Watson and Evelyn Rawski, 20–40. Berkeley: University of California Press, 1988.

Ricoeur, Paul. *Lectures on Ideology and Utopia*, edited by George H. Taylor. New York: Columbia University Press, 1986.

________. "Imagination in Discourse and in Action." In *Rethinking Imagination: Culture and Creativity*, edited by Gillian Robinson and John Rundell, 118–135. London and New York: Routledge, 1994.

Ruichangxian bowuguan 瑞昌縣博物館. "Jiangxi Ruichang faxian liangzuo BeiSong jinian mu" 江西瑞昌發現兩座北宋紀年墓. *Wenwu* 文物, no. 1 (1986): 70–72.

Russell, T. C. "Coffin-pullers' Songs: The Macabre in Medieval China." *Papers in Far Eastern History* 27 (1983): 99–130.

Sanmenxiashi wenwu gongzuodui 三門峽市文物工作隊. *BeiSong Shanzhou louzeyuan* 北宋陝州漏澤圓. Beijing: Wenwu chubanshe, 1999.

Sariti, Anthony William. "Monarchy, Bureaucracy, and Absolutism in the Political Thought of Ssu-Ma Kuang." *Journal of Asian Studies* 32, no. 1 (1971): 53–76.

Schneewind, Sarah. *A Tale of Two Melons: Emperor and Subject in Ming China*. Indianapolis, IN: Hackett, 2006.

Schootenhammer, Angela. "Characteristics of Song Epitaphs." In *Burial in Song China*, edited by Dieter Kuhn, 253–306. Heidelberg: Forum, 1994.

Seidel, Anna. "Buying One's Way to Heaven: The Celestial Treasury in Chinese Religions." *History of Religions* 17, no. 3–4 (1978): 419–431.

________. "Tokens of Immortality in Han Graves." *Numen* 29 (1982): 79–114.

________. "Imperial Treasures and Taoist Sacraments: Taoist Roots in the Apocrypha." In *Tantric and Taoist Studies in Honor of R. A. Stein*, edited by Michel Strickmann, 291–371. Brussels: Institut Belge des Hautes Etudes Chinoises, 1983.

Shen Zongxian 沈宗獻. "Songdai minjian sici yu zhengfu zhengce" 宋代民間祀祠與政府政策. *Dalu zazhi* 大陸雜誌 91, no. 6 (1995): 23–41.

________. *Songdai minjian de youming shijieguan* 宋代民間的幽冥世界觀. Taipei: Shangding wenhua, 1993.

________. "Songdai sangzang faling chutan: Yi *Tiansheng sanzangling* wei jichude taolun" 宋代喪葬法令初探–以《天聖喪葬令》為基礎的討論. In *"Tianshengling" lunji: Xin shiliao, xin guandian, xin shijiao* 天聖令論集 新史料新觀點新視角, edited by Gouli Taiwan shifan daxue, lishi xuexi 國立臺灣師範大學 歷史學系, 155–197. Taipei: Yuanzhao chuban youxian gongsi, 2011.

Shi Jiazhen 史家珍 et al. "Fu Bi jiazu mudi fajue jianbao" 富弼家族墓地發掘簡報. *Zhongyuan wenwu* 中原文物, no. 6 (2008): 4–18.

Shi Tao 石濤. "Songdai de yuyong Daojiao" 宋代的御用道教. *Shanxi daxue xuebao* 山西大學學報, no. 4 (1998): 57–61.

________. "Songdai dui Daojiao de guanli 宋代對道教的管理. *Shanxi daxue xuebao* 山西大學學報 23, no. 1 (2000): 30–37.

Shiba Yoshinobu. *Commerce and Society in Sung China*, translated and edited by Mark Elvin. Ann Arbor: University of Michigan Press, 1970.

________. "Urbanization and the Development of Markets in the Lower Yangtze Valley." In *Crisis and Prosperity in Sung China*, edited by John Winthrop Haeger, 13–48. Tucson: University of Arizona Press, 1975.

Sichuansheng bowuguan 四川省博物館. "Sichuan Guangyuan shike Songmu qingli jianbao" 四川廣元石刻宋墓清理簡報. *Wenwu* 文物, no. 6 (1982): 53–61.

Sima Qian 司馬遷 (c. 145–86 BCE), *The Grand Scribe's Records,* vol. 2: *The Basic Annals of Han China,* edited by William H. Nienhauser Jr., translated by Tsai-fa Cheng et al. Bloomington: Indiana University Press, 2002.

_______. *Records of the Grand Historian: Han Dynasty,* vol. 2, translated by Burton Watson. New York: Columbia University Press, 1993).

Smith, Jonathan Z. *Imagining Religion.* Chicago: University of Chicago Press, 1982.

Smith, Paul J. "State Power and Economic Activism during the New Policies, 1068–1085: The Tea and the Horse Trade and the 'Green Sprouts' Loan Policy." In *Ordering the World: Approaches to State and Society in Sung China,* edited by Robert Hymes and Conrad Schirokauer, 76–127. Berkeley: University of California Press, 1993.

Smith, Richard J. *The Qing Dynasty and Traditional Chinese Culture.* Lanham, MD: Rowman & Littlefield, 2015.

Song, Jaeyoon. *Traces of Grand Peace: Classics and State Activism in Imperial China.* Cambridge, MA: Harvard University Asia Center, 2015.

Song Sanping 宋三平. "Shilun Songdai muji" 試論宋代幕祭. *Jiangxi shehui kexue* 江西社會科學, no. 6 (1989): 104–107.

_______. "Songdai de fenan yu fengjian jiazu" 宋代的墳庵與封建家族. *Zhongguo shehui jingji yanjiu* 中國社會經濟史研究 52, no. 1 (1995): 40–47.

Stahl, Helga. "Su Shi's Orthodox Burials: Interconnected Double Chamber Tombs in Sichuan." In *Burial in Song China,* edited by Dieter Kuhn, 161–214. Heidelberg: Forum, 1994.

Stevenson, Daniel B. "Protocols of Power: Tz'u-yün Tsun-shih (964–1032) and T'ien-t'ai Lay Buddhist Ritual in the Sung." In *Buddhism in the Sung,* edited by Peter N. Gregory and Daniel A. Getz, Jr., 340–408. Honolulu: University of Hawaii Press, 1999.

_______. "Text, Image, and Transformation in the History of the *Shuilu fahui,* the Buddhist Rite for Deliverance of Creatures of Water and Land." In *Cultural Intersections in Later Chinese Buddhism,* edited by Marsha Weidner, 30–70. Honolulu: University of Hawaii Press, 2001.

Su Bai 宿白. *Baisha Song mu* 白沙宋墓. Beijing: Wenwu chubanshe, 1957.

Tackett, Nicolas. *The Destruction of the Medieval Chinese Aristocracy.* Cambridge, MA: Harvard Asia Center, 2014.

Tao, Jinsheng. *Two Sons of Heaven: Studies in Sung-Liao Relations.* Tucson: University of Arizona Press, 1988.

Teiser, Stephen F. *The Ghost Festival in Medieval China.* Princeton, NJ: Princeton University Press, 1996.

_______. *The Scripture on the Ten Kings and the Making of Purgatory in Medieval Chinese Buddhism.* Honolulu: University of Hawaii Press, 1994.

Tillman, Hoyt C. *Confucian Discourse and Chu Hsi's Ascendancy.* Honolulu: University of Hawaii Press, 1992.

———. "The Treaty of Shanyuan from the Perspectives of Western Scholars." *Sungkyun Journal of East Asian Studies* 5, no. 2 (2005): 135–156.

Twitchett, Denis, and Paul Jakov Smith, eds. *The Cambridge History of China*, vol. 5, part 1: *The Sung Dynasty and Its Precursors, 907–1279.* New York: Cambridge University Press, 2009.

Waley, Arthur, tr. *The Analects of Confucius.* New York: Vintage, 1989.

———, tr. *Ballads and Stories from Tun-huang: An Anthology.* London: G. Allen & Unwin, 1960.

Wang Shanjun 王善軍. "Songdai de zongzu jisi he zuxian congbai" 宋代的宗族祭祠和祖先崇拜. *Shijie zongjiao yanjiu* 世界宗教研究 77 (1999): 114–124.

Wang Shengduo 汪聖鐸. "Songchao li yu Fojiao 宋朝禮與佛教. *Xueshu yuekan* 學術月刊 252 (1990): 52–58.

———. "Songchao li yu Daojiao" 宋朝禮與道教. In *Guoji Songdai wenhua yanjiu taolunhui lunwenji* 國際宋代文化研討會論文集, edited by Sichuan daxue, Guoji zhengli yanjiusuo 四川大學古籍整理研究所, 35–49. Chengdu: Sichuan daxue chubanshe, 1991.

———. *Songdai zhengjiao guanxi yanjiu* 宋代政教關係研究. Beijing: Renmin chubanshe, 2010.

Watson, James L., and Evelyn S. Rawski, eds. *Death Ritual in Late Imperial and Modern China.* Berkeley and Los Angeles: University of California Press, 1988.

Wechsler, Howard J. *Offerings of Jade and Silk: Jade and Symbol in the Legitimation of the Tang Dynasty.* New Haven and London: Yale University Press, 1985.

Wei Jun 魏峻 and Zhang Daosen 张道森. "Anyang Songdai bihuamu kao" 安陽宋代壁畫墓考. *Huaxia kaogu* 華夏考古, no. 2 (1997): 103–104 and 55.

Wright, David Curtis. *From War to Diplomatic Parity in Eleventh-Century China: Sung's Foreign Relations with Kitan Liao.* Leiden and Boston: Brill, 2005.

Wu Hung. "Beyond the 'Great Boundary': Funerary Narrative in the Cangshan Tomb." In *Boundaries in China*, edited by John Hay, 81–104. London: Reaktion, 1994.

———. *Monumentality in Early Chinese Art and Architecture.* Stanford, CA: Stanford University Press, 1995.

———. *The Art of the Yellow Springs: Understanding Chinese Tombs.* Honolulu: University of Hawai'i Press, 2010.

Wugenburger, Jean-Jacques. *L'imaginaire.* Paris: Presses Universitaires de France, 2003.

Wyatt, Don J. "In Pursuit of the Great Peace: Wang Dan and the Early Song Evasion of the 'Just War' Doctrine." In *Battlefronts Real and Imagined: War, Border, and Identity in the Chinese Middle Period*, edited by Don J. Wyatt, 75–109. New York: Palgrave Macmillan, 2008.

Xu Jiadong 余家棟. "Jiangxi Boyang Songmu" 江西波阳宋墓. *Kaogu* 考古, no. 4 (1977): 286–287.

Xu Jijun 徐吉軍. *Zhongguo sangzang shi* 中國喪葬史. Nanchang: Jiangxi gaoxiao chubanshe, 1998.

Yamauchi Kōichi 山內弘一. "Hokusō no kokka to gyokko" 北宋の国家と玉皇. *Tōhō gakū* 東方學 62 (1981): 83–97.

———. "Hokusō jidai no kōshi" 北宋時代の郊祀. *Shigaku zasshi* 史學雜誌 92, no. 1 (1983): 40–66.

———. "Hokusō jidai no shingyoden to keireikū" 北宋時代の神禦殿と景靈宮. *Tōhō gakū* 東方學 70 (1985): 46–60.

———. "Hokusō jidai no taibyō" 北宋時代の太廟. *Jōchi shigaku* 上智史學 35 (1990): 91–119.

———. "State Sacrifice and Daoism during the Northern Song." *Memoirs of the Research Department of Toyo Bunko* 58 (2000): 1–18.

Yang Qianmiao 楊倩描. "Songchao jiaosi zhidu chutan" 宋朝郊祀制度初探. *Shijie zongjiao* 世界宗教, no. 4 (1988): 75–81.

Yang Weisheng 楊渭生 et al., *LiangSong wenhua shi yanjiu* 兩宋文化史研究. Hangzhou: Hangzhou University Press, 1998.

Yang, Xiaoshan. "Ritual Propriety and Political Intrigue in the Xuande Gate Incident." *T'oung Pao* 98, no. 1–3 (2012): 145–177.

Yao Meiling 姚美玲. "Tang Song maidiquan xiyu kaoxi" 唐宋買地券習語考釋. *Yuncheng xueyuan xuebao* 運城學院學報 22, no. 1 (2004): 57–60.

Yokomasa Katsunobu 横正克信. "Sōdai no uchidōjo ni tsuite" 宋代の内道場について. *Taishōdaigakuin kenkyū ronbunshū* 大正大學大學院研究論文集 20 (1996): 93–105.

Yü, Ying-shih. " 'O Soul, Come Back!' A Study in the Changing Conceptions of the Soul and Afterlife in Pre-Buddhist China." *Harvard Journal of Asiatic Studies* 47, no. 2 (1987): 363–395.

Yu Yunguo 虞云國. *Xishuo Songchao* 細說宋朝. Shanghai: Renmin chubanshe, 2004.

Zeitlin, Judith T. "Spirit Writing and Performance in the Work of You Tong 尤侗 (1618–1704)." *T'oung Pao* 84, no. 1 (1998): 102–135.

Zeng Qinghua 曾清華. "Jingyanxian BeiSong Huang Nian silang mu qingli jianxun" 井研懸北宋黃念四郎墓清理簡訊. *Sichuan wenwu* 四川文物, no. 1 (2002): 95–96.

Zhang Bangwei 張邦煒. "Songdai sangzang fengsu juyu" 宋代喪葬風俗舉隅. In *Di er jie Songshi xueshu yantaohui lunwenji* 第二屆宋史學術研討會論文集, edited by Di er jie Songshi xueshu yantaohui mishuchu, 79–92. Taipei: Zhongguo wenhua daxue, 1996.

Zhang Xiqing 張希清. *Songchao dianzhang zhidu* 宋朝典章制度. Changchun: Jilin wenshi chubanshe, 2001.

Zhao Jun 趙俊 and Cheng Zhaowen 成兆文. "Daodejia de lixiangguo: Song Ming Daoxue neizai zhuiqiu chuyi" 道德家的理想国—宋明道學内在追求芻議. *Lanzhou daxue xuebao* 蘭州大學學報, no. 2 (1999): 111–115.

Zhao Shigang 趙世綱. "BeiSong Yang Chengxin muzhi ba" 北宋楊承信墓志跋. *Kaogu yu wenwu* 考古與文物, no. 1 (1985): 55–58.

Zhenjiangshi bowuguan 鎮江市博物館 and Liyangxian wenhuaguan 溧陽懸文化館 "Jiangsu Liyang Zhuze BeiSong Li Bin fufu mu" 江嘛溧阳竹簀北宋李彬夫妇墓. *Wenwu* 文物, no. 5 (1980): 34–39.

Zhou Suping 周蘇平. *Zhongguo gudai sangzang xisu* 中國古代喪葬習俗. Xi'an: Shanxi renmin chubanshe, 1991.

Zhou, Yiqun. "The Status of Mothers in the Early Chinese Mourning System." *T'oung Pao* 99, no. 1–3 (2013): 1–52.

Zhu Duanxi 朱端熙. "Songdai de sangzang fengsu" 宋代的喪葬風俗. *Xueshu yuekan* 學術月刊, no. 2 (1997): 69–74.

Zito, Angela. *Of Body & Brush: Grand Sacrifice, as Text/Performance in Eighteenth-Century China.* Chicago: University of Chicago Press, 1997.

# Index